UP AND DOWN AND AROUND

By the same author

Reflections on Reaching the Age of 150
  (Pamphlet)

The Publishing Experience
  (University of Pennsylvania Press)

HARPER'S
MAGAZINE
PRESS

CASS CANFIELD

UP
AND DOWN
AND AROUND

A PUBLISHER RECOLLECTS THE TIME
OF HIS LIFE

A HARPER'S MAGAZINE PRESS BOOK

Published in Association with Harper & Row, New York

LIBRARY OF CONGRESS CATALOG CARD NUMBER: 73-156512

STANDARD BOOK NUMBER: 06-121540-6

To Jane; anchor

Samuel Taylor Coleridge listened to the tale of a sailor, back from a two-year trip around the world in a whaling ship. One or two episodes emerged vividly clear—but Coleridge compared the sailor's incoherent story to looking at the reverse side of a tapestry, lacking pattern or coherence. So go one's recollections, although, now and then, an echo sounds clear in the forest of memory.

"Never believe anything a writer tells you about himself. A man comes to believe in the end the lies he tells himself about himself."
GEORGE BERNARD SHAW

"There is a time when all of us must rise above principle."
ADLAI STEVENSON

"Experience is the word we use when we recognize the same mistake twice."
EARL WILSON

"Nous sommes la triste opacité de nos spectres futures."
VICTOR HUGO

"Man does not live by words alone although he occasionally has to eat them."
ADLAI STEVENSON

"You may not be what you think you are but you are what you think."
ANONYMOUS

"Facts are the brute beasts of the intellectual domain."
OLIVER WENDELL HOLMES

Contents

II. UP AND DOWN AND AROUND

III. WORLD WAR II

IV. YEARS OF CHANGE

V. FOOTLOOSE

Groups of photographs will be found following pages 48, 144, and 208.

Acknowledgments

I am deeply grateful to Elizabeth Lawrence, long an editorial colleague at Harper's, for her invaluable help while I was writing this book. I am also indebted to Beulah Hagen, Edward Streeter, John Fischer, Gregg Sims, Marguerite Hoyle, Jane Canfield and Kitty Benedict for constructive criticism. My sincere thanks to Richard Passmore for his expert help with the final revisions.

The writing of *Up and Down and Around* was facilitated by the perceptive questions put to me by Isabel Grossner, who was assigned the task of taping my replies for the Columbia Oral History program. Much of the typing was done by Ruth Hill and Jacqueline Brettell; it was the former who urged me to write this book. Some of the material is taken from my A. S. W. Rosenbach lectures, *The Publishing Experience*, which were published by the University of Pennsylvania Press.

I am sorry that space forbids my mentioning a number of writers beyond those included here whom I would have liked to include and with whom I have worked happily over the years.

At the close of business on a Friday in the 1920's snow was falling and, as the home-going Wall Street crowd milled around the lobby of the Singer Building, a plump, balding youth stumbled down the stairs. He looked awful, he felt awful.

And with every right, for he was suffering from a running cold; besides, he was exhausted from the effort of having opened every office door in one of the two or three tallest buildings in New York. Although he had not accomplished this feat in a day —his normal pace was five floors a week—wear and tear had begun to take their toll. He was fresh out of Harvard. In spite of his exhaustion, he grinned as he descended the last step of the stairway, for he had just reached a decision. This was to be his last day as a bond salesman. His lagging gait turned into something like a caper as he bounded into the street.

This man is the central character in Up and Down and Around, *who has just reached another decision: to write about himself. I look forward to this undertaking with the same delight as when I faced the prospect of entering every office of the Singer Building, ready to inflict my bonds upon unwilling victims.*

I
GROWING UP

"Rosy-Fingered Dawn"

I was born on Park Avenue at Thirty-sixth Street, and lived until recently nearby on East Thirty-eighth Street. Today the fashionable center of Manhattan is uptown, but at the turn of the century when I was born it was south of Grand Central Station. There my father, Augustus Cass Canfield, and my mother, Josephine Houghteling, pitched their tent. Brought up in France, he had come to New York from Detroit, she from Chicago.

Our house was not far from Forty-second Street, where the father of our country was once in serious trouble, due to the fact that the British Expeditionary Force, under General Howe, having just successfully staged history's largest amphibious operation up to that time, had landed their troops at Thirty-eighth Street and the East River. George Washington was sitting very erect on his fine horse, fuming at the cowardice of his men, who had turned and run after taking one look at the mass of invading redcoats. He dismounted and, in a rage, stomped on his hat. Thereupon, a young aide timidly tapped him on the shoulder and told his commander that unless he mounted quickly, General Howe would catch up with him. This might well have happened except that Howe, according to legend, instead of advancing, enjoyed the tea hour with Miss Murray (from whose family Murray Hill got its name) and tarried with her. Had the British commander pressed his advantage, the American Rebellion might have been stamped out then and there.

The Canfields cut quite a figure. Their victoria, drawn by

spirited chestnut horses with two men on the box, wearing cockades and sitting bolt upright, was smart. So were they. He, a charming gentleman of leisure; she, a Charles Dana Gibson beauty whom Oscar Wilde had called the most beautiful woman in America. They had enough money to live in style—just enough.

Our big brownstone house, in the same block as Pierpont Morgan's, was at the northwest corner of Thirty-sixth and Park; it was near the city reservoir, where the New York Public Library now stands. I remember leaning out of the window, my two older sisters beside me, watching the Thirty-fourth Street Armory burn to the ground in the middle of the night. I was four; Mary and Laura were eight and nine. New York at the time was an ugly city compared with today; no trees on the streets and row upon row of brownstone houses—modest precursors of the Seagram and Lever buildings.

Another vivid, early memory was of rollerskating—everywhere. It was glorious; I covered the ground at ten to twenty times the speed of traffic, which was even worse then than today. On Fifth Avenue one could be stuck for an hour, the carriages hardly moving; and when there was ice and snow, the horses often fell down, blocking the streets. At the Twenty-third Street crosstown intersection there was often a snarl. That was an enticing place for me; I would gaze in wonder at the Flatiron Building, then the tallest in the city, I believe. And on the west side of Fifth stood the magical F. A. O. Schwarz toyshop; also R. H. Macy and Eden's Musée with the remarkable mechanical chess player who beat almost every challenger. In Central Park the rollerskating conditions were perfect; there I would meet my friends for hockey games. Sometimes we'd be challenged by a local gang and would engage them in a stone-throwing contest until the cops chased us away. What good times we had!

But soon this happy city mouse was moved to the country, to Roslyn, Long Island, where Charles McKim, a partner of Stanford White, had built us a large, attractive brick house, which was named "Cassleigh." By that time—some years before the watershed of World War I—we were enjoying the "pleasure" of motoring; we had a Panhard and snorted as inferior rattletraps like Cadillacs, Pope Toledos and Stanley Steamers clattered by. On rainy days we put up the curtains, which prevented all but 90 percent of the rain from pouring in; otherwise we were very comfortable, wrapped up in rugs and heavy dusters, except for blowouts, which inevitably occurred every few miles, and halts at every steep hill because of lack of power to mount them. But there was always a way around—miles around.

I learned to drive a car when I was ten and so by now should be a most dependable chauffeur, especially as my instructor was Ralph de Palma, who became a famous international racing driver. Despite this superior training, I am considered by friends and, particularly, family to be highly unreliable at the wheel.

My father had graduated from the Columbia School of Mines and had gone on to study naval architecture in order to design his own yachts, among which the *Sea Fox* was the fastest ocean-going schooner of her time, winning many Atlantic races. She ended up as a rum-running wreck in the Prohibition era. Daddy lived for his boats, but they failed to arouse corresponding enthusiasm in Mother; yachting was apt to make her seasick. One day she said to him, "The *Sea Fox* or me." End of yacht. Father took to a motorcycle and would set off from Roslyn for Mineola with his golf clubs. The going must have been bumpy, for there were only dirt roads on Long Island in the early 1900's; the region was changing rapidly from truck farming into a resort area. I regarded his motorcycle expeditions as adventurous, and they were; he chugged along over good fox-hunting country, the area of the Meadowbrook Hunt. Although he and Mother didn't ride horseback, we children hunted on our ponies; mine was a lovely creature called Camera.

So I found a substitute for rollerskates and was happy—until my father died. We were in Aiken, South Carolina, at the time—a horsy hunting resort. Daddy caught pneumonia riding home in a buggy after playing tennis. What a lovable, gentle character!—shy, but a man of unusual charm.

One night sometime earlier in Roslyn, when I was suffering from a stomach-ache—and raw knuckles caused by sharp raps from one of our savage German governesses—I overheard my parents conversing. She: "Lift him from the bed and put him on the sofa." He: "No, I might wake him." She: "Nonsense, he'll go right to sleep again." I remained in bed; Daddy remained on the couch in his bedroom.

Another time, in Aiken, Mother asked my father to dismiss two black minstrels who were strumming and singing outside. He strode out and told them to scat, but handed them a dollar, with the result that the volume of sound trebled, to my mother's heightened exasperation. She demanded immediate action, whereupon Daddy observed gently, "Oh, but I don't want to hurt their feelings."

It was shortly thereafter that he died, at the age of fifty-two. I was playing with an electric train in the living room, when Mother admonished me with the warning that my father was very, very ill, that any sound might kill him. I stopped, but within minutes had the train rolling again. Then I heard a cry, looked up the stairs and saw Mother weeping. "Your father is dead," she said. I never got over that and for years believed that I had killed him.

Mother, Josephine Houghteling, was *sui generis*—beautiful, determined, courageous. Although she dressed superbly and spent large sums on works of art, she was generally careful with her money. One morning, at the newly built Plaza Hotel, where I had devoured a huge breakfast with the gusto of a seven-year-old, the bill mounted way up to fifty cents. Mother complained vehemently to the manager; whatever the outcome, it was evident that when she decided upon a course of action, nothing would deflect her.

Mother's Kingdom

In Roslyn Mother reigned over "Cassleigh." Her chef, an artist named Monsieur Gillet, would be summoned to her bedroom every morning and the meals discussed, item by item. (In her travels Mother would extract from reluctant hoteliers their most secret recipes.) This ordering session would be followed by others: with the head gardener, who specialized in yellow roses—which I still like most—the chauffeur, the butler and Eugene, the handyman.

Once, "Cassleigh" buzzed with activity; Edith Wharton, who was visiting us, was in the throes of producing the dramatic version of her famous novel, *The House of Mirth*. The telephone rang incessantly. Unhappily, the play was a flop on Broadway. I found Mrs. Wharton forbidding, elegant and unbending, but even as a child was aware of her cleverness and wit; in fact, she was unremittingly clever. How this citified woman could have written a simple masterpiece of country life like *Ethan Frome* remains a mystery to me. *The House of Mirth* was certainly more typical of her; in this novel the beautiful heroine, Lily Bart, is banned from society because she was seen leaving the Fifth Avenue house of the Trevors when Mrs. Trevor was known to be away. Not only was Lily modern, but, in rereading this story, I was struck by the fact that, although the social mores of 1905 differed from ours now more than did those of the Egyptians in the time of the Rameses, the "jet set" of the time was doing about everything they do now. They were constantly on the move, going to Europe on fast, five-day steamers and motoring to Long Island for weekends. At one of their weddings the mother of the bride rightly complained because a "cinematograph man" took movies of her daughter in church.

Things were changing fast in the first decade of this century. For instance, the ferryboat from Long Island City to New York was about to be replaced by a bridge; bad news for Mother's friends who had invested heavily in land near the ferry, expecting a sharp rise in values. Real estate is always a gamble; many years later the elevated railway on Third Avenue was about to be torn down. A big operator, "Grampy Lee," grandfather of the Bouvier girls, once surprised me with the observation that nothing would induce him to invest in Third Avenue. This mistake must have cost him dearly.

In the early 1900's the Wright brothers were determined to

achieve the impossible and fly once around a small field in Mineola, Long Island. They achieved this miracle, and their flight covered a distance equal to that of the interior of a modern 747 plane. Their performance created among the spectators, who included the Canfield children, an excitement as great as did that of Lindbergh, twenty-five years later. Not long after this momentous event, I listened to the comments of my elders; they were skeptical about the future of flying machines, mainly because they questioned the reliability of the gasoline engine. Frank Griswold, a close friend of the family, distrusted it for a different reason. An ardent horseman, he predicted that the gasoline motor would poison the atmosphere and intensify traffic problems. Seventy-five years earlier the Duke of Wellington had similarly disapproved of the iron horse (the railroad), observing, "It will only encourage the lower orders to travel and so make them restless and unhappy."

The reaction to another innovation, the bicycle, was different. It was welcomed by everyone except book publishers, who forecast that this invention, together with the motorcar, would consume the time people had previously devoted to reading. They had something here—but not much—for today men, women and especially children read more than ever before; this in spite of radio and television.

My Ancestors Missed the Boat

Recollections of my tribal origins are dim. My father's ancestors missed the *Mayflower* and Plymouth Rock, but they got here about a hundred years later, becoming farmers and blacksmiths. They settled in New England and acquired all the Puritan sins and virtues. One of them, Captain Jonathan Cass, fought in our Rebellion. Because of his achievement I belong to the Order of the Cincinnati, the descendants of officers who took part in the Revolution. It's interesting to note that the Order of the Cincinnati was attacked in an early Congress as a self-perpetuating aristocracy and a serious threat to the Republic.

After a while the Cass family packed up and moved to Chicago. My grandmother was a Cass; she married into the Canfields. Of the early-nineteenth-century Casses, Lewis, who attended Exeter Academy, was the star of the clan. He studied law and drifted into politics, becoming, in 1813, Governor of Michigan Territory, a tract covering much of what is now the Northwest. His particular contribution was his ability to deal successfully with the Indians. In the War of 1812, when our General Hull surrendered his sword to the British C.O., Cass stepped up smartly and broke it in two. One of the pieces was preserved as a family relic until a roistering Harvard classmate of mine, doubled up with laughter, hurled it far down the tracks from the back platform of a train leaving Grand Central Station.

After Lewis Cass had finished his Michigan stint he became Secretary of War under Jackson and later Secretary of State under Buchanan. He ran unsuccessfully for President on the Democratic ticket against Zachary Taylor. Less famous than Henry Clay, he became a great compromiser on the slavery issue and continued to compromise until he refused to yield on the issue of Fort Sumter and was consequently dismissed as Secretary of State. President Buchanan insisted that to strengthen the garrison, as Cass advised, would aggravate the friction between North and South.

Lewis Cass's playboy son, Lewis, Jr., spent some time in Europe in our diplomatic service and became one of the many lovers of Pauline Bonaparte, immortalized in marble by Canova. He lived in great luxury; when attending the opera he would order two seats, one for himself and another for his accouterments, which included mother-of-pearl opera glasses, still in my possession. In 1895 another ancestor, my father's father—an Army engineer—drew the first plans for the Sault Sainte Marie Canal linking lakes Superior and Huron.

To Lewis Cass, Jr. I am indebted also for gold dinner plates and the heavy, ornate Capo di Monte breakfast set Napoleon used on his famous lightning Italian campaign. To his father I owe an unfinished painting by Benjamin West, often reproduced in schoolbooks, portraying the American peace commissioners at the Treaty of Paris following the Revolutionary War. The British negotiators refused to pose, so the right side of the picture is blank. It now hangs in the Department of State Building, the gift of my son Cass, Jr. and myself.

When Mother moved East, she left Chicago for good. Of my grandparents I have no memory; I never saw them. Only my Uncle James Houghteling stands out in my memory, a fine, solid man of Dutch and German blood who made a modest fortune from a Chicago investment firm. I remember his visiting us in Roslyn, and taking a pleasant walk with him. Upon returning to the house, Uncle James told Mother that I was obstinate, argumentative and spoilt. I got quite a dressing down.

Dr. Blake's Scissors

Dr. Joseph Blake, a great surgeon, was called to our house in Roslyn. He showed up without the standard medical kit; he relied mainly on a pair of scissors. My appendix, about to burst, was the reason for his visit. The operation was successful—Blake's scissors did the trick.

As I was recuperating, a large box appeared holding three trays of tin soldiers; they came from "Monsieur Canon," Frank Gray Griswold, an admirer of Mother's. I've never forgotten those gaudy soldiers nor the trained nurse who took care of me; when she left, I wept miserably. This was my first completely absorbing human relationship, and after her departure I was desolate. I couldn't believe that she'd deserted me. Then sister

Laura came to the rescue and brought me some measure of comfort. I was seven.

During my convalescence I read *Peter Rabbit*. I owned a typewriter with a keyboard shaped like a plate, which you pushed around until you found the right key; I typed out the whole of *Peter Rabbit* and could recite the story by heart. Other gems of my literary education included *The Rover Boys* (forty volumes) and the early Zane Grey Westerns, which were great favorites. These books left an indelible impression.

Sister Mary was a tomboy and made a man out of me, a thin, backward shrimp. Mary was also a racing man—she and I raced in automobiles made of packing cases built by the obliging handyman, Eugene. We competed in the two-hundred-foot cellar of our house in Roslyn, a dangerous pastime because of the deep coal pits lining the "course." In the final championship Mary won by inches and was awarded a silver cup. She and I would enjoy having lunch with the Italian workmen on the place; they'd treat us to salami and cheese provided out of their $1 daily wage; a bit less than the $16 received by carpenters today for an hour or so's work! They were a cheerful, friendly, hard-working lot, and we became fast friends.

Sister Laura had a special gift for teaching and was able to make difficult subjects clear to me. Once, after missing three weeks of grade school, I was told to make up several centuries of English history. Thereupon Laura instructed me for a couple of hours, and, to this day, I recall everything she said, in spite of the fact that I was a slow learner. To compensate for this lack I would argue interminably; my two sisters christened me *"l'avocat des causes perdues."* Laura gave me even more practical help. Sitting on her bed one day I mentioned casually that I'd just swallowed a scarf pin—an extra-long coral number from Naples. She could feel it in my throat, but, like an obstinate champagne cork, it wouldn't come out. Nevertheless, her ministrations and the physic she gave me were effective. Finally, the pin emerged through the Grand Canal and I breathed again.

Mother took a place in the Adirondacks one summer and

brought the chef along as well as a full complement of servants. Arrived there, Mary exclaimed, "Oh, how lovely to go camping and rough it!" Mary was a good companion but was easily bored and would sit at the gate of our quarter-mile driveway in Roslyn in the hope of seeing some action; this amounted to a car passing by every half-hour or so. She became, in fact, distinctly temperamental, and would madden her German governesses—one after another. Still, she added to the liveliness of the place and was very pretty, although contrariness and a spirit of revolt were part of her nature. Laura was the dignified one—highly intelligent, serious, but with a subtle sense of humor.

Mother would have us children appear for lunch and tea, suitably attired for these occasions. I had to dress in a Little Lord Fauntleroy costume and was ordered to kiss the ladies' hands—it was enough to put me off women for life! But our lives were not altogether formal, although we were attended by liveried footmen; they had to be over six feet, and Mother's inability to find men of the proper height, as the years passed, was taken as a portent of the dissolution of American society. Mother was gay and quick, with a wry wit; she enjoyed having people around her so that on weekends the Roslyn house was full of guests. It was a big, comfortable place with one wing reserved for visitors. We had no near neighbors; the closest were the Pendletons, about two miles away.

The pattern of life at "Cassleigh" was that of an English country house. On weekday evenings Mother would read aloud to Laura, Mary and me. In the mornings she'd summon us to her bedroom where she breakfasted, and one by one we would kiss her. Following this ceremony, she'd get dressed—an elegant routine, for she had a beautiful figure, enclosed in corsets laced in by a strong maid. Her dresses were lavish, and, as a child, I spent many tedious hours at Worth in Paris watching the models and the endless fittings. How bored I became! This was the Paris of Vuitton trunks lining the corridors of the Ritz, of smart carriages, of Voisin's restaurant—now defunct—and of the perennial Maxim's. One of Mother's maids, Julie, had been with her for many years, an exceptionally nice woman. Mother dismissed her because she felt that she and Julie had become too intimate—like the captain of a ship getting rid of his executive officer.

I remember, as an eight-year-old, sitting in a London drawing room where Mother was entertaining some important British political figures at tea. I listened to their comments and opinions on the Boer uprising some years previous. They all agreed, even then—over fifty years ago—that, although Britain finally won that war, the British Empire was doomed and would not endure for long.

Our neighbor's son, George Pendleton, was a bully and worked his aggressiveness out on me. One of the few times I've ever prayed intensely was to implore the Almighty to help me get the best of George. And I also prayed that my nasty, sly, mouse-colored horse would quit pitching me over his head. The creature knew me well; he would wait for a downhill lie and, picking his moment, would toss me forward so that I'd land in the road with a thud. It was both painful and humiliating.

At home, I spent much time around the stables playing with the coachman's boy, Dudley Gibbons; we used to spend hours painting an unfortunate cat different colors. Dudley's father, Tom, was a genial Irishman who had been with the family for many years.

Once I noticed Dudley's baby brother, Billy, sticking his tongue out at me from an upper window, protected by a mosquito screen. Quick as a flash I drew my gun, took careful aim and fired a B.B. shot at him. It penetrated the wire and embedded itself in the child's right eye. Tom Gibbons called a doctor immediately. He removed the pellet but said that he would have to take out the child's eye on the following day, adding that he expected Billy would lose sight of the other eye also. That evening I sat silently at home, dreading the moment when Gibbons would call my family and announce the tragedy. But the telephone never rang, and in due course Billy's injured eye healed. To this day I am infinitely grateful to Tom for keeping this skeleton in the closet.

13

Consuelo and Other Visitors

A striking visitor to Roslyn, whom I spied from beneath the staircase as she entered the house, was Consuelo Vanderbilt Churchill. At thirty she was a most beautiful creature, with a lovely, swanlike neck. Some years before she had borne a male heir for the Duke of Marlborough despite difficulties with her mother-in-law, who had hounded her during the early months of her marriage, inquiring anxiously and repeatedly about the progress of her pregnancy. "Why do you keep asking about this?" Consuelo would ask. In reply, the dowager duchess exclaimed: "Why, my dear, don't you understand? Unless you produce a male heir, that bounder, my grandson Winston Churchill, will become the Duke."

Had he, we in the United States might now be subject to Hitler's whims. For a duke must be a member of the House of Lords, and, as such, cannot sit in the House of Commons. Accordingly, Winston Churchill, who, as Prime Minister, saved the day when Hitler was preparing to invade England, would not have held that office because by custom the premiership goes to a member of the House of Commons.

Among other guests at "Cassleigh" was Morton Frewen, Churchill's brother-in-law, and a much beloved charmer who lost his friends pots of money. He was ahead of his time; his ventures—like railroads across the Andes, wireless telegraphy, the tungsten bulb—were farsighted but still in the experimental stage. And there was Seymour Leslie, a brilliant fellow, cousin of Churchill; Bourke Cochran, the eloquent Irish politician, who taught Winston Churchill the art of elocution; and Thomas Fortune Ryan, who later bought "Cassleigh."

A tall, rather grim beau of my sister's would occasionally

visit us: Sumner Welles was to achieve eminence in later years as Under Secretary of State and become, in my opinion, the ablest diplomat of his generation.

Mother would move to Roslyn from town in the early spring, leaving me with Herbert L. Picke, the headmaster of the day school I attended. He and his wife would put me up in their small apartment, where I thoroughly enjoyed myself; Picke was a foster father to me and I was devoted to him. Among the pupils at Picke's school on Fifth Avenue was "Neely" Vanderbilt. The poor boy never had a chance. One afternoon his mother, Mrs. Cornelius Vanderbilt, called mine and said, "A dreadful thing happened today; my chauffeur failed to call for Neely at school so that he had to come home in a common taxi!"

The Vanderbilts' Fifth Avenue house was famous for its large, elaborate and exceedingly dull dinner parties; I attended one after the First World War and was stopped short by the war memorial to Neely in the front hall. There were his war mementos, enclosed in a vitrine, all his Army equipment—even his toothbrush—on prominent display. Not particularly moving as Neely had escaped from the war unscathed.

I suppose that even in those far-off days inflation was a problem. At all events, Mother decided to sell "Cassleigh" and make her base in New York City, where she would not have to manage such a large establishment. In due time she bought 783 Park Avenue from Oakleigh Thorne, a well-known collector of French eighteenth-century furniture and objets d'art. It was a beautiful house and Mother added many fine things to the Thorne collection.

Vision on a Bicycle—
School in Switzerland
and Mother's Remarriage

In the summers we'd often go to Bar Harbor. When I was about ten, a nine-year-old vision with streaming blond hair, "Dutchy" Smith, would glide down the hill every day on her bicycle, on the way to the swimming pool. I would wait for her and longed to speak to her, but lacked the courage to do so; she became an obsession. However, the whole summer passed without our exchanging a word.

Mother took long trips with her friends during the winters. Once, when she was on the Nile in a dahabeah, I was parked at the Institution Sillig in Vevey, Switzerland. On my first weekend at the school the headmaster took the boys on a fifteen-mile hike up to Les Avants in the Alps. To this day I remember vividly my exhaustion as I staggered back into the town after that walk. The next morning I had pleurisy. To have taken a ten-year-old boy, fresh from the city streets, on such a jaunt seems to me to have shown something less than good judgment! At Sillig's we studied endlessly, without letup beyond an hour's recess; I did badly, except in history, and was duly chastised by Mother. But she did notice my good mark in history and asked me what period I'd been studying. Well, I couldn't quite answer that. This naturally surprised her, and when I was unable to identify even the country involved, she couldn't believe it. I had simply done as I was told from day to day and had learned three pages of history at a time, by heart. That was the French system of education in those days.

On our way back to New York from Carlsbad, when I was eleven, we stayed at Divonne, near Mont Blanc. There "Monsieur Canon" gave me an enormous packet of stamps which totally absorbed me, so that I didn't take in the fact that Mother was about to be called "Madame Canon," or, more accurately, Mrs. Frank Gray Griswold. She was very happy, not radiant; that was not in her character.

Frank Griswold was an unusual person; he devoted most of his life to sport, but at the same time was extremely well informed and an authority on certain subjects—salmon fishing, fox hunting and polo. He wrote a number of books on sport, wine, food and cigars. At the age of eighty he learned Spanish by correspondence course and produced a very respectable book on El Greco.

His memory reached way back; he could recall driving, as a small boy, with the coachman to fetch drinking water from a well for his family's house in New York. And he remembered the excitement during the Civil War when newsboys shouted in the streets: *"Extra: Monitor routs Merrimac!"* He was shrewd; he sold one of his horses and realized $3,000 on it. This sum, in his view, was insufficient for investment and too large for day-to-day spending, so he talked to some of his friends at the Union Club and asked whether any of them knew of an interesting speculation. One of them suggested that he go and see a young inventor in New Jersey who had been trying to raise some money. Mr. Griswold visited him and was shown around his small shack, where my stepfather noticed a machine with a big, protruding horn. The inventor, asked what it was, said, "I call that a gramophone, but it's just a toy—it will never have any commercial value." Mr. Griswold was shown further into the workshop and was told of the work being done on the electric bulb and the problems of finding the right filament for it. The inventor's name was Thomas Edison, a genius with endless curiosity and persistence; in his search for the right filament he even tried limburger cheese! My stepfather invested $3,000 in what later became General Electric; he never took his money out of it, and over the years it multiplied many times.

He laid claim to a discovery. When he was training Pierre Lorillard's horses in England, he'd often see Edward, Prince of Wales, who became Edward VII. The Prince wore a velvet smoking jacket on informal occasions; he'd also leave the lowest button of his vest unfastened because his excess weight made it too tight. This set a fashion that is still followed. In Tuxedo Mr. Griswold would attend stag dinners. At one of them, he asked his friends, "Why do we endure tail coats on occasions like this? Why not cut off the tails?" His suggestion, based upon Prince Edward's smoking jacket, was adopted and so a new costume came into being—the "Tuxedo."

I would attend rehearsals at the Metropolitan Opera, of which Frank Griswold was a director. The rehearsals, with great stars like Toscanini, Geraldine Farrar, Pavlova and Caruso taking part, were exciting to watch. Toscanini knew the opera scores by heart so that he never had to look at the music, Geraldine Farrar would become temperamental, and Caruso, a remarkable man of many talents, would alternately play the buffoon and storm about in anger. One evening at a supper party he tossed off some striking caricatures; two of them, of Gatti-Cassazza and Toscanini, now hang in my study.

Mr. Griswold declared that there were only two places in the world where he could eat—at home and in the Brook Club. Gourmets are curious folk; another one, William Burden, can find food to his taste only in certain French provincial towns and in Belgium—apparently nothing in Paris, London or New York satisfies him.

Jehovah's Groton

Mother had not entered me for Groton School, so it was up to me, with Mr. Picke's help, to get in by competitive examination. This I achieved by a hair.

I started as a second-former. On my first day the diminutive Tom Coward, who had been at the school the previous year, strode up to me at recess and said, "So you're the new kid?" I scarcely had the opportunity to courteously assent when his fist smashed into my nose and left me flat on the ground staring at the sky—hardly a gentle introduction to Groton, but standard procedure. At all events, "Timmy" Coward became a good friend and, later on, a competitor in the publishing field.

The masters at Groton were an odd and interesting lot. At the top of the mountain stood Jehovah—Endicott Peabody; below him were many talented teachers. Among them was Ichabod Crane, a martinet who looked the part with his piercing eyes and cropped black beard. He taught mathematics and would make us stand in the corner when we were stupid. In my third-form year he presented us with a problem in geometry—Original No. 5—which stumped the whole class. But I worried at it as a dog does a bone and finally solved the puzzle; never have I experienced such a feeling of triumph. Crane complimented me and gave me confidence by saying that I would achieve what I wanted in life.

W. A. G. (Wag) Gardiner, a rich, old, eccentric gentleman who was fond of puns, instructed us in Greek from what he called a "little, brown book" (published by Little, Brown & Company). Although we couldn't follow his learned discourse, Wag somehow imparted to us a love of the classics and made us as familiar with the Greek gods and goddesses and their outrageous doings as with neighbors in an adjoining backyard.

Jimmy Regan was as unusual, subtle and inquisitive as he was charming; he had eyes in the back of his head and hearing like a lynx. It was impossible to put anything over on this slender, alert Irishman. He would read aloud to us from delightful books of the period—*Monsieur Beaucaire, Stover at Yale* and the works of William J. Locke.

Gladwyn was the tyrant in charge of our Spartan dormitory, where we slept in cubicles and washed in a big common lavatory, lined with tin basins in which we'd immerse ourselves upon arising. For some reason, I was always late, a failing duly noted by Mr. G. He'd give me black marks, a half-dozen at a time, and in order to work these off, I would have to run around the circle in front of Hundred House. I ran and ran, rain or shine, early in the morning, during recess and after sundown; without my familiar figure the circle would not have been the circle. In fact, I made a record; no boy since 1884, when the school was founded, had ever run so many laps.

Herr Griswold, who taught us physics, was of German extraction. I remember walking around the circle with him in the spring of 1915 when the papers were full of stories about the German gun aimed at Paris, later called Big Bertha. It had a range of seventy miles and a trajectory thirty-five miles in height. I asked Herr Griswold about this extraordinary weapon, and he made this observation: "I've been making some calculations, and believe that if a projectile could be fired with enough force to reach a height of one hundred miles we would create a floating satellite that would go around the world forever." Remarkable that this physics teacher in a preparatory school, in 1915, should forecast the present age of astronauts.

With the Reverend Endicott Peabody, who was a great and strong personality, my contact was remote. He seemed to me a good deal like the Old Testament Jehovah, for whom one has a healthy respect but whom one fears. He ran an excellent school, and his severity was leavened by the "parlor nights" over which his charming, gentle wife presided. We attended early-morning chapel daily and evening prayers before bedtime, in addition to church on Sunday. The rector usually delivered the sermon and, of course, read the lessons; Jehovah passing on the word of God was grimly impressive: "Mene, Mene, Tekel, Upharsin." His sermons castigated divorced parents—an unfortunate theme since fully one-third of the boys at Groton were the children of fathers and mothers who had gone their separate ways.

The effect of all this churchgoing is hard to evaluate. From Groton there emerged two main types: "Good Grotties"—those marked for life by the rector, and on the whole well marked—and wild men—the drinking contingent seeking escape. Religion affected all of us and was apt to produce either conformity or revolt, but in my case the reaction was quite neutral. What I did acquire was a love of the Biblical language and of the

Psalms; to hear them read always gives me pleasure. And I think that having some kind of religious sense is like having a poetic sense; people who are without feeling for what is beyond natural phenomena are the losers.

Years after leaving school I heard Jehovah Peabody speak at the Century Club in New York; before a highly sophisticated audience he thundered against Sin and those dens of iniquity, the night clubs. He pictured these usually dull pleasure haunts as hell holes of Sex. As a result, I hurried to one of them with a friend and watched, with little excitement, pot-bellied business-men sitting morosely with their girl friends, soaking up whisky.

Russell Codman was a close chum at Groton; he and I spent much time together. We invented a foolish game, which involved a rubber ball and the side of a building; this we would play endlessly to the annoyance of Mr. Cross, the physical director, who felt that the Codman-Canfield combine lacked school spirit. At the end of the school term, when I encountered Cross as I was packing to go home after a happy year, he remarked to me jovially: "Well, I may not be seeing you again," to which I replied politely that I was sorry to hear that he was leaving Groton. "Oh, no," he said, "I expect to remain here indefinitely." I was puzzled, but promptly forgot this curious exchange.

Fired!

In Paris the family occupied a beautiful suite on the roof of the Hotel Crillon, overlooking the Place de la Concorde. One day a bellboy appeared at the door with a cable addressed to my mother: "Regret, since your boy lacks proper school spirit and fails to conform to our Groton pattern, his return undesirable. Endicott Peabody."

Lightning flashed, thunder rolled, the skies turned black

and the end of the world was at hand. Although Mother was taken by surprise, as I was, she quickly girded her loins and went forth to battle. Jehovah quailed and, after a spirited exchange of cables, I was reinstated at Groton, on trial for six weeks. I really deserved to be fired as I'd entered the school by competitive exam and was therefore expected to stand in the top 10 percent of the class; instead, I was at the foot, with Codman.

During those six weeks I worked hard at my studies and found, to my surprise, that I actually enjoyed them. Without doubt, any task, no matter how boring, becomes interesting when one applies oneself to it; the invaluable lesson I learned at that time was to concentrate. Concentration is worth more than all the knowledge of a scholar and much more than a brilliant mind. I ended the year in fifth place and led my class the year after; in that position I was of course ahead of Quentin Roosevelt. That I should beat Quentin was what Mother really wanted. "What a disgrace it would be if a Roosevelt got ahead of a Canfield!" she would exclaim.

It is hard for me to measure the effect of this period. First, out of fear of my parent and, second, from ambition, I had turned myself from a clown into a very solemn youth—a "for God, for Country and for Yale" type who obeyed every rule without question.

In fact, I became an automaton. I would watch the reactions of every teacher and, especially, of every sixth-former because the latter were the most important in the student hierarchy. I turned into a machine, without spirit, without originality and without joy; I read nothing aside from what was required, saw nothing, heard nothing. Yet, as an actor, I did quite well and have ever since daydreamed of being on the stage. With Edgar Scott, Jr., I played in *The Private Secretary*, a famous repertory play, first at school and later at a New York theater, for charity. We performed successfully, and Frank Crowninshield, the attractive editor of *Vanity Fair*, said that we could have gotten by on Broadway.

In athletics I tried my best but failed to achieve signal success; I was not first-rate at football and baseball. To compensate for this relative failure a boy named Slater Washburn showed me how to become a "regular guy," which stood for conformity and not sticking your neck out. Regular guys were deadly bores.

In time I got over my obsession with lessons, dropping from No. 1 in the form to No. 5. I then took part, violently, in the extracurricular school activities. Dr. Peabody considered me the busiest boy in the school; true, I had hardly time to sleep.

We spent the summer of my fourth-form year at Dark Harbor, Maine; from there I set out by myself on a boat trip. I was sixteen and had by then reacted against the conformity of my life at Groton. Nothing much happened on this three-day expedition but, to me, it was fascinating and I remember every moment of it as one does a place associated with an intense emotional experience. The three days seemed like an eternity and, on my return, I kept looking at my face in the mirror, trying to detect the immense change that must have taken place as a result of my solitary journey. An introverted adolescent, I was utterly absorbed in my reactions and impressions; I *had* to discover just what made Sammy run. A couple of years later, some weeks spent in a Plattsburg, New York, officers training camp knocked this nonsense out of me.

Top Hat and Tails at Sixteen and Life before the 1914 War

I remember with dismay the train trip from New York to Groton when the Christmas holidays were over, and recall the joy of the journey the other way, when we would read "wicked" humorous weeklies like *Life* and *Puck*. Manhattan seemed to us schoolboys a magic place. Even as a second-former I went to dances and would go to the theater to see the delicious Maude

Adams and Elsie Ferguson, and musicals like *Babes in Toyland* and *The Wizard of Oz*. Jazz was making its debut then with "Alexander's Ragtime Band" and "Waitin' for the Robert E. Lee"; the tango and the Vernon Castles were the rage. It was a gay time, but a tragic event occurred in 1912. One afternoon when we were playing baseball at school someone rushed onto the diamond and shouted, "The *Titanic* hit an iceberg and sank!" Unbelievable, with her watertight compartments and Marconi wireless. But she *did* sink, to the amazement and shock of the whole world.

As a fifth-former I attended the "Metropolitan" dances at Sherry's at Forty-fourth and Fifth Avenue, arriving there in top hat and tails. On more adventurous occasions I'd go with a friend to Bustanoby's cabaret, the hangout of Lillian Russell and Diamond Jim Brady. Ham Coolidge and I, who were to become prefects and, as such, primary guardians of school morals, did not report this misdemeanor to Jehovah. Had we done so, we'd have been sent out to pasture.

I was growing up, but since Dutchy Smith—the bicycle girl— no female had aroused my youthful interest. One thing I remember especially during the summer of 1912 at St. Moritz was a conversation between a bald Russian count and Mother. A horsefly lit on the highly polished surface of his head, and as they talked the creature tarried, drawing blood from the noble dome. A few minutes later, when the count had departed, I asked Mother why he hadn't brushed off the fly. She explained that he was far too much of a gentleman to consider such a thing.

Sister Mary's attitude of revolt had become fixed, and when in a temper, she would hurl verbal brickbats at Mother. As a teenager she disliked the daily round in New York and later, as a young lady, would leave our house to live on her own. However, she would soon return, drawn back to the security of home. We were having tea one afternoon when Mary rushed into the living room, dressed for dinner. Asked where she was going, Mary explained that she had a date with the editors of *The New Republic*—Herbert Croly, Walter Lippmann and Willard Straight. Mother stopped her: "You mustn't go out with people like that." It was a sad event. Mother was a strict conservative and had apprehensions about people outside her circle —especially liberal ones; this led her to act in a way which deeply affected my sister. Mary burst into tears and, without a word, hurried back to her bedroom.

We spent a summer in Vulpera, near the Engadine Valley in Switzerland; I can still hear the sound of the rushing stream far below the hotel. Here girls came back into my life. I was fifteen and followed one of them, several years my senior, up a mountain carpeted with wild flowers. She told me that I was a sweet little boy, an observation that was not at all what I wanted to hear.

"There Is Nothing Like a Dame" and a Rude Interruption

I was still an innocent a couple of years later when, with eight or ten boys of my age, I went on a camping trip in Wyoming. Afterward, the group was shepherded to the St. Francis Hotel in San Francisco.

Baisley Elebash, the sophisticated youth of our party, was sitting with me in the café of the hotel, and at the next table were two pretty young women some years older than we were. While it wouldn't have entered my head to attempt a pick-up, Elebash accomplished this with ease. The ladies joined us and we took them to the World's Fair then going on and had a delightful evening. One of the girls was called Miss Hartshorne. She attracted me and made me feel foolishly immature, for she talked impressively about authors and literature. And when I tried to keep up with her conversation, I found that I lacked the knowledge to do so.

On the way back to the St. Francis I summoned up all my

courage and dared to put my arm around Miss Hartshorne's waist. I shall never forget that moment. Two days later found our party of boys at the Grand Canyon, where we rode to the bottom of the chasm and back again. I suppose it was a wonderful sight, but I saw nothing; all my faculties were concentrated on Miss Hartshorne.

A fortnight later I was staying with the family in Bar Harbor. Mother had taken a cottage there and, by a strange twist of fate, Miss Hartshorne was next door! What Dante went through, quite a few years earlier in Florence, was as nothing to the tumult in my young breast. I envisaged idyllic walks in the beautiful Maine woods with the lady of my dreams. Well, nothing happened at all; I didn't even exchange a word with her. My adolescent shyness, combined with fear of Mother's ridicule, stopped me from doing anything except mope. What agonies youngsters suffer in their teens!

We spent the summer of 1914 at St. Moritz, which was lively and amusing. There were attractive girls there—Margaret Luce in particular—and I had a good time with them. Hans Badrutt's Palace Hotel was then the most brilliant resort in Europe, complete with an indoor tennis court. The great John Barrymore was staying at the Palace and became absorbed in the amateur theatricals—tableaux—put on for charity. He'd rehearse us day after day as if for a Broadway production of *Hamlet* and so showed, by his attention to detail, that he was a professional to his fingertips.

We heard there about the Black Hand and Pan-Slavism; news came of the assassination at Sarajevo, and the political situation in Europe looked ominous. However, Mother and the girls seemed safe at the hotel, so my stepfather and I set off for Paris, since I was due back at Groton. We saw many soldiers on the way, particularly Swiss, who maintain one of the best armies in Europe. Our trip passed without incident. On arrival, we dined at Voisin, one of Marcel Proust's favorite eating places, and were struck by the waiters' hopeless attitude toward the war. In reply to our questions they would just shrug their shoulders and mutter, "The Germans will be in Paris within a week." Actually, they only just missed the mark. As my step-father and I returned to the hotel, we heard a shot; Jean Jaurès, the prominent labor leader, had been assassinated, causing a political sensation.* France appeared to be on the brink of disaster.

My stepfather realized that we'd better return quickly to St. Moritz and the family. The railroad stations were black with troops, their sweethearts, wives, old people, children; the confusion was indescribable. We fought our way onto a freight car, as crowded as the Black Hole of Calcutta, and started moving after some hours. Nobody could tell us where we were going; there was no water, no food—just sweating soldiers, dreading the prospect of facing the German juggernaut.

We bumped along at five or six miles an hour, making endless stops, and, after two and a half days, reached the Swiss border. At St. Moritz the family was happy to see us, although our incipient beards made us almost unrecognizable. Now we had to concentrate on getting home. Although dollars were no longer accepted because of the wartime confusion, Badrutt willingly extended us unlimited credit. But how were we to get to New York? The answer was provided by an American businessman who chartered a steamer from Naples. We were told that this was the last boat to sail for the United States.

Screaming headlines greeted us in New York, headlines about the Battle of the Marne and Galliéni's taxicabs, commandeered to transport poilus to the front; headlines more astounding than any I can recall except, perhaps, those reporting Pearl Harbor, years later. I felt mad exultation over the German defeat.

---

* Since the 1890's Jaurès had been a socialist leader in the Chamber of Deputies and was the founder of the newspaper *L'Humanité*. He took the side of Dreyfus in the famous Dreyfus Case which rocked France before World War I.

Summit: Sixth Form

Now the sixth form, at Groton, the summit. My classmate Charles Fuller had committed a crime; during vacation he'd smoked a cigarette! The news spread so that Jehovah learned the worst, and consequently Fuller, who had been appointed Brooks House prefect, second-in-command to the senior prefect, was deprived of his stripes. So I became the Brooks House prefect. My main duty in this capacity was to supervise some eighty boys; the prefects really ran the school.

I just made the football team; my mother and sisters watched me play against St. Mark's, our archrival. We won the game and the family congratulated me; yet they, and others, speculated on what I'd been doing during the play. Small wonder for although, as center, I did have to pass the ball back, I accomplished nothing notable except to make one pass several feet over the halfback's head, thus losing thirty-five yards for our side.

The week before, we'd played Milton Academy. Opposite me, at center, was a certain "Tubby" Clark, a lad with the strength of Samson and the heft of a Mack truck. Groton had been gaining ground steadily and had reached Milton's two-yard line; first down, it looked like a cinch. Fuller, as quarterback, signaled for a line play and we got the ball to the three-inch line; he signaled again and we gained half an inch. Once more he called for a center rush, but I was getting tired—I weighed only 130 pounds. I protested, but Fuller had his way and we were pushed back. I landed flat on the ground, unconscious, and remained so for hours—Tubby had been too much for me. He was a great athlete and at Harvard played on the varsity football, hockey, track and baseball teams.

The Groton motto—*"Cui servire est regnare"* ("Whose [God's] service is perfect freedom")—had its effect on the inmates; it inspired such men as FDR, Sumner Welles, Dean Acheson and Arthur Woods to enter public service and serve their country. Arthur Woods, later Police Commissioner of New York, taught at Groton. He once gave me this advice: "When you coast downhill on a bicycle and encounter a pair of gateposts close together, don't think about the danger of running into them; instead, see yourself gliding between them." A good tip for, if you fear an obstacle, the chances are that you'll run straight into it.

Woods became a protégé of Theodore Roosevelt, advocate of the strenuous life. Teddy enjoyed long walks. One day, accompanied by his wife, John Burroughs, the famous naturalist, and a Mr. Bingham, he climbed Mount Monadnock, a small mountain in New England. He reached the top, beaming with satisfaction and puffing strongly from his exertion. At that point Bingham exclaimed to Burroughs, "Look at Teddy; how easily he managed that climb!" John Burroughs replied, "Well, yes, but Mrs. Roosevelt was standing quietly on the summit when her athletic husband finally reached the top."

Harvard, 1915

At Harvard I roomed with Ham Coolidge and Charlie Fuller in one of the new freshman dormitories. Soon I made new friends, all of them private-school boys. Many of the men in the dormitory were from public schools, but birds of a feather flock together and, although there was no antagonism between the two groups, we didn't mix. Too bad; by such exclusiveness both groups missed a lot. Today this gap hardly exists and the private-school boys are in the minority. Furthermore, the importance of the college clubs, which contributed to this separateness, has greatly diminished.

The dormitories were comfortable and the suites, with sitting rooms, usually held three people. These we furnished ourselves. I visited the Harvard Co-op at once and bought furniture and looked over some textbooks; there were no paperbacks then, and no clothbound books there aside from the required classroom reading. Next, I visited my faculty adviser, Freddie Schenck, a clever young man who recommended the courses I should take. I wanted to study subjects related to what was then going on in the world, but Schenck objected, telling me that the *New York Times* should supply me with that kind of information. He favored, instead, courses far removed from contemporary events and preoccupations of the time—the study of Shakespeare, life in the medieval period, the history of Greece. I took his advice and decided on the humanities as my field of concentration—history and literature.

During the holidays I would go to Bernard Shaw plays; they made a deep impression on me. Shaw, so far ahead of his time, opened my eyes to the social problems of the day.

At this stage I considered myself far too intellectual (Miss Hartshorne, backstage) for sports and maintained a fine aloofness from such activities, until big Ham Coolidge took me by the scruff of the neck, shook me as a cat would a mouse and made me drop my pose. I gave in, and next day went out for football. At Soldiers Field an extremely nice coach greeted us rookies—Leverett Saltonstall, later a U.S. Senator. My bald head (I had gone bald by the time I left Groton) attracted attention and my teammates respectfully addressed me as "Sir," thinking that I was Saltonstall's assistant. I rushed enthusiastically at the tackling dummy; Saltonstall liked my youthful zeal and put me on the team, at center, although I weighed only 132 pounds. My alternate was "Sliver" Bates, 247 pounds; Sliver filled up the line all right, but his movements were somewhat leisurely.

After a couple of weeks of practice the freshman team faced their first opponents, the Worcester Technical School. I cast no aspersions on the integrity of these gentlemen, but it was apparent that some of them were in their late twenties and had been playing football for some fifteen years. As we ran onto the field before the game, the immediate future looked grim, especially for me, the newly appointed captain of the Harvard eleven. The whistle blew and, before the end of the first quarter, the score stood 42–0 against us. Then the gods took pity on me and caused a 215-pound Worcester linesman to drop (accidentally?) on my ankle. It broke with a loud crack and, infinitely thankful, I was carried off the three-yard line where the Worcester fiends were preparing their final charge. Before the sun had set on that brisk October afternoon, eight of our team, supposedly the cream of the prep-school crop, were carried off the field. Ham Coolidge's ankle had been broken in just the same way as mine.

A required freshman course was History I, "Western Civilization"; we spent hours in the Widener Library doing the assigned reading for it, which I found stimulating. One of my professors was William L. Langer, later to become head of the Harvard history department. Little more than ten years later he agreed to my request that he edit a twenty-volume series, The Rise of Modern Europe. Langer remains the editor, lively and creative as ever.

Another required course was "English A," and I drew a congenial Herbert L. Picke type of teacher. He made us write a daily composition, and I enjoyed working for this man because he liked my papers and thought they showed some originality. I remember only dimly the great Samuel Eliot Morison, the renowned historian, but clearly recall "Frisky" Merriman, who made even the tortuous history of South America fascinating. Our courses in literature were conducted by Dean Briggs, Lowes Dickinson, Barrett Wendell and Bliss Perry, a remarkable group—one couldn't but respond to them.

Harold Laski taught English Constitutional history; like Wag Gardiner he was incomprehensible, at least to me. Laski was too clever and assumed knowledge on the part of his students which most of them lacked. The professor I found most stimulating was Irving Babbitt, an ardent classicist who lectured brilliantly on the Romantic Movement only in order to demonstrate its futility. Its protagonists, Rousseau, Byron, Wordsworth, *et al.,* were to him a worthless lot; only Voltaire had his unqualified approval. He defined the Romantic attitude with rolling phrases: "The never-ending pursuit of the ever-fleeting object of desire." Another Babbitt utterance I liked: "The elemental ground swell of naked human desire."

My courses were not confined to the fields of history and literature. They were crazily varied and included such subjects as freehand drawing, at which I excelled since, with the help of a few rolls of toilet paper used for tracing, I was able to duplicate any great artist's drawing.

Harvard at that time was open, or nearly so, to any graduate's son; getting by was not hard, although far more difficult than ten years previously. Now things have changed. Being the son of a graduate is no guarantee of acceptance and standards are higher than ever, perhaps because Radcliffe girls have become very much a part of the university. In my day association with girls was kept to a minimum and liquor was king. Of course, a few of my classmates spent some of their leisure with women, usually respectable ones rather than tarts, but this was rather frowned upon. The real, *echt* clubman favored girls with his presence only occasionally.

In the winter of my freshman year I took up rowing for the first time. Rowing in the indoor tanks was boring and totally exhausting, but when the ice melted, we went out on the Charles River. This was bearable, yet I really loathed the sport. For a while I rowed on the first crew, but was soon demoted to the freshman four-oar. We toiled away—a galley slave life—until we were sent to Red Top, near New London, to train for the Yale races. That was fun—to be so young, healthy and foolish. No smoking, of course, but our coach, a genial Boston businessman, believed in giving the boys champagne on Saturday nights to prevent their becoming overtrained. Joy!

Our big day came in June. We were nervous because we had heard much about the mighty prowess of the Yale boys and feared defeat. Sister Mary perched in one of the launches, following the races. We did well; after a dead-heat start our four-oar drew away from the Yale crew, ending up seven or eight lengths ahead. Whistles blew, sirens tooted, flags waved, and we were very happy. The next day was, of course, the real McCoy—the varsity race. Again Harvard won easily. We all succeeded, forthwith, in getting uproariously tight.

Porcellian

The club I joined at Harvard was the Porcellian (P.C.), the happiest but hardest-drinking group I've ever encountered. I got a fine start there as a drinker and have calculated that my total consumption of hard liquor to date would fill a tank 10 × 13 × 2 feet. My intake of wine would fill a small pond of the same two-foot depth and twice the area. The approved method was to drink one's fill without showing any sign of it.

The P.C., dating from 1789, was originally named the Gentlemen's Society; it then became the Pig Club. No one has ever been permitted to resign, although Endicott Peabody tried. The members, four to eight per class in my day, have always been chosen for their congeniality. Period. Among them have been athletes, campus leaders, gentlemen of leisure and eccentrics. A number of distinguished men have belonged: Louis Agassiz, Theodore Roosevelt, Owen Wister, Oliver Wendell Holmes and John Jay Chapman.

Chapman was an odd and extremely talented individual. Once, in Maryland, he announced his intention of delivering an antislavery speech after a lynching; he hired a large hall for the purpose, but only one old Negro woman appeared. His oration was so outstanding that it was printed in *The Atlantic*.

Chapman had both conscience and high standards. After a P.C. dinner, having consumed quantities of champagne, he

33

horsewhipped a classmate for making derogatory remarks about his fiancée. Deeply ashamed of his behavior, he rushed to the fireplace and thrust his hand into the flames until it was burnt to a stub. "If thy right hand offend thee, cut it off."

I found it interesting to read the Porcellian Civil War records from an old journal of the club; it appears that the young gentlemen of the period didn't fancy fighting for the Stars and Stripes; instead, for $500 each, they hired substitutes. But in World War I the ROTC was respectable and there were no campus riots; in fact, we took no interest in politics and scarcely read the newspapers.

At the club I introduced red wine to supplement the hard liquor and champagne. I obtained an enormous Great Western jug, placed it on a high shelf and affixed to it a rubber hose with a spigot; my notion was to educate my barbarian clubmates. I felt that, at last, we were set for gracious living and so was not shocked by the fact that, following the installation of the massive jug of wine, our consumption of liquor in the club broke all records. Each member was assessed periodically for what, in my opinion, he consumed—no nonsense about signing for each drink. Later, at Oxford, I was reminded of this easygoing custom by Anthony Eden's lordly manner about financial matters; he would not bother to enter shillings and pence on his checks but would pay his bills to the nearest pound.

As I have suggested, alcohol played a large part in our lives at Harvard—too large. If anyone broke one of the myriad rules of the club, he would be fined a quart of champagne by the boss—the deputy marshal. After a "business" meeting the table in the clubroom would often be completely encircled by empty bottles, perhaps fifty of them.

Once a year we had the "Day by the Book," an exercise for which the members trained for weeks. It involved the following:

Before breakfast: Honiarty and gin.
At breakfast: one quart of champagne—fiz, we called it.
Thereafter, one martini every hour till lunch, when two
    martinis were called for.

For lunch, one bottle of fiz; the afternoon routine was the same as the morning's.

Two preprandial martinis.

By that time most of the candidates had collapsed. The finest contestants, the favorites, were constantly rubbed down and showered by their trainers.

At dinner, more fiz, and until midnight, the closing time for the contest, one Scotch and soda each hour.

In my time only one candidate was able to stand and communicate as midnight struck. It was not I, although, as a strong contender, I was one of those "seeded." Eddie Morgan was the only one to survive. Among other things, he enjoyed the chase and, after one of our Saturday night dinners, would command his friend, Suydam Cutting, to jump out the window and so get a two-minute head start on the hounds, i.e., any of the diners who fancied a nocturnal adventure. Morgan would spend the two minutes going to the kitchen and fetching an extra-large carving knife. Equipped with this formidable weapon, Eddie would lead the hounds in a terrifying pursuit of the hapless hare over the roofs and spires of Cambridge. Fortunately, Cutting was fleet of foot and was never caught.

In spite of such pastimes we managed to do some studying. Life at Harvard was certainly enjoyable, and I found it both lively and stimulating. We had a good time without venturing much beyond the Harvard Yard—ski trips were almost unknown and very few of us had cars.

First World War

Although we didn't really know what Woodrow Wilson's Mexican War was about and didn't much care, it provided the opportunity for a junket and a little excitement. So we signed up as volunteers and drilled in a Boston armory. I was the rawest of raw recruits and would about-face smartly at the command, "Right face." Some of us reached Mexico, but the majority were left at home, as I was.

One day the news broke that the *Lusitania* had been sunk. I was sitting on the Boston Common with my sister Laura, who was living near Boston at the time, having just married the Reverend William Wood—not at all the kind of fashionable marriage Mother had planned for her. I agreed with her that the wanton sinking of the *Lusitania* meant that this country was bound to join the Kaiser's war sooner or later. Laura was elated; I wasn't—I wanted no part of it.

How could I be neutral in the face of this shocking affront to the civilized world? "Too proud to fight," in Woodrow Wilson's words? Although I believed from my study of history that war was utterly futile and hence was a pacifist, I was a rather emotionally volatile young man. Had there been campus protest riots at this time, I would have led the demonstrators to the barricades. So it was natural that I should perform a complete somersault in due course and attack anyone who hesitated to urge U.S. participation in the war against Germany.

It struck me that in wartime Harvard the students knew and cared too little about what was going on in the world. Accordingly, with the help of some of the younger faculty, I started and organized discussion groups on various political subjects; as many as a thousand boys and some teachers attended them. The idea caught on and had quite an effect on undergraduate life, but, when the war ended and we went back to what's called a normal life, these discussion groups disbanded.

In addition, I joined the Harvard Regiment in order to train to be an officer. A Colonel Azain, a seasoned veteran of trench warfare, a Lieutenant Morize and Jean Giraudoux, who later became famous as a playwright, were assigned to train the members of the regiment.

On one of our field exercises we were told to dig trenches, and I could not persuade Lieutenant Morize to give us the proper dimensions. After much questioning, he said, "If you were a Frenchman, I'd tell you to the inch, but you're Americans and I shall tell you nothing." He went on to make the observation that Frenchmen would pay no attention to such specifications and would adapt the dimensions to the terrain. Morize patiently explained that one doesn't dig the same trench in solid rock as in mud.

Colonel Shannon, a fine soldier and a West Pointer, commanded the Harvard Regiment; its performance was admired in military circles because we showed the results of the excellent training given to us by the experienced French officers. Following the final field exercises, Shannon gave the whole corps of some thousand cadet officers a banquet and I was flattered to be placed on his right. He recommended me and another man for the rank of colonel in the U.S. Army and expected that his recommendation would be accepted by the authorities in Washington. Fortunately, it was turned down, for the effect of a silver eagle upon a youth still under twenty-one would have been disastrous.

My activities in the Harvard Regiment came to the attention of Professor Archibald Cary Coolidge, an expert on Russia and the Near East, who had been invited by Herbert Hoover, along with a Catholic prelate and a well-known engineer, to serve on the first American mission to the Soviet Union. When Coolidge asked me to accompany him as his aide, I accepted with enthusiasm, bought my equipment for the trip and practiced up on revolver shooting. We were to set off on a Monday, but on the preceding Sunday I received a telegram from the President's office calling off the mission on account of chaotic conditions in Russia—this was only a few months after Lenin had seized power in 1917. I was sadly disappointed and abandoned any idea of entering our Foreign Service.

At the U.S. officers training camp in Louisville, Kentucky, I chose artillery rather than infantry since I had already received infantry training at Harvard. It was stiflingly hot in Louisville and we had to dogtrot between classes, a torture that, nevertheless, put us into fine physical condition. Discipline was extremely strict, but we'd be let off on Saturday;

with a couple of equally lost and forlorn buddies, I wandered about the streets. One night we ended up in bed above a poolroom and were devoured by giant bedbugs. In the morning, feeling battered and walking unsteadily as if from a monumental binge, I was surprised and delighted to run into my friend Margaret ("M.P.") Luce of St. Moritz days. She was looking extremely smart and invited me to her father's fine plantation. There I had a great time riding with her on thoroughbreds over beautiful Kentucky grasslands.

The camp routine was hard—every shred of our individuality was suppressed—and we were happy when the three months' training period was over. We were a tired-looking lot as we entrained for various places to take up our assignments.

In San Antonio, Texas, I was put in charge of a company of regular Army cavalrymen with the assignment of training them to become artillerymen. Although I could ride tolerably, I was unable to sit a trot and must have struck those hardened soldiers, some of them Philippine veterans, as utterly unfit for command. The only thing I could do was to throw myself upon their mercies and kid them; this worked and we got on.

After a few weeks we entrained for Camp Kearney, California, near San Diego; I was posted to Battery A, 48th Field Artillery. It was a pleasant place; on weekends my two superior officers and I would set off for Coronado Beach and dance happily with the admiral's pretty daughters to the tune of "There are smiles that make us happy, there are smiles that make us blue."

In every battalion, as in any group of people, there is apt to be approximately the same proportion of bright individuals, of lazy ones, of clowns, of ambitious men, of athletes and of bad actors—and their opposites. It's remarkable how constant are these ratios.

One sunny morning the General commanding the division inspected our regiment; he asked endless questions about minute parts of the harness and the anatomy of the horse. Being a conscientious young man—I still didn't inhale cigarette smoke, in obedience to Mother's command—I'd memorized the artillery manual and so knew all the answers, but my buddies, many of them old cavalry types, did not. The General was furious and ordered all present to learn their manual at once; in addition, he insisted that the officers in the regiment, from majors down, take instruction from me in equitation. Accordingly, they had to submit to the indignity of taking orders from a green shavetail. Five hundred unbroken, wild horses from the prairies were assigned to me for training, and I had to see that they were properly fed and nursed when they were ailing. The artillery manual didn't help me here, although I did learn from the opening sentence of that holy writ that "Horses are nervous animals."

At last we got orders to proceed to Vladivostok to fight with the Czechs and White Russians against the Bolsheviks; we were about to sail when the Armistice was announced. Shortly before, the Germans, in a last desperate spring offensive, had broken through the Western front, defeating General Hubert Gough's Fifth Army, and, opening up a big gap in the line, had gained about thirty miles in a couple of days—as against the few hundred yards won by the British and French at the cost of over a million casualties in the First Battle of the Somme. Things looked grim. This was the Kaiser's last gasp, similar to the Nazi attack on Bastogne in World War II. Another disturbing event that year was the outbreak of a "flu" epidemic which swept the world and killed many civilians as well as soldiers.

We never reached the transports; orders were canceled and we were returned in due course to civilian life. Our war was over, and in a few months we were demobilized. Until the Armistice I'd never had any trouble with my battery, but thereafter the men were hard to control; everyone wanted to return home, as in all our wars. The disintegration of the armed forces was rapid, and a year after the end of the fighting our Army was almost totally demobilized.

Dead Man Revived—
Last Days at Harvard

I returned to Harvard for my senior year, which passed quickly. That year we would occasionally go to New York and spend an evening on Broadway. On one of these outings I was accompanied by my friend Freddie Stagg, a strikingly handsome ladies' man who didn't downgrade his power to attract the opposite sex. As several good-looking girls walked past, I made a bet of $100 with Stagg that he would be unable to pick up one of these strollers within ten minutes; he laughed scornfully at my wager and advised me that the operation would take only a moment. Well, he *was* extraordinarily good-looking, with piercing eyes and black, glistening hair, but, as we covered block after block, nothing happened and the girls repeatedly turned him down. Finally, time was up and he had to hand over the $100; New York was quite a moral place in the post–World War I period.

I knew another character, Dick Ames, the equal of Stagg in charm. When still a freshman he would go to the *Ziegfeld Follies* in Boston and, in a top hat, meet the chorus girls at the stage door. One of them, Marion Davies, later to become William Randolph Hearst's mistress for many years, was his constant companion; I envied Ames's sophistication and aplomb. Sometimes I'd put on a top hat myself and wait, like Ames, at the stage entrance—but without result.

We Harvard lads would be invited to dances by engraved invitation, which we would answer or not, according to our mood. We considered it a great favor to the hostesses to show up. Mr. Otto Kahn gave a party for his beautiful debutante daughter, Maude, ordering a special train to New York for us spoilt collegians. I decided that the trip was not worth the trouble—an error, for splendid favors were given at the ball: gold knives for the men, Cartier vanity cases for the girls. Besides, there was extraordinary entertainment: Caruso sang and Pavlova danced.

Jerry Preston and I were having drinks one evening at the Meadow Club in Southampton, Long Island. As the hour approached midnight, the barman reminded us that we were about to enjoy our last Scotch; the Prohibition law was to go into effect at 12 o'clock. Consternation! We, who had been such good friends, concluded that our intimacy was ended, for what would we have to say to one another without liquor? Distressed, we left the bar for the house on the dunes where we were staying. We spent a restless night. In the morning, as we struggled up with dry throats and bloodshot eyes, we heard a loud rap on the door. A smooth fellow, nattily dressed in a black silk suit with shirt to match and a white tie, entered the room and asked, "Don't you boys want a drink?" Didn't we! He was a bootlegger—a brand-new breed—and, without much ado, he produced several cases of liquor so that by lunchtime we'd recovered our spirits, and then some. Thus we kept our precious friendship, firmly based on Scotch whisky. After all, alcohol provides a fairly reliable peephole upon men.

On Commencement Day we had a party. The next morning we awoke in Claverly Hall near the Harvard Yard on the so-called Gold Coast, feeling dusty. My friends got up with some difficulty but soon were cheerfully performing their morning ablutions. However, one of them—George Parker—remained prone on the floor, his face white as chalk. In alarm, we called a doctor, who arrived with the standard black satchel. Things looked bad, for Parker had apparently stopped breathing; the doctor, bewildered, looked into his bag and drew from it a pair of forceps. With these he reached deep down into the patient's throat and, lo and behold, out came a large Havana cigar. Soon, the patient breathed once more and, before long, was capering about the room looking for a morning eye-opener.

After graduation from Harvard I was ready to start real living; the next move was to Newport, where Mother had rented a house. Life was gay there, although the old Newport hands complained that the great days were over. Nearly every evening there was a formal dinner and a lavish ball in spite of the forebodings of the plush hostesses in their marble "cottages." Newport was finished, they wailed.

I continued to lead the life of Riley and ended the summer a fat, jolly ne'er-do-well. Mother was worried, I think, but not a care creased my youthful brow.

II
UP AND DOWN
AND AROUND

"I Can Resist Everything
Except Temptation"

My next project was to enter Oxford; of this idea my mother
disapproved, thinking, with reason, that I was likely to become an idler. But I persisted and, having inherited an annual
income of about $3,000, at the age of twenty-one, did what I
chose. On many matters Mother and I didn't agree; our
values were different, yet she was generous enough to understand my point of view.

I had reached the conclusion that I was designed to be a
workhorse, not a loafer—that I would, indeed, tend to over-
concentrate in some particular field, rather than the reverse.
Accordingly, it seemed to me wise to attend Oxford for a year
and then go around the world.

My stepfather recommended the Cavendish Hotel in London, an establishment erratically run by the famous Rosa
Lewis, cook for Edward VII and mistress of Lord Ribblesdale.
Rosa, a woman then in her fifties, gave me and my two friends,
who were also headed for Oxford, a lively welcome, ordering
champagne for us and her many guests. In a trice we three
Americans, Jerry Preston, Tuffy Pyne and I, felt completely at
home and were having a fine time.

As we stood at the bar before dinner, a cable was handed
to me—from Frank Gray Griswold; it was terse: "Beware of
London sirens. Papa." The company crowded around to help
me read the message and a mighty shout nearly shattered the

windows; my new-found friends became helpless with hysterical laughter. One of them, Euphemia Lamb, Augustus John's model and mistress, was particularly amused and promptly took me to her bedroom.

At the end of a few days at the Cavendish we three innocents abroad were each handed a bill for two hundred pounds. We had been treating the mob, including Rosa and her butler, to champagne morning, noon and night. We slunk away, pockets empty, but it's only fair to record that never again—over many years of frequenting her hotel—did we have to pay Rosa another shilling.

On my first evening in Oxford I strolled through the dark, damp streets, feeling depressed; there seemed to me little gaiety here, little song and laughter, in contrast to Harvard. The next day I encountered a Britisher who courteously invited me to his "digs" and offered me a glass of sherry; I thought that I'd made a friend. Shortly thereafter I ran into him by the Ashmolean Library; he gave me one look and turned away—a startling example of British reserve.

Oxford was cold but beautiful, and the graceful buildings enchanted me. Unfortunately, we couldn't get rooms in New College but found pleasant lodgings in Turl Street, where down the hallway lived two Englishmen and a diminutive Scotsman, Ian Wilson, who later became the custodian of the King's great stamp collection. It was Wilson who seemed to rule that roost.

He pretended to be greatly concerned that I acquire at Oxford what he called "pōrlish" but, after a while, gave up the hopeless task of turning me into a suave, sophisticated type. Nevertheless, Oxford toned down my ebullience—no one can live in that ancient, mellowed place without its having some effect. What I learned at Oxford, in particular, was to read—from the best in classical and modern literature.

The other occupants of the Turl Street rooms, down the hall, were Adrian Holman and a tall, languid fellow, a war veteran, rather Edwardian in appearance. His name was Anthony Eden, of whom I have grown very fond over the years. When I asked him what courses he was taking at Oxford, he replied that he was doing a bit of reading in Oriental languages. This struck me as a casual kind of education; at Harvard we were required to take sixteen courses in order to graduate. I failed to realize, at the time, that the study of Oriental languages meant that the student was required to learn about the cultural and historical development of the nations of the East as well as mastering their languages.

Anthony Eden often spoke at the many undergraduate debating societies which have traditionally been a training ground for future Prime Ministers; in preparing their papers for these debates, students took far more trouble than for their classroom assignments. Anthony eventually became Prime Minister; he still appears rather languid in manner but, obviously, has great hidden reserves of energy and ambition. Eden's Waterloo came with Suez in 1956. He was very ill at the time and left England for Panama, where he wrote me in reply to a letter I'd sent him after the debacle. He mentioned certain mistakes he'd made over the years but said he was sure he'd been right in this instance—Suez! Maybe he was, in the long run.

On another occasion, some years later, Eden made a shrewd observation to me: "If I had to deal with the Vietnam tangle, I would summon Joseph Stalin from his grave to help me negotiate, for he was the cleverest bargainer of us all."

My tutor at New College was Ernest Barker, an eminent teacher in modern history, a course ending at 1815; beyond that events were considered contemporary. Barker was sympathetic and highly intelligent, but he never sharpened his wit at the expense of his students as did Laski, nor did he assume knowledge which they didn't possess. Every week each of us— a group of about six—would read a paper; mine were clumsily written, and, in contrast, I was struck by the grace of style of the essays by my English fellow students. A graduate of Harvard, several years older than most of these Britishers, I was ashamed, but Barker reassured me by observing that the content of my essays showed more depth and hard work than those of the others. For preparation we studied in the Ashmolean Library, where we read source books rather than textbooks—Plato's *Republic,* Sir Henry Maine's *Ancient Law,* Machiavelli's *Prince* and the like.

We attended lectures as we pleased—quite different from Harvard, where one's scholastic work was checked and one's behavior ignored. At Oxford the students' conduct was carefully watched; we were fined tuppence if we returned to our rooms after ten in the evening and fourpence after eleven. For miscreants who did not reach their lodgings by midnight the penalty was expulsion.

On the Oxford varsity "rugger" football team the captain held his arm in a sling; it had been shattered in the war. His arm still bled, but this brilliant, broken-field runner was the star of his team. Our New College eleven would sometimes play the varsity, which was coached by an elderly clergyman, an old "Blue," who would bicycle to the field from a nearby village. The first eleven was chosen after the various college teams had played one another for several weeks, the best men being selected for the varsity—an astonishingly amateurish, informal way of doing things in contrast to the professionalism of American college football.

Springtime Sap

An Australian, an Englishman and I spent the long Christmas holiday in Paris; they were congenial companions and we were as jolly as grigs. We roistered around and would entertain ourselves in the evenings, after having dined well, by sneaking up on Frenchmen as they entered one of the many pissoir kiosks, which dotted the streets in those days, and yanking their legs with our umbrella handles, once they were safely inside relieving themselves. This action would produce howls of protest from the victims and equally loud howls of laughter from the perpetrators.

The Australian picked up one of the fancy girls sitting

Lewis Cass, my great-great-grandfather

The site of the New York Public Library at Forty-second Street and Fifth Avenue was a reservoir when I was a child

Mother with Laura, Mary and me

My father, Augustus Cass Canfield

The *Sea Fox,*
the yacht my father built

Edward Steichen, Courtesy of the photographer

Mary Cass Canfield

Laura Canfield Wood

Painting by Ellen Emmet Rand

Frank Gray Griswold

Jehovah—the Reverend Endicott Peabody, headmaster of Groton School

The Louis XV salon in the former Griswold house at 783 Park Avenue

The author, aged fifteen

Temples at Talifu
in the interior
of China, 1920

Cecil Beaton

Katharine Emmet Canfield

around the Café de Paris one evening and disappeared with her, not returning to our hotel rooms until the next morning. I ordered breakfast and was surprised when the Englishman refused to eat with us; he explained to me later that he'd been so shocked by our friend's behavior that he couldn't bring himself to speak to him. He added that, although as head boy of the school at Harrow, he'd had his pick of the younger ones, the idea of spending the night with a tart was more than he could stand! His homosexual reaction astounded me, but I learned something about adapting my views to the contrasting standards of various nationalities.

I enjoyed Oxford and made many friends there, but the winter had been damp and cold and I felt the need of a change. In the spring, during Easter vacation, I took a trip to Italy with an American friend from Montana—Bruce Hopper—who was studying at Oxford on an Army scholarship. Traveling through Tuscany one early spring day, the weather was so beautiful, the countryside so enticing, that I proposed we abandon ship and not return to Oxford—a wonderful place but bone-chilling. Hopper agreed that we would enjoy ourselves more in the south and perhaps get as much out of travel as from our academic courses. So, on this amiable note, we proceeded to Florence to explore with Baedeker every street, church and museum. We then retraced our steps to settle for a few months in the Latin Quarter in Paris.

At the time there were few Americans in Paris; it was just before the era of Hemingway and other famous young Americans. We lived and ate very well on a couple of dollars a day. And we not only had a good time but learned things that we would not have learned at Oxford. If this suggests that we encountered beautiful women who taught us the art of living, it was not so. We didn't.

Still intent on educating ourselves, we enrolled at the Sorbonne, where we attended rather cut-and-dried lectures on literature. We particularly wanted to learn something about art. To this end—and this is an example of my dead seriousness and painstaking thoroughness at that age—I examined every room of the vast Louvre museum. This took me three hours a day for thirty consecutive days. While some of this time was wasted, I believe that I benefited more from that exhaustive tour than from an art history course.

We made a number of artist friends, one of whom shared a room with Hopper and me in the rue Notre Dame des Champs. We had gay times and often, in the evenings, would sit in the local cafés watching the passing parade; girls would stroll by, rolling their eyes provocatively. We eyed them back but never picked them up nor spent the night with them; why, I cannot fathom!

Despite our economical living arrangements, our funds got low; we even went a little hungry sometimes. One day, pressed to do something about the situation, I strolled over to the Right Bank to the Guaranty Trust to ask about my bank balance; it was nil. As I walked out, thoughtful about this discouraging situation, a vice president stopped me and said, "By the way, we have a letter for you from the Cass Farm Company." Now I had heard of this enterprise in my youth but, since no dividends had ever been forthcoming, I'd nearly forgotten its existence, although I did recall that the Cass Farm was a swamp. The city of Detroit was to have been built on it but, alas, the early settlers chose higher land.

Suddenly I was rich; the letter contained a check for $2,000. We all went out on the town.

Summer found the family once more at St. Moritz, where I joined them. They were understandably suspicious about the turn my life had taken, thinking that I should get to work. For, in spite of the sporting tradition in my family, my mother was emphatic about my making a living, preferably in diplomacy or architecture.

At St. Moritz I was pleased to discover that the sister of one of my closest friends and classmates, Dick Emmet, was staying at one of the hotels. I had known Katharine Emmet for years, and we enjoyed each other's company; she combined grace and beauty with a quick wit. Within a couple of weeks, after some exhilarating tournament tennis in which I took part, we were in Venice floating about in a gondola in the moonlight. In

Paris, a little later, we went to a night club and, driving back to our hotel in a taxi, held hands. After this, I kissed her; at that point I felt bound to her.

Bruce Hopper and I wanted to do more traveling. We had decided on a trip around the world, and in the fall of that year, 1920, we set out. We lacked a carefully laid-out plan but were serious about the trip. Since we had only $3,000 between us we couldn't travel in luxury; nevertheless we spent money freely on books describing the countries we planned to visit. We also made a special effort to meet newspapermen, commercial attachés and consuls who could give us information about the places along our route. Perhaps I got more education from that round-the-world junket than from any other single experience of my life.

Greece disappointed me at the time, perhaps because I expected to find there the lushness and color of the West Indies; in contrast Greece seemed drab and brown in the late summer. We climbed up to Delphi, toiling up the rocky trail by mule. The prospect from the top of the mountain was wonderful and the place had magic—no buses, no swarming tourists, as today— only one small native inn, the museum and magnificent ruins. I remember an awe-inspiring double rainbow, spanning the valley and the high mountains. We stared open-mouthed at this sign from the gods and noticed a line of peasants on their donkeys plodding along the path. Not one of them turned his head.

Constantinople made a strong impression on me. As we reached the city, we were shocked to see General Wrangel's White Russians jamming the ship transports. They were refugees from the advancing Bolshevik Army—soldiers, women and children stood on the decks packed together like sardines. Most of them had not eaten for days, and I saw one poor fellow blow his brains out with a shotgun—a shocking spectacle. But even more shocking was the fact that his companions were so dulled by exposure and exhaustion that they did not even look up when they heard the shot.

Russians in better circumstances served the guests in the restaurants—princesses, counts and assorted nobles earning their living as waiters and waitresses; they were beautiful people, with gracious and elegant manners. I have been asked whether I developed strong feelings about the Russian Revolution as a result of meeting these refugees. I don't recall that I did. I was not sympathetic with the Revolution but did believe that it was not a passing phase, that the changes it was bringing about in Russia would continue for my lifetime, at least. The Russians one met in restaurants would talk—sometimes eloquently—about the experiences, often hair-raising, that they had endured, but they did not theorize about the Revolution. One had the impression of people who had enjoyed life, had cared about their estates and possessions, but were without any social sense. They were seemingly uninterested in exploring the causes of the October Revolution.

Admiral Mark Bristol, the American High Commissioner in Constantinople, was a very powerful figure in the Middle East at the time. Bruce Hopper and I asked to see him, with no introduction. Surprisingly, he gave us a couple of hours of his time and told us much about the whole area. It was an example of the kind of help and courtesy extended to us many times over during our trip.

Then, for a period of three or four weeks, Hopper and I volunteered to help the U.S. Navy in settling Wrangel's refugees; sixty thousand of them were located on a nearby island, where, with great difficulty, separated families were brought together. As a recompense for what we had done, the Navy gave us a ride in a destroyer from Constantinople to Cairo. The trip took two and a half days, as compared with the three weeks then required for passage on the regular steamer, which called at ports on the way. This was a courtesy we appreciated, as boat travel was beginning to lose its charm for us.

In Cairo we stayed at Shepheard's Hotel; it was New Year's Eve, 1920. At the bar we encountered two Oxford friends who asked us whether we could shoot; we answered yes, more or less, and so were accepted as their companions for the evening. Gradually, it dawned on us that we were with British Intelligence men assigned to eliminate certain Egyptian nationalist subversives engaged in a plot to overthrow British rule. It was at this time that the Wafd Party (an Egyptian independence movement) was engaged in an insurrection to eject the English.

We proceeded with our friends to the native quarter. Up a dark alley we saw shadows, with which we exchanged a fusillade; we then entered a deserted house and sat there in total darkness. More shadows down the street, to the right, to the left and on the rooftops; it was time to shoot our way out for, obviously, we would soon be surrounded. We made a racket like Verdun. Bullets whistled by, whining and ricocheting. We ran at remarkably high speed, and, as we reached the Shepheard's bar, dawn broke. Happy New Year.

I remember boats, boats and more boats, from Italy to Greece to Constantinople to Cairo and, following that, three long hot weeks on the Red and Arabian seas en route from Alexandria to Colombo in Ceylon. On one lap of our sea journey Hopper and I made friends with a Welsh miner who introduced us to Brooks Adams' *Law of Civilization and Decay,* one of those books written to last forever. We talked endlessly, arranging the future of mankind.

Colombo was as hot as the Red Sea, and it was a relief to reach the Himalayas at Darjeeling, a very British summer resort and an escape from the sweltering heat of the Indian plains. A short walk took us to a high point from where we could see Everest at sunrise.

We found India fascinating and contradictory, more exciting to me than any other country; in Benares we watched the burning bodies on the banks of the Ganges, black with vultures awaiting the corpses. We stared at the Monkey Temple and the sacred cows jamming the narrow streets. As one of the strolling cows looked depressed, I gave her a playful poke. This foolish act infuriated the Hindu crowd, which became menacing; Hopper and I were lucky to get away alive.

In Hyderabad we failed to meet the Nizam, which I regretted, because Harold Laski had told me that he then owned more gold than the Bank of England.

The Long Walk

After the trip to Colombo, Hopper and I became tired of long sea voyages and consulted maps to find some place where we could walk as a variation from our ocean travels. This search started amateurishly; I first thought we might walk from Calcutta into Burma but found that the area was filled with swamps and jungles and infested with tigers. Then it occurred to me that we might try crossing the Malay Peninsula, only seventy miles wide at one point. But crossing it on foot meant hacking one's way through jungles, covering only a few hundred feet a day. It was impossible to carry provisions in this area and there was no food available; so we abandoned that idea, too.

In Rangoon we did some research in the library. It looked as if we could go far up the Irrawaddy River, north of Mandalay, and from there strike across southern China from a town called Bhamo. Alternatively, we thought that we might try to navigate the upper rapids of the Yangtze River, which had never been done up to that time and, so far as I know, never has since. Or we could keep going from Bhamo in an easterly-southeasterly direction, to the city of Yünnanfu, and from there strike down to Canton. This latter trip would amount to about fifteen hundred miles.

We could find no large-scale maps. Strangely enough, our best guide proved to be Marco Polo, who made the journey to Canton from Burma in the thirteenth century; the places he mentions in his travel diaries still bear the same names.

We purchased some equipment, including rifles, because we were told that before reaching the Chinese border we'd need them to ward off tigers, which occasionally seized men along the jungle trail. We then consulted our Consul in Rangoon and asked him for some sort of document authorizing our trip. He flatly refused, saying that nobody had considered taking the journey we had in mind and that, furthermore, in southern China the routes were controlled by bandits so that we would probably be seized and held for ransom. Being young and foolish, we disregarded the Consul's advice and went on our way without any kind of *laissez-passer*.

We were joined by another American, Harold Fleischauer, whom we'd met in India. The three of us took a boat up the Irrawaddy and, at the hamlet of Bhamo, acquired an interpreter and eight mules loaded with canned goods. But the going was harder than we'd anticipated; we were in the foothills of the Himalayas and had to climb a five-thousand-foot mountain every day. And we had to traverse chasms a thousand feet deep spanned by rope bridges swaying in the wind. The countryside was beautiful; along the trail wild rhododendron bloomed in great profusion. Oddly shaped hills, dotted with ancient, abandoned temples, offered a sharp contrast to the broad valleys where tiny women in bound feet struggled to walk, ankle-deep in water, in the vast rice paddies or worked the huge crimson fields of flowering poppies.

The trails—ancient Chinese roads—were so rough that one couldn't ride a mule but had to step from paving block to paving block, which had been displaced over the centuries; it was like walking over huge cobblestones thrown up by an earthquake. Consequently, we soon got rid of the canned goods and the interpreter, whom we didn't like anyway. We proceeded with a couple of coolies and one mule, loaded down with money —pierced copper coins strung on twine. We used them to buy food—rice, greens and a chicken now and then. This diet kept us going, but during the first few days we felt hungry.

Almost every night we'd reach a small village and stay at an inn; usually, we traveled with a caravan of about twenty mules and seven or eight muleteers who were carrying goods along the ancient trade route. We'd all sleep in a large room with a mud floor; the coolies and muleteers would recline on a ledge around it while we'd lie on camp beds in the middle. Without exception the Chinese coolies smoked opium. Within a

55

few minutes the air in the unventilated room would become so thick with heavy blue smoke that one could hardly see and breathing would become difficult. After enduring this for two nights I began to smoke opium myself, two or three pipes as against the seven or eight consumed by the coolies. The effect on me was like drinking a couple of strong Scotch and sodas after a day of heavy exercise, except that it was more subtle. Instead of wanting to talk, as one is apt to under the influence of alcohol, one felt withdrawn. I enjoyed this repeated experience but have never had the slightest desire to smoke again. Opium didn't produce for me De Quincey type dreams; I probably didn't get the full effect from it because the exercise of walking had put me in excellent physical condition. The dreams don't occur until one has smoked for quite a while.

The expedition would have been even more interesting had we known the language; but unfortunately our conversation with the natives was limited to a few words, just sufficient for our elementary needs.

Once I became separated from my companions and was lost for twenty-four hours. I had no money, but in spite of that I was fed and lodged. The villagers couldn't have been more hospitable and displayed rare courtesy; I have no doubt that, had I started from the western border of China, I could have walked across the entire country without speaking the language or having any money to pay for my keep. The poorer one looked, the safer one was. The important thing was to carry no gun, as is the case in any dangerous area, for what the natives want, above all, is firearms.

The route we traveled, which has now become the Burma Road, was controlled by bandits, as the Consul had foretold. Though no arrangements had been made and we carried no official papers, the chief of each large village would provide us with an "army" of six or seven barefooted men carrying guns with cartridges that often didn't fit. They'd travel with us for ten days or so until we reached another village, where we'd acquire a new army. Our coolies, also, would leave us after two to three weeks, and no offer of money would tempt them to continue onward. For the coolies traveled the same trail as had their ancestors, and to venture further meant, in their minds, sudden death, since they believed the world to be square and that one step too far would surely cause them to fall off the edge and thus drop into infinity.

After three hundred miles, about half the distance to the city of Yünnanfu, we three good companions decided to part. Hopper and Fleischauer hankered to navigate the upper reaches of the Yangtze, but I felt that I couldn't afford the time required for this. We separated, and I went on my way alone. One of the reasons for leaving my friends, which I did with much regret, was to find out what it would be like to be alone for several weeks, to have no one to converse with. I enjoyed the solitude and, with some books, partially filled the vacuum of loneliness. Still, it was a welcome relief to encounter, in a remote village, an extremely cultivated and agreeable Catholic priest living in solitude. He spoke Chinese perfectly and, indeed, had the look of a Chinese; he was a part of the village.

The priest's conversation was stimulating; although he had not seen a white man for some twenty years, he had kept up with recent books and with what was going on in the world. We talked late into the night, and he seemed well satisfied with his missionary efforts for, in spite of the fact that he had been unable to convert any Chinese to Christianity, he had improved the health of his villagers, as well as their education. Some time later, when I reached the coast, I met some Protestant missionaries who lived with their families and hence were bound to maintain a way of life quite separate from that of the Chinese. They were good, dedicated men; yet, in contrast to my Catholic friend, they had had little impact upon their "parishioners," whom they had tried unsuccessfully to convert and from whom they seemed far removed.

I was concerned about a particular spot on my route, a mountain pass where, I had been told, bandits had recently captured and were still holding a missionary for ransom. I stopped before reaching this place, with my two coolies and my "army." We had some tea and rice and a nap. Upon awakening, I found that the soldiers had disappeared, having come to the reasonable conclusion that bandits were probably in the pass and that there might be danger. Since I paid them only the equivalent of a quarter for every ten days of duty, they probably decided that the game wasn't worth the candle. There was nothing to do except go ahead, so the coolies and I walked into the pass. Pretty soon, heads appeared behind the rocks—and rifles. We waved and shouted "Hello" in Chinese and English. After a disturbing interval, our greeting was answered; the bandits came down the hill and we all had a nice get-together. Doubtless I looked too poor to be worth robbing.

The explanation for the presence of so many bandits was the political situation in China at the time. Each province was then ruled by a local general who waged intermittent war with his neighbor; when he could pay his troops, he would; when he couldn't, his men would desert and have nothing to do except turn to banditry. Most of them were quite decent characters, but they had to live.

Once I nearly had my throat cut. I had reached a village where there was no inn and was taken in by one of the inhabitants. It was one of the many malaria spots I encountered on this journey. When I said good night to my coolies, one of them made the sign of a cross on his throat and pointed in the direction of my host. The warning kept me awake, so that when he appeared a little after midnight, holding a long carving knife which glistened in the moonlight, I was ready for him. I flashed my searchlight, sprang from my bed and hollered bloody murder. This heroic action had the desired effect. Mine host disappeared; the coolie had saved my life. The would-be murderer was taking no risk because there were no police and no way for me to communicate with the outside world. My body, stripped of the money belt I wore around my waist, would have lain forgotten and unnoticed.

I was lucky to get through this trek in good health, luckier than Hopper. He and Fleischauer did not succeed in navigating the upper Yangtze River, but they had many hair-raising experiences attempting to get through the most dangerous rapids. As a result of this two-thousand-mile expedition Hopper spent a year in bed from exhaustion.

One evening I reached a town of about 100,000; the inhabitants, who had probably never seen a white man, turned out en masse. I felt like Woodrow Wilson entering Paris in triumph after the 1914 War. A delicious dinner was served to me by the smiling proprietor of a local restaurant—the last word in refinement—except that, when I stretched my legs under the table, they met something soft and warm—it was a huge sow! My shock at this unexpected contact was somewhat cushioned when I was presented, with the proprietor's compliments, with green mint in a beautiful, tiny jade cup.

Yünnanfu, a railway head, was my last stop; after that I floated down the West River in a sampan to Canton. In Yünnanfu, a sizable city under French influence at the time, I was greeted like a king on my arrival by both the French colony and the Chinese officials, but with some suspicion. Nobody would believe that I could have been fool enough to walk six hundred miles from Burma over rough, mountainous country—a fifty-day trek—without some strong motive, such as looking for minerals. Still, they gave me a fine time, and for four days I was treated to champagne with every meal.

An elaborate welcoming dinner. consisting of twelve courses, supplemented with local rice drinks, champagne and the finest French wines, was given for me by the local Chinese potentates. Although the language barrier made conversation between us impossible, we parted bosom friends.

At Canton I took a steamer for Shanghai. An attractive Australian couple joined me in the bar, and we talked and talked. I was full of my travelogue and found it a relief to converse again after many weeks of silence. After dinner my new friends, Mr. and Mrs. Bill Newcastle, asked me whether I played craps; I didn't, but assured them that I would be glad to learn. They told me it was an easy game; indeed, I found it delightful and, with beginner's luck, amassed nearly $1,000 Mex ($500 in our money at the time), but in the early morning hours my luck turned. At 4 A.M., when we quit, I was $600 Mex in the red. I explained that I couldn't pay up at the moment, but that money would be awaiting me at Shanghai. Upon arrival there we had a couple of drinks at the longest bar in the world and then proceeded to a hotel, an elaborate modern building in the heart of the bustling port. As we had hit the town on a Sunday and I couldn't go to the bank to get money, we went to the races, where I lost a bit more. Nevertheless, I was in a most expansive mood. The news of my overland trip from Burma had spread, and I enjoyed being the center of attention. Unfortunately, this was an expensive pleasure since I was expected to treat everybody to round after round of drinks. However, I just signed chits, as one did in the East, so no cash was needed.

On Monday morning, feeling rather hung over, I reached the bank as its doors were opening. The manager, a tight-lipped, meticulous little man, inquired in what denominations I wanted the $1,000 they'd received for me several weeks before. He then asked me whether I would be so kind as to wait for a few moments; I did so, feeling rich and important. The manager returned, shaking his head; the money, he explained, had been returned to New York. Because of the long delay in my arrival in Shanghai, the bank assumed that my plans had been changed. I asked for an advance, but to this the answer was a firm *No*. I couldn't see that this made any real difference to my situation; I would simply tell my Australian friends that they could feel confident about repayment in the near future. I spoke to them and all was well; we proceeded to have a few drinks together to discuss the day's plans. Then I beckoned to the drink boy for the chit; when he appeared, he explained apologetically that the manager had ordered him to accept no more chits from me.

I was now finished in Shanghai. The Australians' attitude changed by 180 degrees and my race track chums avoided me like a leper, for in the Far East nothing is more despised than a white man without ready cash. Well, I thought that certainly the hotel manager, like Hans Badrutt in St. Moritz, would give me unlimited credit, but this was not St. Moritz. The manager pointed out to me that I was traveling with only one, old, battered suitcase and that I presented an extremely unattractive credit risk. So I had the unhappy experience of being thrown out into the street, to the mingled amusement and distress of my friends who watched my undignified exit. My next call was on the American Consul, who gave me a stiff lecture: bums like me had caused altogether too much trouble in Shanghai—the place was full of them. He advised me to apply to one of the ship captains in the harbor for a job as a steward or deck hand and get home that way. This I did, but got nowhere—they took on only Oriental labor.

Unfortunately, I had but very few dollars in my pocket, and these I wished to save as long as possible since borrowing would obviously be impossible, although the Consul had made the unwelcome suggestion that he pass a hat among my racing friends. I then had a good thought—to apply for a job on the *North China Daily News*—and obtained an interview with the city editor of this excellent newspaper. I told him something of my Harvard-Oxford-Sorbonne background, which sufficiently impressed him so that he offered me a job as a reporter, provided I signed on for three years. Never have I felt more elated; I walked out of that office on air. But as I thought about the assignment, I realized that I wanted to settle down in New York —and soon. After a long hassle with myself I decided against accepting the offer, a decision I've regretted ever since. My next move was to cable the family; after that I sat and slept on a park bench, near a sign reading, "Chinese and Dogs Not Permitted." There I remained day and night for three days— waiting, waiting for an answer, with only dry bread to eat. Finally, the happy day dawned; the money arrived; I repaid the Newcastles and took the train for Peking.

Peking exceeded my expectations; the Temple of Heaven, the Empress' Palace, the Wall of China are unforgettable. In contrast, Tokyo seemed drab and black with people, but traveling upcountry in Japan was a delight. The fine, roomy trains rolled through beautiful rice fields which looked much like Japanese prints, with Fuji in the background.

Mother was happy to see me back in New York; she had worried about my unexpectedly long absence. Being of an adventurous nature, she enjoyed the story of my lengthy trip but still entertained doubts about my ever getting to work.

I did—immediately—and within a year married the beautiful Katharine Emmet, member of a famous clan, descended from the Irish patriot, Robert Emmet, who defied British rule in the early nineteenth century and died a hero. Katsy's family was warm and talented; I became devoted to them. We were married in St. Bartholomew's chapel in New York. It was a perfect wedding and the future looked rosy; we were a congenial and happy couple.

Katsy and I took an apartment on upper Park Avenue; it was small and not too attractive, but we were content and without concern about our financial future. Although we didn't have much money, we were young, and looked forward with confidence to the years ahead.

Back to the Overweight Youth

And so we get back to the overweight youth, selling bonds in the Singer Building. This undertaking of knocking on every office door was not as foolish as it may sound. My firm, Harris, Forbes & Company, had given me old lists of customers who had purchased bonds in past years, but I found that most of them had moved or were dead. Consequently, it made more sense for me to cover as much ground as possible each day; by concentrating on one building I saw many more prospects than if I had used the firm's lists.

My job at Harris, Forbes was not according to plan. Upon my return to New York I had called on George Whitney, a Morgan partner several years my senior, whom I'd known at the club at Harvard. Although he was willing to employ me, he advised against my working for J. P. Morgan & Company, pointing out that I wasn't related to any of the partners and that, unless I had superior ability, I'd better find a job elsewhere. When I told him that, at least in my own opinion, I did have some ability, he remained unconvinced, but helped me to get into Harris, Forbes & Company, one of the most solid and reputable underwriting houses in Wall Street at the time.

Having made the decision to quit the bond business after my experience in the Singer Building, I went job hunting again, with the thought of getting into the newspaper field. I wanted something more adventuresome than Wall Street seemed to offer and journalism attracted me. In the course of my search I came to the offices of the New York *Evening Post*. There I ran into a man from my Harvard Regiment days, a faculty officer named Chester Lane, who was now business manager of the paper, and through his help I was hired.

At that time the *Post* was owned by a syndicate of wealthy men under the leadership of Thomas W. Lamont of Morgan's who felt that it was important to keep the *Post* alive. They had appointed an able and energetic Harvard professor, Edwin F. Gay, a noted economist, to be the head of the paper. It was a good newspaper, but small. And that was lucky from my point of view, because I was called on to do many different kinds of work. I occasionally wrote a feature story; I worked in the production department, in the circulation department, and sold advertising. I couldn't have had better all-round training.

One day Mr. Gay called me into his office and told me that he was one of a group interested in starting a magazine of international politics because, in his opinion, there was no first-rate periodical in the field in this country. The magazine they planned to establish was the quarterly *Foreign Affairs*. Gay lent my services to Hamilton Fish Armstrong, the managing editor, and I was charged with raising $125,000 in order to launch the magazine and carry it for five years.

This was not an appetizing assignment, but I concentrated on it doggedly. Without much effort I raised half of the total from members of the board of the Council on Foreign Relations, the publishers of *Foreign Affairs*—from well-known men like George W. Wickersham, John W. Davis, Paul Warburg and Frank L. Polk, who gave me leads to their friends. Thereafter, the spring dried up and for weeks no more money came in. Then a thought occurred to me. Why not buy from an agency—for a few dollars—a list of the thousand richest Americans and appeal to them by mail? Armstrong agreed that, while this was a very long shot, there was no harm in trying.

We took considerable trouble composing a letter of solicitation and got prominent trustees of the Council to sign it. The letters were mailed on a Wednesday, and the following Monday we received some replies—one of them from Howard Heinz, pledging $5,000 a year for five years, the largest contribution to date. At the end of ten more days the entire underwriting fund was in. Our stunt had worked; the mailing had cost less than a hundred dollars. Today, of course, this would be an utterly impossible operation because money-raising has been so professionalized.

The *Foreign Affairs* assignment having been completed, I returned to the *Post* and was told to work on the *Literary Review,* the *Post's* weekly book supplement which later became the independent *Saturday Review of Literature.* It was edited by Henry Seidel Canby, Amy Loveman, William Rose Benét and Christopher Morley, a provocative and stimulating group. My job was to sell advertising, which I did rather successfully; it was in this way that I became acquainted with book publishing. Though I didn't usually see the top people in the publishing houses, I did learn something of their operations and became interested in the book industry.

At this point occurred one of those critical turning points in a man's life. I was apparently a good salesman, for the *Post* offered to put me in charge of their automobile advertising at a salary of $10,000 a year. As in Shanghai, I was torn. I realized that opportunities at that time in the advertising business were limitless. Besides, $10,000 was a tempting prospect to a young married man of twenty-five then earning only one-third of that sum. However, I finally decided that advertising would not interest me as a life's work and declined the offer.

Book publishing seemed more suited to my interests than advertising or newspaper work. I really didn't aspire to become city editor on the *Post,* although his was an absorbing—but harassing—life; and I felt that I lacked the talent to become a top-flight reporter-commentator. So I considered the possibility of acquiring a financial interest in a small-town paper, but, while that would have offered interesting possibilities in politics as well as in publishing, I wished to work in New York.

I then started looking for a job in the book business; several firms I called upon had nothing for me. But I did get an offer from a small, rather unsuccessful house on condition that I put money into the company; however, this wasn't what I wanted. It was at this point that I called on Thomas B. Wells, the editor of *Harper's Magazine* and chairman of the board of Harper & Brothers. He agreed to take me on as a salesman at $3,000 a year.

The Early Harpers

The House of Harper had existed for over one hundred years; pretty old, but not in relation to the beginnings of publishing, which started under the Ptolemies. It was founded in 1817, two years after the Battle of Waterloo, when New York City boasted one hundred thousand inhabitants, fewer than Niagara Falls today. New York was then a small, bustling town which resembled a steepled and gabled Dutch village, sprouting from the Battery at the tip of Manhattan Island. Lacking the social or cultural pretensions of Boston, Philadelphia or Charleston, and despite the swine wandering along its unpaved streets, New York was destined to become the chief financial center of the nation, and its major port.

To this lively little town the four brothers Harper, born on a Long Island farm, came to start their printing and publishing enterprise. Except for their primitive printing press and bookbinding operation, the brothers' activities, conducted without benefit of typewriters or telephones, bore almost no relation to what now goes on in publishing, so the lessons to be learned today from the early years of the firm are limited. Their system of book distribution was as primitive as their production facilities.

The young Harper brothers quickly developed a thriving

business. They started in Cliff Street with a few thousand dollars' capital and made their way through character, energy and shrewdness. By the end of the 1840's they were printing approximately two million books and pamphlets a year; they had built an establishment which, with 350 employees, exceeded, in the extent of its operation, that of any American competitor. In 1853 a devastating fire destroyed their building and the four original brothers built a "showplace" in Franklin Square, the first iron-frame business structure in the city, which attracted many tourists from overseas. Even then, the firm's operations were unbelievably old-fashioned by today's standards. Nevertheless, what we now regard as primitive methods were in some ways highly effective and make publishers of the present era look slow and unadventurous. Today it usually takes seven months—almost as long as for a baby to be born—from the acceptance of a manuscript to placing a book on sale, whereas the early Harpers would accomplish this in twenty-four hours!

At a time when British books were not copyrightable in the United States, publishers paid as much as $7,500 to obtain a set of imported proofs ahead of their competitors. There was then, as now, pressing need for adaptation to change, and the Harpers did their share of pioneering. Along with other nineteenth-century publishers they put out paperback books, which flourished for a time and then disappeared as the result of a price war. Beginning in 1850, they also launched several magazines, of which *Harper's Magazine* alone has survived.

Leading novelists of the century, mostly British, gave luster to the Harper list: The works of Dickens, Sir Walter Scott, Thackeray, the Brontës, George Eliot, Trollope, Thomas Hardy and many others appeared in book form after serialization in one of the firm's magazines. By 1890 the *National Cyclopaedia of American Biography* could say, as it did, that "Harper and Brothers have grown to be the largest publishing house in the United States and probably in the world."

An elementary lesson in finance is that in a partnership business, as Harper's was until 1896, the interests of the partners cannot be paid off in cash when their connections with the firm are severed for one reason or another—at least not indefinitely.

Toward the end of the nineteenth century the Harpers disregarded this business axiom, feeling, no doubt, that a house of such long standing was bound to go on forever. So, mainly as a result of withdrawals of capital when the second-generation Harpers died or retired, the firm suffered from a serious cash shortage which led to its going into receivership in 1899. This would have been the end of the road had not J. Pierpont Morgan stepped in with loans to the company, making continued operation possible. These loans were finally liquidated, but the House of Harper owes a debt of gratitude to Morgan for his generous attitude and for his acting on the conviction that the end of the Harper publishing enterprise would have been a serious loss to the cultural life of the country.

I recall a nice story about the nineteenth-century Harper's. At a meeting of their board of directors, to which none but the family was admitted, the thorny question arose as to what to do about the Harper horse which operated their press. Its assignment was to walk around and around a pole—like oxen in India drawing water from a well. The horse had reached the age of retirement, and the problem confronting the august board was what future plans were to be made for it. By unanimous vote the decision was reached that the horse should be put out to pasture so that he could enjoy the rest of his days in peace.

Accordingly, Dobbin was honorably retired. He should have been happy but, instead, began to fade away. It happened quickly and something had to be done at once. The problem was presented forthwith to the Harper board; it was a puzzler. What could be done to make the horse happy? The solution was hard to find, but one of the Harpers hit upon it. Why not attach Dobbin to a pole so that he could walk around it as he had been accustomed to do when he operated the press? The plan worked, and the faithful horse put on weight, was content once more and regained his health.

Moral: Don't retire before your time; if you have spent years walking around a fixed position, you had better keep on doing it.

Mr. Morgan was a great leader and a very strong personality. During the Panic of 1907 he summoned the leading bankers of

New York to his library and invited them to put up the funds necessary to ride out the crisis. When they hesitated, Mr. Morgan locked the door and told the group that the meeting would continue until the money was forthcoming. He named a sum which he was willing to put up on behalf of Morgan & Company and then proceeded to tell each of his visitors how much he would have to produce. The meeting soon ended when all the money required had been pledged.

During the period of heavy indebtedness to the Morgan firm, Harper affairs were run by George Harvey, later to become U.S. Ambassador to England, and then by Clinton T. Brainard, head of McClure's Syndicate. No two men could have been in greater contrast: Harvey, the brilliant, erratic publisher, a showman capable of maintaining a majestic front without a cent behind it, who brought to the house all the books of Mark Twain and new works by Woodrow Wilson, William Dean Howells and Henry James; Brainard, the watchdog, who established strict financial controls and lost, in the process, such authors as Joseph Conrad and Sinclair Lewis. Neither Harvey's freewheeling nor Brainard's rigid brakes were successful, and in 1923—shortly before my joining Harper's—the firm was reorganized.

A second lesson in publishing operations: Beware of the impulsive, free-spending editorial genius. Beware, equally, of the penny pincher with little knowledge of books.

With the reorganization of the firm, it was moved from Franklin Square to the present premises at 49 East Thirty-third Street and two good publishers with long experience took over, Thomas B. Wells and Henry Hoyns. The latter was primarily a businessman. They worked well together and provided the company with a good foundation for rapid growth.

This was the situation when I was employed by Harper's in 1924. The place appealed to me; it was an old, respected firm with a fine backlist. And I was impressed by the way it had come through its recent financial difficulties. Actually, the common stock was considered by Wells and Hoyns to be practically worthless; but it looked promising to me, and I was glad, early in my apprenticeship, to acquire 200 shares. Because of my very junior position I couldn't obtain more; and I received that amount as a bonus in return for investing $10,000 in a new 8 percent preferred stock Harper's was floating. I believed then, as I do now, in having an interest in the business in which you work.

My training as a salesman for Harper's began by my being assigned to the warehouse, where I was supposed to familiarize myself with the books published by the firm. Harper's was really living on its backlist at the time. Mark Twain and Zane Grey were among the top money-makers; among other familiar authors were John Kendrick Bangs, Rex Beach, Henry James, Conan Doyle, Booth Tarkington, Henry Van Dyke, Thomas A. Janvier, Hamlin Garland, Lew Wallace of *Ben-Hur* fame, Sir Philip Gibbs, Mrs. Humphry Ward, William Dean Howells, Woodrow Wilson, Albert Bigelow Paine, Rupert Hughes, and British novelists like Compton Mackenzie, Thomas Hardy, H. G. Wells and Gilbert Parker. One cannot omit from such a list that delightful writer, Lafcadio Hearn, who made a solid niche for himself in Harper history with his magnificent letters of abuse, unprintable in his day, protesting Harper business practices:

Yokohama, Japan, 1890

HARPER'S:

I am informed of your desire to show a conciliatory disposition. Good!

Your resentment seems to be, then, wholly artificial—a mere trick to extort money. Mine, I assure you, differs from it in the same manner that I myself differ from you—in being honest. It only dies with the man.

Please to understand that your resentment has for me less than the value of a bottled fart, and your bank account less consequence than a wooden shithouse struck by lightning.

And you can now begin to comprehend that there are two varieties of resentment.

LAFCADIO HEARN

1890

HARPER'S:

Having in my last, convinced you of my sincerity, allow me to advise you that you will find it to your interest to settle your responsibilities. As for myself, you are far from having done with me yet, although I am done with you. You will have excellent reason to remember me.

Liars—and losers of mss.—employers of lying clerks and hypocritical thieving editors, and artists whose artistic ability consists in farting sixty-seven times to the minute—scaliwags, scoundrels, swindlers, sons of bitches:—

Pisspots-with-the-handle-broken-off-and-the bottom knocked out, ignoramuses with souls of slime composed of seventeen different kinds of shit.

Know by these presents there exist human beings who do not care a thimbleful of piss for "their own interests," and if it be indeed to their own interests to deal with liars, scoundrels, thieves, and sons of bitches.

Know also there exists one particular individual, whose name is at the end of these words, whom all the money of all the states of the United States of America and Mexico could not induce to contribute one line to your infernally vulgar, beastly, Godey's-Lady's-Book-Magazine—you miserable, buggerly, cowardly, boorish, brutal sons of bitches.

LAFCADIO HEARN

Though the backlist was of first importance, new and promising life came with the reorganization. The Harper Prize Novel Contest had been established in 1923 and was first won by Margaret Wilson for her novel, *The Able McLaughlins*, which subsequently won the Pulitzer Prize. Edna St. Vincent Millay had recently appeared on the list, along with Fannie Hurst and Anne Parrish. It was mainly Eugene Saxton, an editor who came from George Doran and had also been editor of *The Bookman,* who brought new blood into Harper's editorial veins.

While I was looking around, trying to get my bearings and acquire some knowledge of the firm's operations, I was lucky to get a marvelous break. Hoyns received a cable from Wells, who was then in London on a literary scouting trip, stating that a replacement was needed at once to run the small London office. He suggested that the young man, Canfield, be considered because of his Oxford background, explaining that several more seasoned candidates had declined the job. Mr. Hoyns called me into his office on a Friday afternoon in the spring of 1924 and offered me the post. When I accepted immediately, he advised me to think things over during the weekend, which I didn't need to do. Katsy and I were delighted by the prospect of a few years in London, and it was obvious that, for me, this was a great opportunity.

The London Years

Katsy and I, with our infant, Cass, Jr., set off for England, and from 1924 to 1927 I was manager of Harper's London office. In that interval our adopted son, Michael, was born.

For what it had cost us to live in a small apartment in New York we enjoyed a commodious and pleasant house on Wilton Crescent with a butler and maids. Katsy was knowledgeable in literary matters, and, besides being a woman of great beauty, she was a superb hostess. We loved being in London and were happy there; we had American friends living in England with whom we often spent weekends, and the Channel gave easy access to vacation spots on the Continent and North Africa.

The Harper office was on Albemarle Street just off Piccadilly, next to the establishment of John Murray. It was there that in the 1820's the police had to be summoned to maintain order on the day Byron's *Don Juan* was published. No motion picture first-nighters ever witnessed a bigger crush.

The Harper London business, although started before the Civil War, was insignificant. Of the half-dozen employees, Percy L. Buck, the sales manager, was easily the star performer. Not only did he do his job well; he was, besides, an amusing and bizarre character whose difficulties with the English language produced hilarious malapropisms matching those of Sam Goldwyn:

The Americans are giving phantasmal discounts on the Continent.

26th November 1924

Now, my dear Mr and Mrs Cass Canfield, we must
begin with a little candour as to my present state and
condition. I am just going away and until I go I am
absolutely drowned in urgent work which must be finished
before I go. Therefore I desire to postpone the pleasure
of meeting you until afterwards, and I hope you won't mind.
(Tommy Wells would say that this is just like me. So it is.)
I shall be delighted to make your acquaintance, and still
more delighted if I can be of any use to you.in your job of
getting hold of London.   You will find people very decent
here — on the whole.

You shall hear from me in due course.

Believe me,

Cordially yours,

Arnold Bennett

Cass Canfield Esq.

A letter from Arnold Bennett, shortly after my arrival in London as
Harper's representative.

That book has fallen into disusitude.

That jacket is too seweralienist [surrealist] for my taste.

Mrs. Buck is suffering from sequestrations of the blood.

Mrs. Buck's condition is worse because she has been lying dormant so long.

Up to the last, the obstreporist said she had a chance. [Buck was not referring to his wife.]

As for my duties, they were two: first, and most important, was the scouting activity—finding English books which we could publish successfully in the United States. The second was selling those Harper books which had not been placed with British publishers—in other words, the books of limited appeal in England. The scouting, in particular, offered real possibilities because Frederick Slater, the man who had preceded me in the job, had confined his activities to selling books and managing the small office.

Determined to break into publishing circles, I set about it with my customary persistence, much in the way I had set about selling bonds. I wrote to twenty-three individuals—publishers and agents—inviting each of them to lunch. All of them accepted, but it was not until after this long succession of luncheons that I was asked out by anyone. Such caution, or reserve, in social relationships is one of the many qualities which distinguish British from American ways. It may help to explain why, until recently, English publishers have not fraternized to the extent of their American counterparts. Odd though my approach may have been, the luncheon meetings proved fruitful, and in the course of years I developed many warm friendships with these British colleagues.

One of the most colorful personalities in the London publishing group was Victor Gollancz. The Gollancz office in Covent Garden looked like a barn—and still does. There Victor reigned supreme, shouting his orders to terrified girls who scurried about like frightened mice. Despite this, he was a lovable and stimulating man—an original character and an original publisher. The jackets of his books were all alike—heavy lettering on yellow paper; he advertised with great effect in the same space in *The Observer* Sunday after Sunday. Although his list was a varied one, his particular interest was that of representing the intelligent Left; his campaign against capital punishment was both intensive and successful. He certainly influenced public opinion, but I wonder whether this is a book publisher's function. It seems to me that his primary role should be rather that of a catalyst who provides means for the expression of any responsible viewpoint.

Gollancz wrote and edited books himself, one of which—*From Darkness to Light,* an anthology of inspirational writings—we published in this country with little success. His scouting practices were as original as everything else about him. Instead of making the usual three weeks' visit to New York each year, he would come for two months with his wife, Ruth, who helped him greatly in his publishing activities; other British publishers timed their scouting trips so as not to overlap his. He would devote a day to each American publisher whose list he admired, ferreting out every editor he could lay his hands on. In this way he'd acquire the English rights to the most promising books.

Stanley Unwin was a publisher of the old school—hard, fair and acquisitive—the author of that famous book *The Truth About Publishing*. He claimed the world as his oyster, particularly the Continent of Europe, which he was the first to exploit intensively. I admired his shrewdness and enterprise but had many run-ins with him over exclusive sales territories. After World War II Unwin persuaded the British Publishers Association to pass a ruling that in contracts with U.S. publishers and authors the British Empire and Commonwealth be defined, then and forever, as of the year 1947. I protested this arbitrary rule to the president of the Association, who admitted, with a twinkle in his eye, that had the British Empire been so defined as of the year 1776, American publishers' operations would have been confined largely to locally produced books.

In those early London days Charles Evans of Heinemann was the man with the nose for fiction; his list was remarkable. Charlie was pure editor, without much interest in business, but he had with him the very able Alexander Frere, who never lost an opportunity of telling his friends that books and authors bored him. Despite this, Frere successfully edited Somerset Maugham, Graham Greene and many other famous writers.

Another outstanding editor was Martin Secker, who could boast of such authors as Compton Mackenzie, Francis Brett Young, Frank Swinnerton and Hugh Walpole. His office, near the Thames Embankment, was minute, and I remember there only one aged gnome who supplied stock to booksellers. I don't believe that Secker bothered much about a book once it had been published; in consequence he lost many of his authors and his firm was eventually sold to Fredric Warburg and renamed Secker & Warburg. Warburg, the author of a memoir, *An Occupation for Gentlemen,* has built up a successful list of unusual distinction.

There were other notable publishers who were part of the English publishing scene in the 1920's: Allen Lane of the famous house of John Lane, publishers of *The Yellow Book* in the nineties, who earned himself a knighthood by starting the Penguin paperbacks in the mid-thirties; Walter Hutchinson, a wild man who published about a thousand books each year under a variety of imprints; Billy Collins, the supersalesman among London publishers, and a very good editor as well.

One of the leading London literary agents then was A. S. Watt, with whom my relations were difficult because of an encounter Watt had had with Clinton Brainard, the former president of the Harper firm, of whom we were not proud. Brainard had purchased all publishing rights to Captain Cook's book on the discovery of the North Pole and had paid a million dollars for the manuscript. When it became highly questionable whether Cook had ever seen the Pole, this transaction began to look dubious. Brainard solved his financial commitment by saying to Mr. Watt in his office, where a coal fire was burning, "I cannot feel bound by our contract in the circumstances." He proceeded to throw the contract into the flames and added, "And *now,* Mr. Watt, what in hell are you going to do about it?"

I believe that it was the same Mr. Watt who acted as agent for an important British journalist, A. G. Gardiner. When Mr. Gardiner approached his old-fashioned publisher, J. M. Dent, with his manuscript, Dent asked him what was the subject of the book. It was a life of Christ, the journalist explained.

Now, in those days many publishers wished to deal directly with their authors and resented an intermediary. Accordingly, the aged Mr. Dent was outraged that his author had used an agent—so much so that tears of anger and disappointment ran down his cheeks as he said: "And to think, Mr. Gardiner, that with the life of our Saviour you saw fit to employ an agent! It is more than I can bear."

British publishing has changed over the years. Although it is thriving today, one cannot but regret that the passion for mergers has left a minority of important independently owned firms, among them the indomitable André Deutsch, Collins, Unwin and George Weidenfeld—a relative newcomer to the publishing field who produces an idea for a book every minute, and whose large list is one of the most varied anywhere.

London was a gay place in those days, with many gray toppers appearing in St. James's Street. There were lots of parties, at which we invariably wore silk hats and tails; we did so even when dining out with intimate friends. I avoided the great hostesses, particularly those who collected literary lions—like Lady Colfax—because they made me feel uncomfortable. But there was abundant social life for us without them. Our circle of friends was made up largely of authors, publishers and agents; this has been a good deal the pattern ever since. The London theater was wonderful: Noel Coward electrified audiences with his plays; I still remember the impact of *The Vortex,* his first big hit. And the American-born Astaires were dancing beautifully in musical comedy.

I soon found myself becoming accustomed to British ways and manners. As George A. Dorsey, author of *Why We Behave Like Human Beings,* once said to me, "The English get on with each other without friction, without ever raising their voices." In time I was inclined to judge English books and plays from the British point of view and became overadjusted to the local scene—a habit often acquired by ambassadors, which explains why they ought to be shifted frequently from post to post.

In the pursuit of literary talent I followed a questionable formula: I made a list of prominent British authors and wrote each of them a letter of invitation to join the Harper list. Needless to say, this gambit, which was not in the gentlemanly publishing tradition, failed. Nevertheless, in time, armed with letters of introduction, I did meet many of the literary great. A number of the authors I came to know were added to the Harper list—Richard Hughes, E. M. Delafield, J. B. Priestley, Philip Guedalla, Sheila Kaye-Smith, Susan Ertz, my old acquaintance Harold Laski, Julian Green, J. B. S. Haldane, Hesketh Pearson, Julian Huxley, H. M. Tomlinson—and many of them became close friends.

Only one or two American publishers maintained London representatives at that time and the competition was far less than it is now. Moreover, the stream of books ran in the direction of the United States rather than the other way, as it does today. The trick for an editor was, obviously, to winnow out manuscripts with special appeal to the American reader. In this endeavor I was greatly helped by Katsy, whose literary judgment was excellent. The decision to accept or decline wasn't always an easy one to make, for often a book with a very local British background would be avidly read by our public, and vice versa. A case in point was Sinclair Lewis' *Main Street,* which was a wild success in England.

A valuable asset to me during the years in England was my friendship with Tom Wells, whom I admired and liked enormously. He would come to London every year for a month or so, and I found him—though he was many years older than I—a fine companion, with a warm sense of humor and a biting wit. His inquisitive, unconventional mind was in awe of nothing. Together we'd enthusiastically make the rounds of London and Paris restaurants and night life. In the succession of able editors of *Harper's Magazine,* Wells was outstanding, as was Frederick Lewis Allen. Yet Wells did have an occasional blind spot, as when a young Yale graduate came to him in the twenties seeking financial help in starting a news weekly. Wells dismissed the fellow, explaining that the chances of such a periodical in competition with the well-established *Literary Digest* were hopeless. The young man was Henry Luce, the magazine he was showing to a few prospective investors was *Time.* But every editor has a few blind spots, and Tom Wells was one of the great in his publishing era.

Knowing and working with English authors was a rewarding

experience, and I learned much then that was useful to me later. I have always admired British writers as meticulous craftsmen with an inborn sense of style and grace. H. M. Tomlinson, perhaps best known today for his classic *The Sea and the Jungle,* was a first-rate stylist. His novels were admirable, but with his poetic sense he was at his best in describing his own impressions as he traveled to far places. He told me an anecdote about the period when he worked on the *Daily Chronicle.* It was in 1909 and he had been sent to Folkestone, along with twenty or thirty reporters from other British newspapers. Their assignment was to watch for the arrival of a man who was attempting to fly an airplane from the French coast to the English. The reporters celebrated on their arrival at Folkestone, and in the early hours of the morning, after many drinks, one of them said, "It's ridiculous, our getting up at five o'clock in the morning. This Frenchman is never going to reach the British shore." So they all went to bed—with the exception of Tomlinson, who was the only one to see Blériot arrive on the first cross-Channel flight in history. He was that kind of conscientious, careful, imaginative reporter. And he was a very wise man, with an irresistible, sly sense of humor.

Seven Pink Gins:
J. B. Priestley
and Some Other Authors

J. B. Priestley, one of the cleverest men I have known, became a close friend. But the way in which I acquired his work for the Harper list was hardly proof of my editorial genius. Priestley had a young agent, an able man called A. D. Peters. Peters telephoned me one day in London, saying that a young fellow named Priestley wished a contract for a novel. I told Peters that I had read some of the author's essays and thought them extremely well written, but, being very young and therefore very sure of myself, I added that I would have to see the manuscript of his novel before making a commitment because essayists, in my opinion, were seldom good novelists. Since Peters was eager to obtain a modest advance for his client, who needed money at the time, he suggested that I come and have a drink with him and Priestley at the Rainbow Tavern on Fleet Street. As it turned out, I had several, and after seven pink gins a hundred pounds seemed like very small change indeed. So I confidently announced, "We'll take the novel." It was *Adam and Moonshine,* which did quite well. Shortly thereafter came *The Good Companions,* an international best seller and a Book-of-the-Month Club selection. So did alcohol triumph over bad judgment.

Priestley is considered by some to be the *enfant terrible* of British letters. But, while he is apt to tell reporters home truths in a thick Yorkshire accent and while he admits that he's a champion grumbler, he is the best of companions. Reporters in this country used to find him anti-American; he is not at all so, and has shown his sympathetic understanding of the United States in such books as *Midnight on the Desert.* Nevertheless, the publisher's task of shepherding him around New York and points west was sometimes tricky. On one occasion, in the late twenties, we thought we had safely navigated him through the perils of R. H. Macy's book department when Priestley, having made a good impression, exclaimed to the chief buyer, as he was departing: "You have a fine store but what a *dirrty* shop."

Many years later Priestley, having been divorced, was feeling lonely and so was ready to welcome the companionship of a pretty woman. In Mexico City, at a UNESCO cultural conference, he found himself sitting opposite Jacquetta Hawkes, an attractive lady who is also a noted archaeologist. Jack took an immediate dislike to her and, when the meeting broke up, took pains to tell her just what he thought of female bluestockings. Jacquetta answered him with spirit and they enjoyed their violent argument; so they decided to meet for cocktails the next day

Drawing by J. B. Priestley on endpaper of his novel *The Good Companions*. Priestley in the center, flanked by the author and his wife. Priestley's inscription reads, "The Good Companions in New York."

for Round 2. Time passed, and their arguments became less heated. Within months they were married and have lived happily ever after.

Very different was the attitude of Ronald McCrindle, Susan Ertz's husband, who encouraged his wife in her career as a novelist. Her first important success was *Madame Claire* and she has continued to write entertaining and perceptive fiction. Today she is one of the few authors capable of creating a sense of romance.

John Dickson Carr was one of my friends in London. A prolific author whose suspense stories are known world wide, he has kept countless people awake nights reading them. Carr wrote a fine biography of Conan Doyle, in which he tells how Doyle watched the mailmen deliver letters in Davos, Switzerland; he noticed that they traveled rapidly over the snowy landscape, standing on long sticks. Doyle put on a pair of these appliances and so discovered the joys of skiing; this was in the eighteen-nineties. He then invited a few of his friends from England to take part in this new sport and boldly prophesied that, within a generation, perhaps hundreds of people might travel to Switzerland to ski.

My friend E. M. Delafield achieved fame with her *Provincial Lady* books, two of them Book-of-the-Month choices. One of the things that struck me about this delightful lady was that if I kept her waiting for an appointment for even ten minutes I would find her busily writing. When I asked her about her writing habits and made the observation that she must surely have a room at home, probably in a separate building, where she could work without interruption from children, husband, dogs and the like, she replied, "Not at all. I write in our living room with clatter going on constantly. You see, my husband dislikes the idea of my having a career, and if he realized that I was writing professionally, he'd be extremely angry."

Shades of the Victorian past! Here was a woman, turning out book after book—and good books—*sub rosa* because she didn't wish her husband to know that she was supporting the family. Over many years, she must have earned $40,000 annually, sometimes more, from "this little hobby," as she called it.

A writer who opened many doors for me was E. V. Lucas, author of a number of attractive travel-guide books—*The Wanderer in Florence, The Wanderer in Rome* and so forth—and literary adviser to the firm of Methuen. On one occasion he gave me a dinner at the Orleans Club, which was well known for its bachelor affairs, and invited about twenty men from the various arts. I sat next to Max Beerbohm and asked him to tell me about the people at the table, since I knew only five or six of them. Beerbohm answered, "Just observe each one carefully and identify them yourself. Those who look worried and gloomy are writers; the others are painters, architects and sculptors, who work more instinctively and are not obliged to cudgel their brains so much." I did as I was told and picked out the gloomy ones; they were writers, sure enough. I've often wondered whether Beerbohm's recipe would apply in other situations.

An episode occurred during those three and a half years in London which momentarily disrupted my married life. One afternoon in 1926, the well-known Paris agent, William Aspinwall Bradley, telephoned me to say that Georges Clemenceau, the Tiger of France, had just finished an important book—a book about the struggle between Sparta and Athens, intended to show many of the aspects of the conflict between the Germans and the French in the 1914 War. It was his way, Bradley said, of expressing certain views about the war, which Clemenceau couldn't do directly. The project sounded exciting, but, unfortunately, that evening Katsy and I were giving a party for the Prince of Wales (later Edward VIII) on the occasion of the arrival of some of our American friends who knew him well. We'd invited thirty or forty people to a restaurant in Soho, the Eiffel Tower, and I didn't quite know whether I ought to abandon my wife to handle the party alone while I pursued Clemenceau. I finally decided to do so and took one of the very uncertain planes of the day to Paris, missing the dinner party.

The next morning I was ushered into the presence of Clemenceau, who really did resemble a tiger. He was an impressive, rather fearsome sort of person, and my conversational French was, alas, not very good. He told me that he had only one copy of his manuscript, that I should go downstairs to read it and then return and give him my opinion. He obviously expected a large sum for the U.S. publishing rights. Down I went to a little room in his house. I could read French perfectly well and so understood the book, but I was bored. It seemed to me that Clemenceau's manuscript was written in an ornate French style of a type that wouldn't appeal to an American audience, that his allusions to World War I were hard to grasp and rather remote. After finishing the book I was faced with the ordeal of confronting the great man. I don't remember too well what happened next—except the great relief of somehow getting out of that house without having actually said "No," and certainly not "Yes," to its publication by Harper's. The book eventually appeared in the United States but had no success with the American public. I was lucky to have avoided this publishing pitfall but will never forget the ordeal of having to stand up to this very powerful personality.

Although I reached the right decision on the Clemenceau book, I made others that I lived to regret. One mistake was to fall for a series of books called *The Broadway Travellers* which George Routledge and Sons published in London—accounts by early explorers in the Far East. The books were excellent, but they were flops in the United States. Sometimes I wonder whether they might sell if reissued today; perhaps my miscalculation was just a matter of poor timing.

Then there was the occasion of the big fish that got away. Having heard that George Bernard Shaw was thinking of making a change in his publishing arrangements with Brentano in New York, I paid him a visit. He received me briskly, indicated that he was pressed for time and proceeded to give me a long lecture on publishing, a profession he did not admire. The theory he expounded was that a publisher without his own bookstore outlet was necessarily ineffective. After a while I interrupted his discourse and attempted to argue—a fatal mistake since I doubt whether anyone ever won an argument with Shaw. He showed me out in short order, and later I discovered that a shrewder and more experienced competitor, Howard Lewis, of Dodd, Mead, had signed him up on a long-term contract.

Thomas Hardy was an appealing man. When I was taken to

his house in Dorset, he was by then old, with a rather sardonic sense of humor. I don't think he much liked seeing people, apart from a few close friends, but his wife enjoyed the social scene and would arrange to have people call. Mrs. Hardy took the initiative and assumed the burden of the conversation; her husband seemed abstracted. In his later years Hardy was embittered because one of his novels (this is hard to credit in the day of *The Naked Lunch* and *The Story of O*) was banned by Scottish booksellers for indecency. Hardy was so hurt by this that he turned wholly to poetry.

A young writer whom I found interesting was Richard Hughes; I had heard from various knowledgeable literary people that he was gifted and looked him up. In due course we published his *A High Wind in Jamaica,* which first appeared in the United States under the title of *The Innocent Voyage.* This novel has become a classic; it is an extraordinary story about the real reactions of children, as distinct from those attributed to them by adults. Hughes is a Welshman, and on visits to his house in Wales I learned how unique is that country. He introduced me to the term "sermon tasters"—people who attend an early Sunday morning sermon and then bicycle to other churches to hear other sermons, and compare them. The Welsh are indeed a very special kind of people; they speak and sing superlatively and admire eloquence beyond anything.

Hughes's house, set among beautiful sheep pastures, faces on an estuary and, as is evident from his books, he is very much part of this country, which he loves. I learned, while staying with him, that the Welsh exercise the same discrimination about their sheep meadows as do the French with their grapevines. When I commented on the quality of the lamb that was served at dinner, Hughes was pleased and pointed out that it was considerably better than the lamb from an adjoining field.

One is apt to remember a person for a particular quality; I recall Philip Guedalla for his caustic wit. Commenting upon T. E. Lawrence, of Arabian fame, who usually dressed in Arab costume, Guedalla observed that it was curious that such a shy, retiring person should invariably appear on public occasions clad in fancy dress.

Another man who sparkled was Harold Laski, the formidable lecturer in my Harvard days; he gave me many leads in London to talented young people who were writing and contributing new ideas. And there was André Maurois, whom Tom Wells and I saw when we went to Paris, a gentle person, a wise and civilized man. We obtained the right to publish his work when his former publishers refused, on grounds of economy, to use a frontispiece in one of his biographies!

Maurois combined the talent for writing simple, elegant prose with great industry and persistence. As a young man he worked in his father's wool business but soon decided that he preferred a writing career. When he approached his parents about this, he was told that he could not hope to make a decent living in the literary field. In reply, he wagered his father that within two or three years he would be earning more from his books than from working in an office. With the very successful publication of *Ariel,* his life of Shelley, he made good his boast.

At an evening party in Priestley's house I met H. G. Wells. He was a man of great vitality; not only highly intelligent but communicative as well. I asked him about his writing, whether he was overworking—he had mentioned that he was extremely tired. His eyes lit up and he replied, "You know how I become aware of that? When I'm very tired, I answer all my letters." I prodded him to find out just what he meant and he explained, "In a normal state I throw nine-tenths of them in the wastepaper basket because I have the energy to choose what I'm going to do. But when tired, I lapse into routine and blindly fulfill every obligation; I answer everything. That's the invariable sign."

Then there was Hilaire Belloc, a jolly, fat, clever man and a good companion. At lunch the first thing he'd ask for was a large beaker of beer to quench his thirst; after that he could drink his wine for the pleasure of the taste. Belloc liked his food and found the meals on British railroads execrable. He insisted, however, that the champagne served on them was the best to be found anywhere, "because it is continuously and thoroughly shaken as the trains rattle over the tracks," he explained. Belloc loved history and wrote engagingly about it—such books

WHITE HOUSE
WASHINGTON

November 14, 1941.

Dear Cass:-

     I like Gerald Johnson's book much --
and when I have finished reading it I am going
to get him to come to Washington to argue with
me about one or two estimates he makes, not of
me, but of some of my predecessors in the
Presidency! I think Gerald Johnson has done
the best possible job any contemporary could
do. In another fifty years my memory will be
in Heaven or Hell, one way or the other!

     As ever yours,

Franklin H Roosevelt

Cass Canfield, Esq.,
President, Harper & Brothers,
49 East 33rd Street,
New York, N. Y.

FDR's comments on *Roosevelt: Dictator or Democrat?* by Gerald
Johnson, published by Harper.

as *The Ifs of History* and *The Path to Rome;* he also wrote nonsense verses for children—one of the most famous being *Cautionary Tales.* But I think that his literary career suffered because he needed a considerable sum of money each year. This led him into ephemeral, journalistic writing.

Not every gifted person has genius, but J. B. S. Haldane, the scientist, undoubtedly had it. A very large man with enormous energy, he possessed a highly original mind; I remember his saying to me, "I actually get only one or two ideas each year, but if one can achieve that, one is pretty well ahead of the game and of most people in science." He was a research man and had no interest in popular writing, but when he took the train from the country to London, he'd become bored and start to scribble. These scribbles were published as books of scientific essays, which have not been surpassed for interest and grace of style.

Julian Green was the winner of one of our early Harper Prize Novel Contests; I used to see a good deal of him in Paris and of his engaging sister Anne, whom we also published, when I was on the Continent. Julian is American by birth, but utterly French in his point of view. He has always been a first-class writer, interested not only in his own literary output but also in the artistic and literary life of France. His work is as much admired there as it is in the United States. Green's fiction is usually somber, but his evocation of scenes and characters is masterly.

On visits to Paris I would call on Ludwig Lewisohn, who wrote several volumes of memoirs as well as novels. His *Expression in America* remains, in my view, one of the outstanding books of literary criticism. Lewisohn's big success was *Upstream,* an autobiographical work about the struggle of a Jewish youth which attracted wide attention.

The British General Strike, which occurred in 1926, completely tied up the nation until the white-collar class went to work and restored some of the services. I remember watching gentlemen with Eton ties acting as porters in Waterloo Station; other volunteers drove railroad engines and ran buses. I was assigned to delivering newspapers and would report daily, before dawn, at the Horse Guards Parade in London. As time passed, the situation worsened; barbed wire appeared in Hyde Park, and big guns. Winston Churchill went down to the docks in an attempt to quell the rioting. For a couple of days there were no newspapers, and that was hardest of all to bear for no one knew what was going to happen next and everyone feared the outbreak of widespread violence. Finally, a single-sheet government handout appeared—the *British Gazette*—and people breathed easier, but settlement of the issues dividing labor and the government appeared to be insoluble. The strike dragged on for a fortnight, with apparently no end in sight. Then, one day, the skies cleared; a compromise was reached and the workers returned to their jobs. It was remarkable that no bad feeling persisted between the opposing camps in view of the fact that the country had faced a possible revolution.

Much as I enjoyed England—the work there and the associations—the time came, in accordance with the agreement I had made upon taking over the London office, to find someone to take my place. Both Katsy and I were sad to leave, for our three and a half years in London had been happy ones as well as filled with interest; yet we wanted our two little boys to have an American education. With heavy hearts, we packed up and left our beautiful house on Wilton Crescent.

Tom Wells and I talked to a number of candidates to replace me and decided to employ a young man, Hamish Hamilton, three years my junior, recommended by the publisher Jonathan Cape, for whom he had worked. Hamilton is very bright, tremendously energetic, and has an exceptional "nose" for books. There are some people with a special sense of perception that can't be quite defined, who can spot the young author likely to develop and become successful—an even more valuable asset to a publisher than the ability to evaluate manuscripts. Hamilton had this gift, even then. He took on my duties in the London office and performed them extremely well. But, after a couple of years of doing this, he concluded that he wanted to be a publisher on his own. Harper's helped him to start, in 1931, the firm of Hamish Hamilton, Ltd., which is now one of the leading publishing houses in London, with a list of very high quality.

Hamilton and his captivating wife, Yvonne, are among my best friends. He's a dynamic person. A fine athlete, he used to fly out to Henley-on-Thames after work, in a plane held together with string and some rubber bands, and stroke the Thames Boat Club crew. Besides being a good publisher, Jamie Hamilton is a man of wide interests; he is, or has been, among other things, governor of the Old Vic and of the English-Speaking Union, founder and chairman of the Kathleen Ferrier Memorial Awards and member of the Royal Literary Fund.

Return to New York

We returned to New York, my stint in London having come to an end. After a considerable hunt we found an apartment and adjusted ourselves to a simpler standard of living, since our income did not permit the luxury we had enjoyed in England. In compensation, we were happy to rejoin many old friends and I was heartened by my reception at the Harper office. Having been born and brought up in New York, I felt at home again and confident; in contrast, even after three years in London I still felt myself a stranger there, although I had adjusted myself to British ways. Thus I had had to try harder than in my own country to make myself agreeable—a very useful experience for anyone.

Changes had taken place in the home office and more were to come. At the time the powers at 49 East Thirty-third Street were Tom Wells, Henry Hoyns, Eugene Saxton, the editor-in-chief of general books, and the crown prince, Douglas Parmentier.

I admired Saxton as a man and as an editor. He used to visit London once a year during my stay there and would drive me nearly mad by his tardiness; we were late for every appointment. One of the most considerate and gentle of men, nervous and sensitive, he possessed a delicately ironic sense of humor and combined a flair for publishing with an appreciation of good writing. While I had succeeded in bringing some significant British authors to Harper's, it was Saxton, more than anyone, who beefed up the Harper publishing program with important new books. Among writers he added to the list were Aldous Huxley, Glenway Wescott, Anne Parrish, John Dos Passos, Gustav Eckstein, Robert Benchley, E. B. White and James Thurber.

Gene Saxton was one of the best editors of his day. His approach to his job was deliberate; he would read a manuscript and leave it lying on his desk for weeks. Why, I'd ask him, hadn't he made a decision on it? He would reply: "I want to see whether the book sinks in, whether I remember it. Often, on first reading, I may like a manuscript quite well, but if it doesn't make a lasting impression, I turn it down." A good rule to follow.

He had some odd work habits.

In London, we dined late with Eric Pinker, a literary agent, so that I knew there was no time that night for Saxton to read a manuscript which required an immediate decision. But when, the next morning, I said that I considered the book good enough to warrant publication, that I intended to accept it, he calmly informed me that he had read it. This struck me as impossible, and when I pressed for an explanation, Gene admitted that he hadn't slept well, had taken a hot bath in the early hours of the morning and had fallen asleep in the tub. Upon awakening he'd found the water cold. This revived him and it was then that he had read the manuscript.

Eric Pinker got into trouble; he was successfully sued by E. Phillips Oppenheim for $100,000 owed to the author for royalties on his books. Pinker had "borrowed" this money and lost it gambling. He wound up in jail. When he was in the Tombs, in downtown New York, I visited him. I felt rather virtuous for making this effort but was deflated by being thoroughly frisked as I entered the prison. Conversation was stilted behind the bars; the only thing I could think of saying was that when he went to Sing Sing he'd find some agreeable companions there,

Richard Whitney and another friend, both absconders and both good friends of mine.

Pinker's disgrace ended his literary agency in New York, but J. B. Pinker & Son, one of the oldest and most respected firms in London, continued in business—it was headed up by Eric's brother, Ralph. A few months after my encounter with Pinker of Sing Sing I had lunch with Ralph at the Savoy in London. I sympathized with him about his brother's sad predicament and was comforted by Ralph Pinker's statement that the great authors he handled had stuck by his firm. We parted happily, and I pondered upon the contrast between the behavior of the two brothers. So it came as a severe shock when I read in the London *Times,* shortly after, that Ralph Pinker had landed in Wormwood Scrubs, the British counterpart of Sing Sing, convicted of absconding with a hundred thousand pounds!

Douglas Parmentier played quite a role in Harper's. Wells thought, wrongly I believe, that the firm, which then did only about two million dollars' worth of business annually (the yearly volume today is over sixty million), needed a first-class financial man as its head. So Parmentier, a young, personable and socially ambitious man from the First National Bank, who had made a reputation reorganizing movie companies, was hired in the mid-twenties and became president—a position he held until 1929. He was bright and did some useful things on the business side of our publishing operations; besides, he helped Wells modernize *Harper's Magazine,* editorially and typographically. After this creditable performance he naturally expected to play an important part in the book editorial end and on trips abroad proceeded to make publishing decisions of which Saxton and I disapproved. Matters reached a crisis when he offered to the three Sitwells, who enjoyed a special literary and social prestige in London, an annual financial guarantee over a number of years. The commitment was unrealistically large, in the opinion of Saxton, Wells and myself, considering sales of the Sitwell books at the time, and Parmentier was told that the deal must not go through. He was furious and promptly resigned. At this point Henry Hoyns became president and I was made executive vice president, though I remained active on the editorial side. Parmentier offered to sell his stock in Harper's for $80 a share—a high price considering that, a few years before, I had purchased shares at $5. However, I had never shared Wells's opinion about the low value of Harper stock and so bought the Parmentier block. I was pleased to have done so— until the crash of October, 1929.

Hoyns was the manager of the business; besides, he was a supersalesman. So far as I know, his sale of one million clothbound copies of *Ben-Hur* to Sears, Roebuck on a single trip to Chicago established a record that has never been matched. Hoyns had worked for the firm since the time one of the Harper brothers had found him shining shoes on the Staten Island ferry, had taken a fancy to the bright lad and had given him a job in the company.

He had a kindred spirit in Eddie Cullen, a wonderful, salty Irish character, the Cerberus who watched the cash. In his economies, Eddie, as treasurer, could count on being backed up by Hoyns, to whom payment to any author or printer seemed like robbing the Harper coffers. Cullen would always be at his desk at 8 A.M.; nothing could interfere with his routine. The story is told that in the great blizzard of '88 he started, as usual, for the office, but the ferry from Staten Island wasn't running so he ventured forth on the ice. All went well until the chunk on which he was standing broke off and took Cullen out to sea, to be discovered, eventually, near Sandy Hook signaling frantically. That day he reached the office more than an hour late.

Eddie's sayings were memorable:

I can't go to the party tonight; I'm on the bandwagon.

I have no objection to the AF of L, but I cannot stand those IOU's.

I don't like the directors' comments on security purchases, although I wouldn't want them to be stool pigeons.

One of the attractive things about publishing, I discovered early, is that the business and editorial ends are inseparable;

you cannot be a publisher without being very much aware of sales and of how books are made. An editor must be in close touch with the sales manager and with the promotion people.

By present standards, Harper's was a modest organization in the late twenties. The three book editors included William H. Briggs, who had been with the firm a long time, and there were three readers. We then had less than a dozen salesmen on the road; today we have two hundred. The *Magazine* was then a division of the House, and although there existed the beginnings of a college textbook department as early as 1924, it was in the fifteen years following that Harper's developed most of its departments and regained its position as a large publisher operating in many different fields.

The firm of Harper & Brothers, as I found it on my return from England, presented the kind of diversified challenge I was looking for. I was a hard worker and ambitious, and had demonstrated my interest in publishing; I possessed a certain amount of business as well as editorial sense and an ability to deal with detail. Finally—a great advantage—due to my premature baldness, I looked much older than my age. As executive vice president I had a finger in all the publishing operations of the House, including those of the *Magazine,* and I found them all great fun.

Publishing in the Twenties

Publishing in the twenties was exciting; it was a brilliant time for writers and one of rapid changes in the trade. The list of famous books of the period is striking. Theodore Dreiser was being published regularly in the years of this decade, and *An American Tragedy* came out in 1925. Willa Cather's *A Lost Lady* appeared in 1923, Fitzgerald's *The Great Gatsby* in

1925, and Edna St. Vincent Millay wrote several books of poetry in this period. In 1924 Alfred Knopf brought out the first issues of the *American Mercury,* under the editorship of H. L. Mencken and George Jean Nathan. *Crome Yellow* by Aldous Huxley bears the date of 1921; *Antic Hay* followed a couple of years later. There were also Dos Passos' *Three Soldiers* and *Manhattan Transfer* which sold 340,000 copies at the original price within twenty-four months of publication. e. e. cummings' *The Enormous Room* appeared in 1922, and Sinclair Lewis' *Main Street* in 1920.

Lytton Strachey's *Queen Victoria,* the nonfiction best seller in 1922, had been published in 1921; Hemingway's *The Sun Also Rises* appeared five years later. The decade produced an extraordinary number of distinguished authors and books.

In my publishing experience I have come to believe that if a book has quality it is recognized rather quickly by the reading public. Who could fail, for example, to spot the distinction of prose like this from an English novel, *Precious Bane,* by Mary Webb, published in 1926?* I quote from it:

For lambing time is the shepherd's trial. In the black of night, in the dead of the year, at goblin time, he must be up and about by his lonesome. With mist like a shroud on him, and frosty winds like the chill of death, and snow whispering, and a shriek on this side of the forest and a howl on that side, the shepherd must be waking, though the pleasant things of day are folded and put by, and the comforting gabble and busyness of the house and the fold are still, and the ghosts are strong, thronging in on the east wind and on the north, with none to gainsay them.

Certainly, quality counted in the twenties when the vogue for a book was apt to start in New York City, as is true today. I have found the most alert group in recognizing good new writing to be the Jewish audience. The twenties were a time of interesting developments in publishing. The new firms—Knopf;

---

* Well, I did. Mary Webb, in straitened circumstances, went from publisher to publisher trying to obtain funds in order to support herself. Jonathan Cape gave her a little money and published her book; after that the author called on me, and I, believing that a payment to Mary Webb would never be recovered, refused her. Thus we failed to publish *Precious Bane*, which did not appear in this country until two years after its publication in England.

Harcourt, Brace; Random House; Simon and Schuster; Viking Press; Boni & Liveright—were making their mark. All of them developed fine lists and, with refreshing new energy, enlivened the appearance of books and found new ways to advertise and promote them.

It was in 1926 that the Book-of-the-Month Club and the Literary Guild started operations almost simultaneously. They opened up a new market, particularly in rural areas and small towns where there were few, if any, book outlets. For many years, booksellers maintained that the book clubs were cutting into their business, but I've never agreed with that view. Harry Scherman, creator of the Book-of-the-Month Club, got his start in an advertising firm, where he conceived the idea of the Little Leather Library. These books were classics which he sold, in imitation leather, at ten cents apiece. From this venture he learned how to sell books by mail and so evolved the idea of the Book-of-the-Month Club. At about the same time, curiously enough, Harold Guinzburg, head of the Viking Press, had the same conception. I suppose that he and Scherman got it from Germany, where book clubs already existed. At all events, the two—the Literary Guild and the Book-of-the-Month Club—started almost simultaneously. One was a venture tied in with a publishing house; the other, the Book-of-the-Month Club, a separate entity.

The establishment of the book clubs marked a milestone in the sale of books because booksellers lacked both the capital and the profit potential to expand their numbers and effect efficient distribution throughout this large country. Publishers had always been concerned about retail distribution, and the book clubs solved part of the problem, although to this day the sales setup of the book industry seems primitive in comparison with that of other business products.

The booksellers objected to mail-order operations—the direct sale of books by the publishers through circulars sent by mail—as well as to those mailed by the book clubs. Today this opposition by the retail stores has lessened; most of them have found from experience that mail-order sales tend to stimulate their own sales.

The bookseller has always had a difficult time; his low margin of profit makes it difficult for him to employ competent clerks who know something about the thousands of titles they must try to sell. Yet the good bookseller loves his calling and is apt to carry on indefinitely in a difficult business. When he becomes enthusiastic about a particular book, it is extraordinary how many copies of it he can sell. And an able bookseller can transform a "bad book town" into a community that is literate and cares for books as well as buys them.

The mail-order operation is curious. A competent practitioner in this field can often estimate with surprising accuracy the returns he will receive on a sales solicitation by circular. Hence, the alert publisher takes care to find an able mail-order expert who can forecast the approximate sale of a book by mail on the basis of a test mailing in advance of publication.

For example, when Harper's planned an elaborate Encyclopedia of Science, we mailed out a circular describing its content and showing samples of its illustrative material. The result was unexpected; we mailed two different circulars, one to a selected list of prospects, the other to a quite different list. On the first circular the price of the book was given as $19.95; the second listed it at $24.95. Although we expected that our potential customers would buy fewer copies of the book at a higher price, we thought it possible that the profit margin at $24.95 might yield us a greater return than the lower one. On the contrary: *More* people ordered the encyclopedia at the higher price than at the lower one.

Mail order is indeed a strange kind of business operation. When the New York *Evening Post* was selling a set of Mark Twain through large advertisements, with an order form, or coupon, at the bottom of the page, I was consulted about the copy because Harper's controlled the publishing rights in Twain's work. Accordingly, I read the copy with care and told the representative of the *Post* that, in my opinion, the ad was excellent, with the exception of the last two paragraphs, which I could not understand. Their meaning was unclear to me.

At that point the man from the *Post,* who was a mail-order expert, said: "I meant the concluding part to be unclear because I want to give the potential buyer the impression that, if he signs the coupon, he will receive, for only a slight consideration, a magnificent set of books. If, on the other hand, the sales copy were precisely stated, he would become aware of the extent of his obligation and would be less likely to commit himself."

Another development in the twenties, less closely related to book distribution than the book clubs, was the establishment of the *Reader's Digest* in 1922. This magazine began on a very small scale in Pleasantville, New York. At first, the editors didn't pay anything for the material they reprinted, but soon they began paying at the rate of twenty-five dollars an article. Within a few months the *Digest* had twenty or so imitators, not one of which survived, to my knowledge, indicating that DeWitt and Leila Wallace had some magic which none of the editors of the competing periodicals possessed. At present the *Reader's Digest* enjoys the largest magazine circulation in the world. In addition, it operates the world's biggest book club, Condensed Books.

Inevitably, individual publishers and editors put their stamp on the house with which they are associated. To my mind, Alfred Harcourt, in his day, and Alfred McIntyre of Little, Brown & Company combined the qualities most necessary for running a publishing company. Both men had editorial as well as a business sense. Harcourt got his training as a salesman for Holt. Then, with very modest capital, he started Harcourt, Brace & Company with Donald Brace. He was a great editor. There is a story about him which stirs my admiration: The firm of Harcourt, Brace was newly established when Harcourt went to England on a scouting trip. On his return, his partner asked Harcourt whether he'd found anything of interest, to which he replied, "Nothing much. I picked up a book on economics [which didn't sound very exciting to Brace] and a historical biography which might have some promise." The first was Keynes's *Economic Consequences of the Peace* and the second, Lytton Strachey's *Queen Victoria*. And it was at about this time that Harcourt, Brace published Sinclair Lewis' *Main Street*. With these three huge sellers the firm was launched on its illustrious career.

Alfred McIntyre, whom I admired equally, was a rather

dry but striking character with a flair for figures—as nearly perfect an editor-publisher combination as anyone I've encountered; his Little, Brown list was studded with fiction stars and still is. McIntyre's rival in Boston was the urbane Henry Laughlin of Houghton Mifflin, a *bon vivant* and a connoisseur of wines. On one occasion he gave a dinner at the Somerset Club for a number of publishers, including Alfred Knopf, McIntyre and myself. Henry had taken great trouble selecting the wines and produced a sherry he admired, instead of cocktails, since Knopf disapproves of martinis before wine. Knopf tasted it and, when asked by Laughlin for his approval, opined that that particular sherry had seen its best days. The host tried again with a white Burgundy which came from a village he knew in France. Alfred said he liked that quite well, but was Henry familiar with the finer grapes on the hillside opposite? Well, Laughlin was *sure* of the Bordeaux and this, finally, suited Knopf. Indeed, he expressed a favorable opinion of it but asked, "Why in heaven's name didn't you decant a wine of this quality?"

If I've made Alfred Knopf sound querulous, I have given the wrong impression; his observations on the wines were spiced with humor. But, while Alfred is the best of companions, he's a loner where meetings and committees are concerned; he hates them. As for his taste in books, it compares favorably with his excellent taste in wines, and his list has always been widely admired.

Another fine publisher in his day was Ellery Sedgwick, editor of the *Atlantic Monthly*. Once I was in the office of the American News Company, talking to one of the hard-boiled Irish executives there. Turning to glance at someone wandering in the hallway, he muttered, "I wonder who that old bum is; he's been hanging around all day." It was none other than the Boston Brahmin, Ellery Sedgwick. Among his editorial achievements, Sedgwick published Littell's *Living Age,* a literate compendium of the best foreign opinion. It was the precursor of the *Reader's Digest* but enjoyed only a tiny fraction of the *Digest*'s enormous readership. On occasion I'd visit Mr. Sedgwick in Boston. He would answer all my questions about editorial matters, but when I asked him anything about the *Atlantic*'s circulation, he would assert that he took no interest in the magazine's business operations and knew nothing about them. Nevertheless, if I produced an inaccurate statistic, he would immediately correct me, following this with an immensely detailed summary of his business activities. Sedgwick's successor, Edward Weeks, is "a man for all seasons." Sportsman, lecturer, editor, he ran the *Atlantic* until his recent retirement from the magazine. In addition, he directed the Atlantic Monthly Press.

I only just met Horace Liveright, the most colorful of the New York publishers during the twenties, and a lone wolf. He had unusual flair; the Modern Library, later sold to Bennett Cerf, was started by him. The Boni & Liveright list was a leading one and the firm should have been successful, but, because it was ill managed, it folded prematurely. Many men who became well-known publishers worked for Liveright, including Richard Simon and Bennett Cerf. Of the two I have known Cerf better; I admire him for his good humor, his imaginative approach to books, and even for his puns. I've been Cerf's editor for several of his books and have enjoyed the experience.

While new firms were emerging in this period, some of the older ones, like Doubleday, were equally aggressive and up-to-date. Nelson Doubleday, a mail-order genius like Harry Scherman, was feeling his oats then. As a young man just out of college, he approached his uncle, F. N. Doubleday, for a job but came up against a blank wall; "Effendi" told his nephew that he'd have to prove himself to qualify for employment and mentioned that there were crates of unsalable books in the cellar, adding that, if Nelson could move them, he'd be hired. Nelson picked out an old book of etiquette and built a mail-order campaign around it; the campaign was brilliantly devised and caught the public's attention. Questions like "Do you eat olives with a fork?" were printed in large ads in the *New York Times,* whose readers cut out the coupons by the thousand. Nelson was made, and in time became president of Doubleday.

Some Happy Acquisitions

The Bridge of San Luis Rey by Thornton Wilder appeared in 1927 and received prompt critical acclaim. Some time before it had become a best seller* I made up a list of eight or ten promising young novelists and, as a matter of routine, asked my secretary to send them our announcement of the Harper Prize Novel Contest with my business card enclosed. I never expected to hear from any of them and so was quite surprised when Wilder came in to see me. He asked questions about the contest, thanked me for giving the answers and thereupon departed hurriedly. Since he had said nothing about sending us a manuscript I assumed that this was the end of the matter.

Wilder telephoned me a couple of weeks later and suggested that I look him up if I should happen, sometime, to be in the neighborhood of Lawrenceville School, near Princeton, where he was teaching. I found it difficult to hold off making the trip and, after allowing a decent interval, showed up at the school. We talked many hours. It developed that when Wilder

---

* *The Bridge of San Luis Rey* later achieved an enormous sale—an unexpected event in the book world for, as Richard H. Goldstone wrote recently in *Four Quarters,* the novel defied the trend of its time:

While *The Cabala* had been about aristocratic life in contemporary Rome, Wilder's new novel with an eighteenth-century Peruvian setting—all about love but without a love story—was as unlikely a contender for the best seller lists of 1927 as anything that boomtime America could conceive. It was the year that serious readers were buying Sinclair Lewis's *Elmer Gantry,* Dreiser's *The Financier,* and Hemingway's *Men Without Women.* That is to say, realistic-naturalistic fiction was secure in the saddle. But for reasons that have been analyzed yet never explained, Wilder's *The Bridge of San Luis Rey* sold well over a quarter of a million copies in its first year of publication. It also catapulted an obscure and astonished young author into international celebrity.

had received the Harper Prize Novel announcement, he was thinking about which publisher he would choose to issue his future work, having decided to leave Albert and Charles Boni, who had brought out *The Bridge*. In fact, he told me that he wished Harper's to handle all his work on the basis of paying him a 15 percent royalty. I was delighted but did have the sense, as well as the modicum of decency, to say to him, "Fine, but don't commit yourself indefinitely, and don't tie yourself to 15 percent. You may write plays in the future, which could become movies, and on these productions your participation should be a much higher percentage. Let us publish your next novel that's contractually free [this was *Heaven's My Destination*], with an option on another book."

In this way Harper's acquired Thornton Wilder. My continuing association with him through the years has been a source of deep satisfaction, and I was particularly proud and pleased to publish *The Eighth Day* in 1967, forty years after the appearance of *The Bridge*. Wilder is the perfect author. Though he may take many years to finish a book, he delivers it on the date he has promised. And his manuscripts are a joy—hardly a comma needs to be changed.

Reflecting on this episode early in my career as a publisher, I have no doubt that my impulse to protect Wilder's interests was also good business. For it is inadvisable to obligate an author indefinitely; in fact, often the best relationships with writers are those not based on contractual arrangements. Take the case of Aldous Huxley; we had an agreement with him, dated in the late twenties before various subsidiary rights, which did not then exist, had developed. Saxton and I both knew that Huxley didn't wish to be bothered with detailed business arrangements and we operated on that assumption. As his new books came along, we didn't alter the old contract but simply obtained his consent to interpreting the agreement in accordance with changes in publishing practices.

Dr. Arnold Gesell was another valuable acquisition for the firm. When he brought in his manuscript, a study of child behavior, he said that he realized we could not make a commercial success of such a book but that, nevertheless, he hoped we might

Dec 8, 1964

50 DEEPWOOD DRIVE
HAMDEN, CONNECTICUT 06517

Dear Cass:

Many Thanks for your letter.

Yes, it's coming on; the end is in sight.

I didn't foresee so long a work and I'm a little wonderingly amused that I've flagged so seldom — had so few and so short intervals of discouragement and doubt. My father used to wring his hands over what he feared was my "lack of perseverance."

Long sections are now coming back to me from the typist.

I still don't know how it "ends" — how the plot-lines converge and express the ideas that govern the book. Gertrude Stein used to say that you should always leave a portion "open" — don't work too close to a determined schema — if you've built correctly the material itself will dictate its culmination.

I talk of it as being long, but it won't be a long book compared to many others — merely the longest I ever ventured upon.

There's a good deal of painful matter in the book — it's about how we variously confront, endure, assimilate, evade, or accept the tragic circumstances in life, but there are some very funny passages, too. And I like to think that Cass will as much approve the one aspect as he will enjoy the other.

As I draw to its close I must remove myself from civilization again. I leave soon to spend Christmas day with an aged aunt in Florida.... then take a slow ship to Europe (Curaçao to Genoa), then soon after take another slow one back. There's nothing like a tight little, right little cabin, rocked in the cradle of the waves, to work in.

A MERRY CHRISTMAS
Happy New Year

your old friend
Thornton

A progress report on *The Eighth Day* from Thornton Wilder.

accept it provided he paid for the plates. After some discussion I agreed to accept his subsidy and to publish the book, although I felt bound to tell him that such an arrangement was an exception to our general policy. As it turned out, *The First Five Years of Life* sold in the tens of thousands and was followed by a number of other famous books by Gesell. The subsidy was returned to Gesell with grateful thanks.

An exceptional case like Gesell's provides a lesson to be heeded. I was learning that publishing is full of surprises.

It was perhaps a year after the start of my association with Saxton in New York that two gloomy-looking young men came into our office. They appeared dispirited and spoke little; one of them carried a manuscript; the other, a large portfolio of drawings. Within moments our floor was covered with the drawings, and the taller of the two men observed that nobody seemed to like them much. He asked whether Saxton and I thought they were funny. Well, they were certainly strange and we could only observe that we considered them original. This was hardly the enthusiastic reaction the artist was looking for, and at that point the sad young men departed, leaving their material. Their names were James Thurber and E. B. White.* After a second look Saxton and I caught on to the humor of the drawings and warmed to them. Upon reading the text—with delight—we accepted the book, which was titled *Is Sex Necessary?* It became an immediate best seller.

Years later, Thurber, having heard about my involvement with the planned parenthood organization, wrote me:

Planned publisherhood is not the easiest thing in the world, as you know. It's like planned parenthood—you can never tell what's going to happen between covers.

Since that meeting with White and Thurber, Harper's has published many titles by each of these authors. White's books for young people, in particular, have enjoyed unusual popularity. His *Charlotte's Web* has sold over a million clothbound

---

* The drawings littering the floor were then unknown. It was not until *Is Sex Necessary?* was published that Harold Ross used Thurber drawings in *The New Yorker*.

EDITORIAL OFFICES
OXFORD 5-1414

September 11, 1964

Dear Cass:

     The prospects for a Perennial One Man's Meat
are inviting, and Katharine has agreed to introduce
it into her perennial border with the hollyphlox
and the acrimony. Instead of a royalty of 10% of
the wholesale price less 42%, I have been turning
over in my mind the idea of a 42% royalty but
<u>without</u> cross-fertilization, less ten of the little
ones. This would be the equivalent (if my mathematics
are right) of six long ones, if they're the size I
think they are. I am accepting your offer assuming.
I mean, I can't not go along with anything that is as
exciting and challenging as this except.

                Yrs,

                        Andy

P.S. I saw Zane Grey on the street the other day. He
      looked awful.

Mr. Cass Canfield
Harper & Row
49 East 33rd Street
New York 16, New York

E. B. White's whimsical reply to a proposal for putting *One Man's Meat* into Harper's Perennial paperback line. The postscript is his way of commenting on the continued posthumous publication of Zane Grey novels.

copies. When E. B. White handed in *Stuart Little,* the precursor to *Charlotte's Web,* he told me that he had written it for his six-year-old son, but that by the time the book was finished the boy was in his teens and was reading Hemingway!

Thornton Wilder, Thurber and White were indeed happy acquisitions, and I became good friends with each of them. Wilder is a reserved man, who nevertheless likes people and enjoys the world around him. He is a born teacher; his subtle and elegantly written books usually have a moral. During World War II, I encountered him in Italy, where he was serving as a captain in the U.S. Army. It was there that Wilder may have conceived the idea for *The Ides of March,* his remarkable novel about Caesar and Cleopatra.

The late Jim Thurber was as amusing in conversation as in his writing. It was in Paris that I encountered him after a heavy night making the round of strip-tease joints. Thurber's eyesight was very poor, and he remarked on how severe a nervous strain it was for him to go to these places because he was unable to see the nude women.

E. B. White, called "Andy" after Andrew D. White, my wife's great-uncle, who was a founder of Cornell (E. B. White's college), is famous not only for his books but also for the leading role he played as a writer for *The New Yorker* magazine. His wife, Katharine, was an editor and writer there as well. His essays, like those in the book *One Man's Meat,* are comparable to Montaigne's. He lives in Maine much of the time, and his feeling for animals is most perceptive; in writing about them he endows them with human qualities so that they become the reader's friends. White's acumen in commenting on world events has not been surpassed. And his letters are a delight, as will be evident from the one reproduced here.

Prohibition and Bathtub Gin

The Roaring Twenties were what they were because of that national phenomenon, Prohibition. It was a bad time; solid citizens broke the law of the land without conscience in the name of personal freedom. Every proper man-about-town had his favorite speak-easies, his favorite bootleggers. This was the period when excellent food became common in New York; before Prohibition, people dined at indifferent hotel restaurants. It was the speak-easy that introduced good eating. And many of them were glamorous, like Jack & Charlie's, now "21," where, at the pressure of a button, the entire bar could be made to disappear, to the discomfiture of the police. One was admitted only after careful scrutiny through an iron grille and one entered with a sense of mystery and excitement. It was the era of Al Capone and the great gangsters who flourished on the huge profits from bootlegging. Defiance of the law was fashionable and the foundations were then laid for today's widespread and often openly violent attack on the social order.

I remember an evening in our New York house at this time. We were giving a party and, as usual, I got home only half an hour before eight o'clock dinner. Katsy's greeting was chilly and she reminded me that we had no liquor on hand; I told her not to worry, there was plenty of alcohol in the house which I had purchased at the corner drugstore. My first duty was to convert, using distilled water. Unfortunately, I didn't have any and time was pressing, so I turned on the tap and filled the bathtub—might as well make a quantity of gin so that by the end of the winter it would be well aged! In a few moments, with the addition of coriander and oil of juniper, I had plenty; I had only to siphon it off into gallon containers. The bathroom reeked of alcohol fumes, but that didn't bother me.

As it was still twenty minutes to eight, I thought we'd better have some liqueur; with essence of green mint I made a supply sufficient to last for years. Then, with a sigh of satisfaction—it was still ten minutes before the guests were due—I lit a match for a cigarette. That's where I made my mistake for I'd forgotten the inflammable toilet seat, which burst into a sheet of flame. The next thing I knew, I was enveloped in fire and had to scamper out of that bathroom. My hair and mustache had disappeared.

I received the guests and they commented on the excellence of the drinks, which would not have tickled the palate of my stepfather.

On "Pops" Griswold's eightieth birthday I produced for him the finest box of Havanas to be found in New York. He accepted them politely but could not refrain from saying, "But they're the wrong shape," as he returned them to me. Not long after, he died; I mourned him, for in his formal, detached way he had been a good stepfather.

On another evening Katsy and I were hosts to Count Hermann Keyserling, who was visiting America for the first time and was staying at the Ritz Tower while gathering material for a book on this country. Asked what sights he'd seen, he replied: none—he explained that he didn't need to leave his room to *know* the city and understand it. (He did, in fact, succeed in writing a penetrating book on the United States.) There was, however, one place he wanted to visit—Harlem. So we invited him and Mrs. Paul Robeson to dinner, taking care to obtain special permission for her admittance to our apartment house for, in those days, there were strict rules about allowing blacks to enter a white enclave.

Mrs. Robeson was our admirable guide for the evening. She took us to a Negro ladies' club built by Stanford White as a residence for the woman who discovered how to take the kinks out of curly hair. Keyserling was delighted with the place and, as the evening progressed, his enthusiasm mounted dangerously; the beautiful black women sitting around playing bridge fascinated him. For a while he watched them from a distance. Then, as one of them started downstairs, the tall, bearded count followed and, catching up with her, made a pass. Thereupon

Count Hermann Keyserling, nobleman of Darmstadt, Germany, was thrown out into the street on his ear.

It was a night to remember.

The Great Depression

The 1920's, as everyone knows, ended with the Great Depression, to which the publishing industry reacted in its own peculiar way. For a while, after the stock market crash in October, 1929, book sales held up surprisingly well. Publishers congratulated one another that their volume had not been substantially affected as had been that of other products, particularly luxury items. We hoped that, no matter how bad the depression might become, book sales would remain steady. However, as the slump got worse, the publishing business declined sharply. When the bottom was reached just before recovery began in 1933, book sales had dropped by at least 60 percent. And, surprisingly, they didn't really get back to predepression levels until the start of World War II. This applied, also, to the number of titles published annually.

During the depression years I was extremely busy and extremely worried; my responsibility as executive vice president of Harper's, with sales plummeting, was wearing. And at the same time I was president of the National Association of Book Publishers. In 1933 I owed several hundred thousand dollars, and my only collateral at the Corn Exchange Bank was $50,000 in miscellaneous stocks, plus my Harper holdings. Since Harper stock was then not marketable, I have always felt grateful to the Corn Exchange for not calling that loan; had they done so, I would have been a bankrupt.

The elderly president of the Corn Exchange Bank, Walter E. Frew, had told me at a dinner in September, '29, that he expected, within a few months, the worst panic in stocks this country—and the world—had ever seen. He admitted that he was old and perhaps behind the times but expressed the view that the craze for mergers at the time and the "new financial plateau," announced by Roger Babson, were madmen's dreams. I listened to Mr. Frew respectfully and then immediately forgot his warning, only to recall it all too clearly when the stock market crashed the following month.

The only reason that I still possessed $50,000 was that one bleak winter afternoon, when the Atlantic Ocean was very stormy, the S.S. *Bremen* was pitching and rolling to a point that made me seasick. So I thought it might be a good idea to walk up to the sun deck and breathe in some fresh air. On the way I passed the radio room and, just before throwing up over the rail, cabled my broker, "Sell everything." That act of seasick desperation saved what was left of my financial hide.

Prior to purchasing stock from Parmentier I owned only a few shares of Harper's. Following that purchase I committed myself to buying a substantial holding from Wells and Hoyns. Having observed what happened to Parmentier, I had declined to accept executive responsibility unless I was permitted to buy Harper common stock up to one-fifth of the then authorized issue. Since I couldn't possibly pay for that much stock, not having at my disposal anything like the $400,000 necessary for the purchase of 4,000 shares, I arranged to cover my commitments to Wells and Hoyns over a period of years.

Wells was paid off before he retired in 1931, but I couldn't meet my obligation to Hoyns. Summoning up my courage, I went to the office of this redoubtable and extremely careful man; I cast myself upon his mercy and expected the worst. Instead, he said, "Name your figure, I'll accept any price for the stock that seems fair to you." I proposed $90 a share and Hoyns immediately agreed, although my commitment to him was at a considerably higher figure.

The depression reached its low point with the closing of banks in early 1933; by that time our sales had, like those of other publishers, sunk very low. *Harper's Magazine* sales had also plummeted, but, oddly, its profits improved due to large savings in paper and production costs. In the book end we were

"Eight years we spend on this darn tomb, and all we find are some old bound copies of 'Harpers.' " *Drawing by Richard Decker; Copr.* © *1932, 1960 The New Yorker Magazine, Inc.*

This cartoon gave evidence of the durability of *Harper's Magazine,* which was started in 1850.

so hard hit that we were forced to cut salaries by 10 percent on two occasions, although we managed to avoid dismissing employees. It was at that time that I put forward a plan to move our establishment to the country and provide housing for employees who were in a position to break their leases. This would have meant communal living, with a central kitchen, dining room, etc., and would doubtless have saved everyone a lot of money. The plan was never implemented because the economic tide turned in time to avoid this drastic solution.

I remember a trifling incident during the depression. One day, on my way to New York, I noticed a cheerful-looking man standing on the Mt. Kisco station platform; this surprised me for at the time gloom prevailed. I asked him what caused this happy state of mind and he replied, "I've just sold my Park Avenue apartment." That, indeed, sounded like good news; I inquired about the price. "One dollar," he answered. Although this did not seem particularly handsome in relation to the apartment's $50,000 cost, my friend could hardly contain his joy because he no longer had to pay the annual maintenance charges.

This episode reminds me of a British stock, bearing the name of an old, established and renowned shipping line, which was selling at *minus* during the depression. That is to say, the holder of this stock was obliged to pay the purchaser $3 a share to take it off his hands. Obviously, the owner of this "security" was held liable for part of the company's debts.

Expansion

While the effects of the depression were felt for a long time, it was not a period of stagnation for Harper's. Even before the crash the firm had embarked upon new fields of publishing, and it continued to grow through the thirties.

At the time I joined the firm in 1924, our publishing activities—apart from *Harper's Magazine*—were basically confined to trade books, that is, books of general interest, adult and juvenile, sold in the bookstores. We had the beginnings of a college textbook department, but it was hardly more than a promise. In succeeding years we developed many different lines so that our list became one of the two or three most diversified in the book industry. We went on the theory of finding good editors to head the various departments and letting them alone, except for keeping a check on their sales, operating costs and profits.

We developed, so to speak, a federal system, with decentralized authority, which suited the department heads and worked well for the firm. To my knowledge, no other company has done this to the same extent, and I give much of the credit to Henry Hoyns, who ran the business operations with some help from me. Hoyns had the wisdom to know his limitations and did not feel qualified in the editorial area. So he kept his hands off and willingly let the editors make their own selection of books without establishing a committee to pass on their decisions. Hoyns was unusually able. As a boy he had had only a rudimentary school education, but his abilities and his candid self-assessment earned him the presidency of the firm; his was an Horatio Alger story.

In determining what departments to add, and in what order, we were governed by several factors. The growth potential of certain areas of publishing was a prime consideration, but it was also necessary to find the right man in each department to head his operation. We proceeded by instinct to a considerable extent as there were no general publishing figures available at that time. For instance, it was obvious to us that college text publishing was a promising field, so that was the first new department we started. In 1924 Frank S. MacGregor came to Harper's to head it up, and he successfully developed and expanded the department.

As the years passed, MacGregor's functions in the House changed and he gave less time to college publishing in order to help me with trade editorial operations, as well as with general management. His special contribution over the years as editor, and later as president, was his talent for employee relations. He was the barometer of office morale; many a time he made suggestions which improved the efficiency of the staff and gave employees a greater sense of participation in the company's affairs.

In 1925 we obtained the services of Ordway Tead, who came to us from the McGraw-Hill Book Company. He started a line of social and economic books and developed a notable list in the fields in which he was interested, such as business, educational theory and social relations. One of the most famous books he published was Gunnar Myrdal's *An American Dilemma*. Tead was, for many years, chairman of the Board of Higher Education of New York City.

It was in 1926 that juvenile books were made a separate department. Since 1939 Ursula Nordstrom has been head of Harper's junior books department; our list of children's books has been expanded under her editorship, to rank with the best anywhere.

The religious book department was also started in 1926; shortly thereafter, Eugene Exman, a fine publisher, took over. This department became a leader in its field and brought out some of the most notable books to appear under the Harper imprint—books by such authors as Harry Emerson Fosdick, Albert Schweitzer, Martin Luther King, William Ernest Hocking, Reinhold Niebuhr, Robert H. Pfeiffer, Elton Trueblood and Teilhard de Chardin.

Harper's bought the business of Paul B. Hoeber, a medical publishing company, in 1935. Hoeber had made a reputation for publishing excellent books, mostly medical monographs and expensive volumes on special subjects for the profession. Several outstanding medical journals, of which *Obstetrics and Gynecology* and the *American Journal of Pathology* are the best known, were added to the Hoeber list.

So, in spite of the depression and the ups and downs of the economy, the firm was growing like Topsy during the two decades following my employment by Harper's. While I participated in managerial as well as editorial affairs, the main credit for the firm's development belongs to Hoyns, who was backed up by his treasurer, Edward Cullen, and the latter's intelligent young assistant, Raymond Harwood—later to become president of the company. Tom Wells was always importantly in the background until his retirement, and there were many individuals, apart from department heads, who made valuable contributions.

I became president of the National Association of Book Publishers in 1932. A year before that, on Wells's retirement, I had been made president of Harper's, succeeding Hoyns, who became chairman of the board.

The National Association of Book Publishers (now called the Association of American Publishers, Inc. and recently merged with the American Educational Publishers Institute) was the trade association for trade publishers. I devoted about a quarter of my time to working for this organization. There were the regular duties to be performed and, in addition, two projects of far-reaching interest. The "Cheney Report"* had appeared not long before I assumed office; it was an impressive work written by an ex-banker and economic analyst who had been brought in by the publishers to study the book industry. In his long report Cheney examined and analyzed the distribution of books, book-buying habits, pricing, accounting methods, advertising, credit policies. It was my task to appoint committees to evaluate Cheney's findings and try to put into effect those of his recommendations which the publishers considered practical. This work took about two years, and I believe some good came of it. It was worthwhile if only because through it the publishing industry learned something about itself and became more aware of the problems to be solved. The effort to implement Cheney's recommendations led in time—some years later, in 1947—to the preparation of industry-wide figures and yearly statistics that have been an important guide to individual companies.

The other unusual project which absorbed the time of the association during my term as president was the drawing up of the NRA (National Recovery Administration) code for book

---

* *Economic Survey of the Book Industry* by O. H. Cheney, National Association of Book Publishers, 1931.

publishing. It was a complicated operation, well carried out by two men I appointed—Morgan Schuster of D. Appleton & Company, and John O'Connor, then quite a young man and, until recently, chairman of the board of Grosset & Dunlap. The adoption of the NRA code led to better trade practices and rounded out the work resulting from the "Cheney Report."

Europe in the Thirties

Unpleasant warnings came from Europe, but they were not much heeded by Americans when Katsy and I traveled to Germany in 1933, the year Hitler assumed power. We visited the great Löwenbräu beer hall in Munich; the place, filled with hundreds of people, was vibrating with excitement. A five-foot model of the first pocket battleship, the *Scharnhorst,* was about to be unveiled, and I shall never forget the insane furor of this crowd when that took place. It was delirious. As my wife and I started to leave the beer hall, we were recognized as Americans and the atmosphere became tense; we were crowded and jostled—I feared violence at any moment. We reached our car only after a considerable struggle, and three or four of the Nazi students pushed their way onto the running board, ordering us to take them to their various destinations.

Passing Hitler's headquarters one day, we noticed a smart nurse wheeling a baby in front of the Brown House. She briskly raised her right arm in the Nazi salute and, of its own accord, the baby extended its arm with the identical gesture!

Katsy, Cass, Jr., Michael and I went to the Bavarian countryside, where we stayed in a pension owned by a baroness who lived in a castle across the valley. On fine evenings we'd walk to her schloss on top of the hill; and often the little houses in the adjoining village would be illuminated with hundreds of candles and there was dancing in the streets to the gay music of a brass band. The villagers were attractive, and we were told that when a Communist Putsch had threatened some years before they had seized their ancient spears and faced machine-gun fire to defend their baroness. However, these villagers became the most frantic and cruel of all Hitler's cohorts.

From Bavaria Katsy and I went to the Soviet Union. This was not long before the Kirov assassination, which served as a pretext for the "show trials" of 1936–1938 and introduced a violent period of persecution under Stalin. The most vivid memory of that visit is a meeting in Moscow with a Mr. Tomsky, head of the Soviet State Publishing House. Tomsky, an interesting character, had been demoted on account of his liberal views from membership on the Supreme Soviet Central Committee to this position, which was, nevertheless, one of considerable power. Tomsky's knowledge of the American book trade was impressive; indeed, he knew more than I did about what was going on in U.S. publishing circles. When I asked him about Soviet writers and the degree of freedom they enjoyed, he observed that I probably had mistaken ideas on this subject and, by way of informing me, showed me around his establishment. The place was enormous, with a central passageway and cubicles on each side. Over one of the rows of cubicles, in which perhaps thirty or forty authors were working, was the sign: "FICTION WRITERS." Other rows carried signs reading: "BIOGRAPHY," "HISTORY," "POETRY," "BELLES LETTRES."

"Now I don't want you to go away with the idea that we demand uniform production from our writers," Tomsky said. "We're flexible and fully realize that a poet's output cannot equal that of a biographer. Poets are required to produce only 20,000 words a year; historians, on the other hand, 200,000; novelists, 125,000—and so on." This stable of regimented authors was an incredible sight, lined up as they were in stalls and made to write to order. The scene was to haunt me when, in 1937, Tomsky came up for trial, testified and then committed suicide.

Returning to Paris, we encountered a storm which tossed our plane like a feather in the wind. Katsy became very nervous, but I chose to assume a brave front so that when she asked whether I wasn't nervous, too, I replied laughingly, "No, not at all; why should I be?" That bit of hypocrisy reduced her to silence until we were about to land; she then quietly remarked, "Just have a look at your hands." They were blood red; I had been reading a book with a crimson binding, whose stain had come off on the palms of my hands as I'd sweated in terror.

FDR

The depression was easing in this country as Hitler and Stalin started jockeying for power in Europe. FDR, "That Man in the White House," was steering a difficult course, hated by many but trusted by more. Although my family was staunchly Republican, I believed that in the conduct of foreign affairs, since the time of Woodrow Wilson, the Democrats had been the more forward-looking party. The conviction that Democrats were on the side of the angels in domestic matters came to me later, although I was not enchanted with the party in New York City.

I didn't know FDR, although I was vaguely aware of some family connection in the past, when I had occasion to call on him in 1940 because the historian Gerald Johnson was then preparing a biographical portrait of Roosevelt. I was anxious to see the President about getting access to some of his papers. But no appointment could be made with him since he was so absorbed by the increasingly threatening international situation. Nevertheless, the morning after my arrival in Washington, the telephone rang at the Hay-Adams Hotel and a secretary advised me that, if I came right over, the President could see me for five minutes. I rushed to the White House wondering, on the way, whether FDR would take the trouble to turn on his famous charm with me, as he was reputed to do with almost anyone he met; I couldn't imagine that he would put himself out for me since I meant nothing to him in political terms.

I was shown into his study; ship models and memorabilia of various kinds were arranged on the desk. It was my impression that Mr. Roosevelt rose to greet me, but this was, of course, impossible for him because of his paralysis. Yet he appeared to rise from his chair and was certainly most cordial. "Hello, Cass," he said. "How long is it since we last met?"

This stumped me, because I'd never met him; I'd seen him, maybe twice, speaking from a platform a hundred feet away.

He continued: "Now, let's see. You're the son of Augustus Cass Canfield, aren't you?" He talked on and on, seeming to recall details as he went along. He told me that he owed more to my father than to anyone he could think of because it was he who had taught him to sail a boat—the pleasure he enjoyed above all others. As a boy, FDR had spent many days and weekends on my father's schooner. He talked for nearly an hour, mentioning many people whom I could only dimly recall from my childhood—names of my father's friends. By the end of that visit I'd learned more about my father, his outlook and entourage, than I had ever known before. It was amazing.

In the course of my visit the door was opened and Mrs. Roosevelt entered. "Oh, excuse me, Franklin, I don't mean to interrupt, but I want to remind you that Alex Woollcott is due for the weekend. He's coming to dinner Saturday night and we're all going to the theater." FDR retorted that this was exactly what he was *not* going to do, because he'd arranged to go to Shangri-La.

Mrs. Roosevelt, undaunted, pursued her point: "But, Franklin, two weeks ago you *promised* and I told Alex that you'd be there. You simply have to cancel anything else you have planned."

Answer: "Well, I'm not going."

The argument shuttled back and forth, a classic husband-and-wife interchange. Of course the lady won, and FDR finally gave in, saying, "All right, all right, I'll go to the theater."

PLEASE PASS ON THIS COPY OR DISPLAY IT

The British Gazette

Published by His Majesty's Stationery Office.

No. 7.   LONDON, WEDNESDAY, MAY 12, 1926.   ONE PENNY.

ORDER AND QUIET THROUGH THE LAND.

Growing Dissatisfaction Among The Strikers.

INCREASING NUMBERS OF MEN RETURNING TO WORK.

850 Omnibuses In The Streets Of London.

MORE AND MORE TRAINS.

OFFICIAL COMMUNIQUE.

WHITEHALL, May 11.

The situation throughout the country shows a further improvement.

The distribution of food supplies gives no cause whatever for apprehension. There have been a few reports of temporary local shortages in particular commodities, but on investigation it has been found that in the majority of these the reports are inaccurate, and in the remaining cases the necessary steps have been at once taken to make the position secure. Especially large supplies of sugar were distributed yesterday.

The situation at the ports is entirely satisfactory, and there is a growing confidence among traders as to their ability to move goods consigned to them without the direct assistance of the Government.

The distribution of petrol is proceeding more rapidly than at any previous period of the General Strike.

WORK AS USUAL.

Tour Through Agricultural Eng'and.

FOOD FOR THE TOWNS.

(By a "British Gazette" Representative.)

A dash by road through the Eastern Counties of England brings home something of the magnitude of the task which has to be faced in feeding London. All through the day the rumble of great lorries is heard in this powerful agricultural area, including the Counties of Norfolk, Suffolk, Cambridgeshire, Huntingdonshire and Essex, to feed the millions in the cities. In the evening the stream is reversed and this time the empty vehicles are radiating swiftly from London to pick up more of their precious freight, and so it goes on.

In a run from London, via Cambridge and Ely to Huntingdon, I did not see a single breakdown or lorry held up for an accident, and considering the volume of traffic this is a remarkably high standard of driving. The lorries were, without exception, handled with great skill, and their drivers were always courteous in making way for faster traffic, so that the overtaking of a group of a dozen or more of these heavy vehicles held up no traffic for the drivers of lighter or faster cars.

BUSY MARKET TOWNS.

The agricultural people of the district were carrying on their work in a normal manner, and everywhere I heard the opinion expressed that the trouble would soon be over. In

TO-DAY'S CARTOON.

By BERNARD PARTRIDGE.

UNDER WHICH FLAG?

JOHN BULL : "IF ONE OF THESE TWO FLAGS HAS GOT TO COME DOWN—AND IT WON'T BE MINE."

LEGAL ISSUE OF THE STRIKE.

Sir H. Slesser against Discussion.

THE TRADE DISPUTES ACT.

WESTMINSTER, Monday.

On the motion for the adjournment of the House of Commons, the legal aspect of the General Strike was raised.

AMONG THE MINERS.

Uneventful Days in Yorkshire.

MEN ANXIOUS TO RETURN.

No Trouble Expected.

(By a "British Gazette" Special Representative.)

I have just returned to London after a week spent in Yorkshire, the centre of the mining industry, in the West Riding of Yorkshire, the headquarters of the Yorkshire Miners' Association.

I left London hardly by the first train before the General Strike on May 1 was undertaken, and in this district; but it has been entirely uneventful.

Front page of a four-page government handout—the only "newspaper" available during the early days of the British General Strike.

I departed with the papers I wanted, the business part of the visit having taken only a few moments.

A couple of years before this interview I had written FDR on quite another matter. It was when he was pressing for reforms in the operation of the New York Stock Exchange, before the SEC was started. Richard Whitney, ex-president of the Exchange, had been convicted of fraud—a great scandal at the time. During the two or three days following his conviction I naturally expected that FDR, who was scheduled to appear on radio, would mention the Whitney affair as striking evidence that changes in Stock Exchange practices were urgently necessary. But he never referred to it. I then wrote him a letter, on plain stationery so that I would not be identified with Harper's at the White House, expressing my admiration for his not having mentioned Whitney's name in connection with his intention to effect reform in Wall Street. My duty done, I forgot about the letter and certainly expected no reply. By return post, a note came from FDR:

DEAR CASS:

Thank you so much for your letter about Richard Whitney. I do appreciate your writing me, I get few such letters.

Such punctiliousness reflected the character of the man.

John Gunther

The year 1936 was memorable on a number of counts; for one thing, it was the year we published *Inside Europe*, a book that developed over a long period of time and the first in a series that made publishing history.

It all began back in my London days. Having read *The Mirrors of Downing Street* and *Washington Merry-Go-Round*, it occurred to me that, if I could find someone to write inti-

"Isn't it about time another one of John Gunther's 'Insides' came out?" *Drawing by Helen E. Hokinson; Copr. © 1944 The New Yorker Magazine, Inc.*

mately about personalities and events in Europe, the resulting book should be useful as well as salable. Although I knew a very young man named John Gunther who had written an arresting article for *Harper's Magazine* on the Reichstag fire, I doubted whether he had the necessary experience to deal with the whole of contemporary Europe. So I set out to find H. R. Knickerbocker, then the star reporter of the day. I pursued him several months, catching up with him in the bar of the Berkeley Hotel in London.

At once Knickerbocker said, "I'm not your man, try Gunther; he's the only one I know with the brains, the brass and the gusto to write the book you want." Obviously, my next move was to locate John Gunther, which I finally succeeded in doing. He turned me down cold, explaining that he couldn't risk giving up his job as foreign correspondent of the Chicago *Daily News* in order to write a book. I couldn't blame him, but neither would I abandon what seemed to me a good idea.

Years passed. Then, one day, I called on John at the Hotel Chatham in New York. It was early in the morning and my quarry was in a bad way; he was sitting on the edge of his bed with a cold towel around his head—the personification of a man with an acute hangover. He was about to sail for Europe and my breezy entry nearly finished him.

Gunther greeted me with a limp handshake and asked what in hell I wanted—at dawn!

I replied, "That book about Europe," and he fell back on the bed.

Recovering, he said, slowly, "If—you'll—just—get—out—of —this—room—and—let—me—pack—so—I—can—catch—my—boat—at—eleven, I'll do anything you want."

Fortunately, I told him, the contract for the book was in my pocket.

"Oh, I'll sign—but," he warned, "it won't mean a thing."

He did sign and it did mean something for within a year he'd started *Inside Europe,* a remarkable book that was a landmark in its time and sold 150,000 copies in the original edition. Remarkable, too, that anyone without a research assistant could have written a volume covering such a vast canvas.

Gunther's next book was *Inside Asia*. When we discussed this volume in its initial stages, I ventured the observation that, while he'd spent several years in Europe, he'd never been farther east than Beirut, where he had stayed only a few days. He replied that he thought he could bone up on Asia—which he did. As was his habit, he read intensively before starting to write, and talked to academic experts as well as to people in Washington before going on his trip. At one point I introduced him to Nathaniel Peffer, a Columbia professor and an authority on the Far East, and, after a long lunch during which Gunther scribbled like mad on a big yellow pad, I suggested that he cancel his trip to Japan because it couldn't possibly provide him with more information than he had obtained from Peffer.

Gunther was one of the most vivid characters I have ever known, and one of the most indefatigable workers. He was helped enormously by his beautiful and intelligent wife Jane, an acute observer with a gift for factual accuracy.

I remember sitting at a café in the Piazza San Marco in Venice and noticing a lovely young woman striding toward me, followed by a tired, droopy man; they were the Gunthers. John complained bitterly at having been dragged through the Accademia picture gallery—he was done in. . . . A fortnight passed and the scene was repeated, in reverse. This time a bright-looking fellow walked briskly toward us, followed by a tired lady dragging her feet; the Gunthers again. During those two weeks they had been traveling in Yugoslavia, where John had interviewed scores of people. The explanation of the reversal in their roles was that the endless working sessions in Yugoslavia had acted on John like a shot of adrenalin, while Jane had found the experience utterly exhausting.

One of Gunther's remarkable qualities was his timing. Again and again it looked as if one of his *Inside* books would be hopelessly out-of-date by the time it was published, but there was a little alarm clock tucked away somewhere in the back of John's head which never seemed to fail him. He started *Inside Europe* just as Hitler was emerging as a dominant figure; he began *Inside Africa* when the nations of that continent were in the process of breaking away from colonization. An amazing man.

As the subtitle of this book suggests, I've had a good time; but, as in everyone's life, there have been sad periods. One of them is recent; in the spring of 1970 John Gunther died. He was a great reporter, a great friend, a great person. John always hoped for the best; he looked on the cheerful side of things and usually they turned out as he wished. It was perhaps this quality, together with his generous spirit, that made him so endearing, that attracted to him so many people. He had the gift of friendship and, beyond that, the quality of steadfastness. John Gunther never let anyone down.

The success of his many books is evidence of his ability as a writer; Raymond Swing called him the world's foremost political reporter. He was, indeed, outstanding, with a flair for the colorful phase, for vivid portraiture. Harold Nicolson, another admirer, told Gunther's London publisher, Hamish Hamilton, that *Inside Europe* had been most influential in awakening the world to the intentions of the dictators, adding that the free world was indebted to this high-minded, indomitable man of unquenchable energy.

The "Hindenburg"

In 1936 Mother needed to reach Germany by a certain date but found no available sailing to fit in with her plans. But she noticed an ad that the airship *Hindenburg* was shortly to "sail" and forthwith invited Katsy and me to join her on the trip. I exchanged glances with my wife which said, "Oh, all right, but we'll all end up at the bottom of the Atlantic."

After buying the tickets we were instructed to proceed by bus to Lakehurst, New Jersey, where the ship would take off, despite a heavy fog. Upon asking how this was possible, I was told that the airship was like a balloon and therefore rose from the ground vertically. The boarding procedure involved our being weighed, and Mother, who tipped the scales at only 125 pounds, was shocked to be told that she had to pay for overweight on account of her baggage. Although she explained to the stiff German officials that her own weight, added to that of her bags, came to less than the total poundage of other passengers who were not being charged extra, her plea was ignored. Another passenger, drunk and carrying a cigarette lighter, was stopped as he ascended the gangplank and obliged to return to the ground. After a few such delays we got on board and settled ourselves in the dining saloon. Over glasses of excellent Rhine wine Katsy and I could just see, through the big window, her brother, Bill Emmet, smiling at us through the fog. By degrees his smile faded, like the Cheshire cat's; the *Hindenburg* had begun its soundless ascent. In a few minutes we heard a slight purring—the engine had started and we were on our way. Our destination was Frankfurt, Germany. We departed on a Friday night, scheduled to arrive at journey's end in time for lunch on Monday—a leisurely flight in jet terms.

The ship was very comfortable and, for the most part, completely steady; you could fill a glass of water to the brim without its spilling. And there was no vibration. On one side of the craft was the large dining room, thirty by eighty feet, with plate-glass windows looking out to sea; on the other, a miniature promenade deck with deck chairs and space for strolling. Smoking was not permitted except in a small downstairs room lined with asbestos. In the small cabins for two—about the size of British Pullman car staterooms—there was a persuasive sign: no words, simply a picture of a lighted cigarette exploding a large balloon. So you didn't smoke in bed. The *Hindenburg* was held aloft by a number of gas balloons within its outer envelope.

The second morning out, at about 5 A.M., this normally steady ship started to pitch and roll like a big ocean liner in a heavy sea. Although I'm a sound sleeper and of a calm disposition, a combination of nervousness and curiosity made me get up and go to the dining room. It is an odd commentary on my fifty traveling companions that the only other person there was Hugo Eckener, the famous navigator who, had he so chosen, might have been President of the German Reich. (His refusal to consider this office opened the way for Corporal Adolf Hitler.) Eckener had made a number of successful crossings on the *Hindenburg* to South America, but the tricky North Atlantic passage was relatively new to him. Now he was rubbing his hands in pleasurable excitement.

"I've just returned from the control room," he said, "where it was very interesting; the ship behaved beautifully."

When I asked him what he meant by "interesting," he replied, "This is the first time in my experience that an airship has been hit by a wind from one direction on its bow and from the opposite direction on the stern. The only other case I have heard of was that of the *Akron,* a couple of years ago; she broke in two. But," he added cheerfully, "this is a very good ship."

Apart from this freak squall when the *Hindenburg* was in danger of splitting in two, our voyage was without incident. However, as I discovered from asking Eckener countless questions, so many factors were involved in making a safe flight that every successful trip was a miracle of performance.

For the ship was very tricky to handle. With a maximum speed of eighty-four miles an hour, she traveled at a cruising speed of seventy-eight miles an hour at a height of five thousand feet, so that a fifty-mile-an-hour wind on the quarter would make her go crabwise; against a gale wind she couldn't make any forward progress at all. Furthermore, the eight-hundred-foot *Hindenburg* was so light that one man could push her from side to side when she was resting on the ground. And there were only three places in the world where she could land—Buenos Aires, Lakehurst and Frankfurt—for without a specially trained crew of 150 men to grab the lowered ropes she couldn't ground safely. The United States Government, at Harold Ickes'* insistence, would not sell helium to the Nazis,

---

* Harold Ickes was then FDR's peppery Secretary of the Interior. He rightly feared that the Germans would make wartime use of their dirigibles.

so the German airships were kept aloft by hydrogen, which, though serving the purpose, is highly flammable. With the thought that these astonishing facts would interest, if not impress, my mother, I related them to her. She turned to me with a withering look and exclaimed, "I never knew, before this, that I had produced a coward for a son."

We arrived in Frankfurt in due course; the ship was pushed into the hangar by the ground crew and the passengers queued up to land. Not understanding why the line moved so slowly, I questioned an officer about the cause of the delay. He muttered something about its taking time to have papers cleared, but when this reply failed to satisfy me, he finally admitted, "You see, as each passenger disembarks, a compensatory weight must be added so that the ship won't go through the top of the hangar."

That's how delicate was the operation.

This was the *Hindenburg's* last trip east. On her next voyage, back to Lakehurst, she met her end in a violent thunderstorm as she was landing, killing half of those on board. The landing field was charged with electricity; it ascended the wet ropes which had been let down by the airship. The *Hindenburg* exploded, so the persuasive warning signs in the cabins became a grim reality.

Alexis Carrel, "The Reader's Digest" and The Rise of Modern Europe

One of the publishing innovations in the mid-thirties came from the fertile mind of DeWitt Wallace, the founder of the *Reader's Digest*. The magazine was beginning to use condensations of books when, in 1935, Harper's published an interesting volume by a scientist on the nature of man. Although intended for the general reader, it was by no means a light popularization and the advance sales of about 3,500 copies bore out Harper's feeling that the book was destined to reach an intelligent but limited audience.

With considerable misgivings we sold condensation rights in this book to the *Digest*. Hoyns, in particular, was doubtful about the deal, believing that the book's appearance in a magazine in abbreviated form would hurt sales, and he demanded a guarantee against loss. The book was Alexis Carrel's *Man, the Unknown*. Its condensation in the *Digest* appeared a month or two after publication, and immediately the work began to be talked about. Sales, which had previously been modest, took a phenomenal spurt and reached 100,000 copies in cloth.

Unquestionably, the great success of *Man, the Unknown* was due to its use in the *Digest*. Accordingly, I was amused—and silent—when Carrel told me, a few weeks after publication, that if scientists could plan and develop their programs with the scientific foresight we had demonstrated with his book, they would achieve results beyond their dreams.

I often called on Carrel at the Rockefeller Institute, and the talk would turn to various subjects. Once he showed me the artificial heart he had created with Charles Lindbergh; in Carrel's opinion Lindbergh was much more than an inspired mechanic. Had he received the proper training, Carrel believed, Lindbergh would have become one of the outstanding research scientists of his time.

As his famous book suggests, Carrel was fascinated by the occult; he told me about his clairvoyant gardener in the south of France. When Carrel would go to Marseille for the day, the man could tell him on his return home exactly where he'd been and what he'd done, minute by minute. There was no doubt in Carrel's mind that clairvoyance exists; incidentally, he believed that individuals with extrasensory perception were apt to be uneducated. What concerned him was that in spite of the fact that it had been scientifically proved that certain people have the power to read the minds of others, no significant research had been done as to the cause. To him there was no mystery about the supranatural; he felt sure that in time an explanation for it, probably electrical, would be found.

As for DeWitt Wallace, I tried without success to recompense him for having helped to make *Man, the Unknown* a success. So I ventured to suggest to him that there might be a modest sale for his magazine in England and that a British edition of it could be handled through our London office. I went on to point out to him that, with his huge subscription list, there existed a ready-made base for a successful book club. He listened attentively. Whether these ideas had already occurred to him I do not know; at all events, he carried out both of these projects himself in due course, as he had every right to do. His book club has attained a larger audience than any other, and the circulation of the *Reader's Digest* abroad has reached astronomical figures.

Over the years I have been involved with some large-scale editorial ventures; the first was The Rise of Modern Europe, launched in the mid-thirties. The idea, hatched several years before and considered rather bold at the time, was to publish a twenty-volume series on European history from medieval times to the present by American scholars, the books to be designed both for college use and for the general public. Before making a final commitment I had sought the advice of my friend and senior, Alfred Harcourt, since he was, in my opinion, the ablest publisher of his day. Harcourt prophesied that the series would be a flop because, he explained, it would fall between two stools; the volumes would prove too difficult for the general public and not sufficiently scholarly for the college market. Although I respected his opinion, knowing that he was probably right and I wrong, I went ahead anyway.

The first thing was to find a general editor who would mastermind the project and, for this assignment, I approached William L. Langer, my former professor at Harvard. He accepted my offer and has performed this onerous task brilliantly, as I knew he would. After nearly forty years, three of the twenty volumes have yet to be delivered, but to nurse an important publishing project along for more than a generation and see it develop has been one of my enduring satisfactions.

As it has turned out, Alfred Harcourt, although probably right at the time he made his prophecy, misjudged the future. The series has sold well; to date the average sale per volume is over 13,000 in the clothbound edition and 34,000 in paperback. Three factors, as I see it, account for this happy result: first, the line of demarcation between the textbook and the general, or trade, book has become progressively less rigid; second, the development of quality paperbacks has greatly increased student buying and made it possible for college stores, which in the old days sold only required textbooks, banners, ties, shirts and the like, to carry a representative stock of books; third, the education explosion has immensely increased the reading of serious books.

Years later, encouraged by the success of The Rise of Modern Europe books, we started The New American Nation Series. The two projects, together, add up to a small publishing business on their own. It would have been impossible for me to have carried this heavy editorial load without help, over decades, from my assistant, Beulah Hagen. Her contribution has been very great.

Two Novelists Who Turned to Nonfiction

Books develop in interesting ways. One in which I took particular satisfaction was *Reveille in Washington* by Margaret Leech.

I knew of Miss Leech as the author of several good novels, including *Tin Wedding*. When, one evening in the thirties, I found myself seated next to her at a dinner party, I asked her whether she had ever thought of trying her hand at nonfiction— whether she might be open to suggestions. My questions struck a sympathetic chord, and I went on to develop a theory about the writing of history. I made the point that historical books which attempt to cover too large a canvas tend to be dull; that a work dealing in detail with a short period of time is apt to be more lively. Might she consider, I asked, writing a book covering a dramatic fortnight in the life of Abraham Lincoln and describe what happened from day to day, what appeared in the press, the exchanges between Lincoln and his associates—a book that would contain the kind of lively detail that gives a reader a feel of the time? Miss Leech liked the idea and even worked on an outline, but in the end she chose, instead, to write about the Civil War as it was concerned with events and scenes in the city of Washington. She decided to limit the area of her subject rather than its time span. The result was *Reveille in Washington,* published in 1941, which sold extremely well and won a Pulitzer Prize. Another Pulitzer Prize winner by Margaret Leech was her biography of William McKinley. In order to get material for this book, the author went to Ohio to interview the ex-President's relatives; it was Mrs. Clemens E. Gunn who gave Miss Leech Mrs. McKinley's diary, telling her that she could take it away if she wished. "But this is a very precious document," Peggy Leech said to her, "and you should not let it out of your house." However, Mrs. Gunn didn't seem to care much about the diary and Miss Leech took it away with her.

She read the diary with avidity and was particularly interested in the entry on September 6, 1901, in Buffalo, New York, where the President was scheduled to make an important speech. During a reception McKinley was shot by an assassin, Leon F. Czolgosz. For days he hovered between life and death, and on September 14, 1901, he died. His wife had recorded her thoughts as the day for her husband's speech approached. An invalid of rather limited mental range, she was devoted to Mr. McKinley and always referred to him as "My darling." Finally, the great day dawned—and passed; the diary dismissed the shock and tragedy of the assassination in surprisingly few words: "Mr. McKinley was shot today. Too bad."

I believe that *Reveille in Washington* started a trend, but I may be making a dubious claim, as my stepfather perhaps did when he identified himself as the inventor of the Tuxedo.

Nevertheless, in the years that followed the publication of *Reveille,* a succession of volumes have appeared dealing with brief periods of time in limited compass—like *The Day Lincoln Was Shot, A Night to Remember, The Day Christ Died* and others. They are all books whose focus on contemporary detail brings the historical past vividly to life.

Another author who began his career as a novelist and turned to nonfiction was Louis Bromfield, whom I knew well and worked with over many years. He was an unforgettable and vital person, with a special talent for friendship. Bromfield, his wife, Mary, and their three daughters lived in Senlis, outside of Paris. My association with him dated back to my London days. On one of my business visits to New York Katsy had cabled me from Paris to say that I'd better fly over for a weekend to talk with Louis, who was looking for a new publisher following the collapse of the Cosmopolitan Book Company. The failure came as a surprise, for this company, which published *Cosmopolitan Magazine,* was well financed; it was another example of ineptitude by managers ignorant of the fundamentals of book publishing. Witness what happened to Mark Twain and other writers who have attempted to bring out their own books.

I often visited Senlis, where the Bromfields were usually surrounded by throngs of visitors. A first-rate storyteller and reporter, Louis would talk continuously whenever a group gathered around him, and he apparently listened to no one. Yet, after the guests had gone, he could tell you, almost verbatim, what every person had said and just how he or she had said it.

George Hawkins, an engaging Broadway character, was Bromfield's oldest friend and confidant; he'd applied to Louis for a temporary job and never left him. I remember attending a grand Bavarian ball near Senlis where we drank champagne out of beer mugs. During the evening Hawkins came up to me with a rather seedy drunk and, with elaborate formality, introduced him with wildly inappropriate words that have engraved themselves on my memory:

"Cass, get a load of the Duke." The Duke was the Duc de La Rochefoucauld, whose unappetizing exterior gave no hint of the purple blood flooding his veins.

On one of our visits to Senlis Bromfield took us to see Edith Wharton, who lived in a lovely house with a beautiful garden. Mrs. Wharton talked well about the past and her work, and we were attentive listeners; we had to be because it was impossible for us to get a word in edgewise. Later, reviewing the afternoon on the way back to Senlis, Louis quoted Mrs. Wharton as saying: "Josephine's son [meaning me] is a very silent boy, isn't he?"

In the late thirties, when war seemed imminent, Bromfield pulled up his roots in Senlis and bought land in Pleasant Valley near Mansfield, Ohio. Malabar Farm was a delightful, homey place which, under his skilled hands, became widely known as a model farm throughout the country and brought visitors from everywhere. Louis had a green thumb and Malabar Farm inspired him to write books on the pleasure of growing things; they are considered by many to be his best.

A perennial optimist, Bromfield was a very vital person and so all sorts of people flocked to him; he loved his place and his attachment to it led to exaggeration. The farm was indeed a fine piece of land, but his friends learned to be wary of expecting too much there. Louis would tell you about the joy of swimming in a clear, rushing stream and—lo!—the spot would turn out to be a mudhole.

My Family Undergoes Changes

Changes were taking place at home; it was a difficult time. Mother was coming to the end of her life and my marriage to Katsy was also ending.

In 1937 I accompanied Mother on a trip west, to visit Santa Barbara, where, incidentally, she was first married. Even in her seventies she was still active and beautiful, and her health was good except for a slight heart murmur. But her doctor had warned against hard physical effort such as walking rapidly uphill.

I had returned to New York when I received word that she'd suffered heart failure after a brisk uphill walk; taking a train immediately to Santa Barbara, I found her gravely ill. My sisters arrived soon thereafter and we learned from the doctor that the uphill climb had been too much for her. I have always wondered about this: why a person of her unusual balance, courage and good sense should have gone—deliberately, it seems—against her physician's advice. The explanation, I fear, is that she'd decided that she had lived long enough; she dreaded the idea of old age and wanted to live only if she could do so fully.

Just before she died, Mother called me into her room, which looked out on a lovely garden, took a deep breath and said, "You've been a good son." This terse comment from that unforgettable and great lady—her last words—has given me comfort over the years.

Shortly before Mother's death, Katsy and I had reached a crisis in our marriage. One can't pretend that a divorce is anything but unhappy, and it always comes as a shock to one's children. Cass, Jr. and Michael were still very young, and we wanted to spare them as much as possible.

An amusing incident occurred at this time. The four of us had been out in a car one afternoon and were returning to the apartment through Central Park when Katsy, who was a witty woman, said something about my eccentric driving that put me into such a paroxysm of laughter that I had to stop the automobile to recover. Yet the moment had come for breaking the news of our impending divorce to the children. This we did the following morning.

The boys couldn't believe their ears in view of the car episode the day before. "But I don't understand," Cass kept saying. "I don't understand. How can you two separate when Mummy makes you laugh until you cry?"

A good question.

The answer is that in my early years I was so absorbed in work, so concentrated, that Katsy, with her warm, emotional nature, must have felt hungry for a more personal relationship; and so, I suspect, the trouble began. Real communication between us—the basis of any good marriage—was lost.

Time passed and I became engaged to Jane White Fuller, who has been described as possessing the magic of making a cold room warm and a hot room cool. She had been married to a talented man—my old friend Charlie Fuller—but their marriage had been a tempestuous one. When Jane and I came together, we found in each other a likeness of rhythm and tempo, an ability to live together in harmony while we each pursued our own particular interests. To be able to benefit from our earlier experiences, to be given a second chance, was a gift from the gods.

My engagement to Jane was something else to tell my children. With this in mind I went to St. Mark's School to see Cass, Jr., then fourteen, and, after some hesitation and embarrassed gulps, I launched into a long explanation. At one point, having heard enough of my discourse, Cass cut me short, exclaiming, "Well, it's about time!"

Jane and I were fortunate in that her three children—two girls and a boy: Sage, Jilly and Blair—had known Cass and Michael since infancy. They were all about the same age and got on marvelously; as time passed, they became truly brothers and sisters. Still, there's no question that divorce leaves a permanent mark on the young, a scar about which children usually keep silent.

It was on a May morning that Jane and I, accompanied by her father, Ernest White, took the subway to the Municipal Building in New York and were duly married by a judge. Mr. White, a salty, shrewd person, seemed to approve of me, and I felt drawn to him. Being a fine horseman, with a sportsman's virtues and failings, he had his own way of testing my fiber—as I discovered when we visited him at his farm near Syracuse, New York. Upon our arrival he showed us around, drawing my attention to a public golf course he had constructed on the grounds, from which he netted a cool $10,000 a year; in addition, he saved by picking up lost balls in the evenings. Then, having taken me over his place, he inquired with old-fashioned courtesy whether I would enjoy a ride. He said that he would be happy to mount me on an excellent horse—not exactly docile, in fact a bit spirited—but a fine animal. I assured him that I would like this very much.

We had a nice ride. It was only after my safe return that I learned that my horse's mouth was reputed to be made of iron, that he was considered practically unridable. Mr. White had, of course, been giving his new son-in-law a tryout; had I not passed that test, he would have thought less of me. Doubtless the horse had disappointed the old sportsman; it did pull, but not as much as those wild beasts I'd broken in at Camp Kearney. In fact, I felt easy on that ride.

Having shed my temporary bachelorhood, I started to look for a place to live and came upon an attractive house in Murray Hill. One hundred years old, set back from the curb about seventy feet, it had been built as a gatehouse to a farm and afforded a surprising break in the New York scene. I rented 152 East Thirty-eighth Street at once and, a few years later, purchased the property from the Sturges family, which had been its owners for several generations. The house had undergone remodeling by Russell Pettengill, an eccentric and ingenious person engaged in the business of printing design. He had a unique claim to fame; one day, so the story goes, he hit upon a bright idea which he offered to divulge to the Secretary of the U.S. Treasury upon payment of $100,000. As the Secretary wouldn't buy that, Pettengill, without further ado, told him of his scheme. It was this: He proposed that the Treasury reduce the size of its dollar bills. His advice was followed, and the government consequently saved, annually, far more than his asking price of $100,000. (Pettengill did receive $50,000 for his suggestion.)

Jane and I lived in our Thirty-eighth Street house, now designated a New York Landmark, for thirty-one happy years. It was used and enjoyed by our combined family of children. Recently we sold the house and moved into an apartment because we wished to simplify our lives. This we did with heavy hearts.

A painful duty for me, as executor of Mother's estate, was to arrange for the sale of her Park Avenue house. It was too big an establishment for either of my sisters or myself, so we decided that the property had to be disposed of and most of the furnishings put up for auction. In preparation for this we had experts come in to appraise the items; they were a shrewd lot. The young man from Parke-Bernet, the auctioneers, would take a quick look at a room and point to a piece of furniture, saying, "That's a good piece, you might get $10,000 for it." His choice and his valuation usually proved to be right.

Jacques Seligmann, the famous art dealer, paid us a visit; he particularly admired a Chinese porcelain dragon, and when I asked him what he would be willing to pay for it, he replied $7,500. "Seven thousand, five hundred dollars!" I exclaimed. "That's half the price Mother paid for it when she bought it from you many years ago!" His expression never changed and he showed not the slightest embarrassment, but calmly observed, "I just told you it was a fine piece."

The time came, during the depression, when the house had to be torn down. The question then arose about the disposal of the fine eighteenth-century boiseries covering the walls of the living room. They presented a problem because they were too high for the ordinary house or apartment; moreover, although two or three museums had expressed some interest in the boiseries, none would make a commitment to display them. One day the house wreckers told me that they would have to begin operations within a few hours. I had looked into storage cost of the woodwork and found that this would amount to thousands of dollars annually. So there seemed nothing to do but to let the wreckers chop away and use the boiseries for kindling wood.

At that moment Samuel French, an art dealer, telephoned and offered me $10,000 for the woodwork. I was immensely relieved, but my bank warned me that French & Company were hard up at the time so that I might never see the money. Still, the offer was better than nothing. Years passed, and one day a certified check for $10,000, signed by Samuel French, was placed on my desk.

The Paperback Revolution
and Publishing Maxims

It was in 1939 that the paperback revolution took place in this country, some years after Allen Lane had started his famous Penguin line in England. In the half-century before Penguin, paperbound books had not existed except for Tauchnitz editions, sold on the Continent of Europe. However, paperback books were not a new phenomenon, since many publishers had brought out cheap books in similar format in the 1880's and had done well until a cutthroat price war put an end to them.

Penguin established itself in foreign countries and sold quantities of their books in the United States. Upon hearing, some years after Penguin had begun operations, that American Penguin was ready to dispose of half its shares, Harper's bid for them in competition with several U.S. publishers, particularly Houghton Mifflin. To close the deal I flew to London and, with my son Michael, had a long and apparently successful session with Allen Lane, who agreed to come to New York and have dinner with a number of the Harper officers. We affixed our respective signatures to a letter of agreement at the Century Club and, the next day, called in our salesmen from various parts of the country to tell them about this important deal. Lane agreed to be present and this promised to be quite an occasion.

We foregathered promptly at nine o'clock in the morning and I told the men the story of the successful conclusion of complicated negotiations. Then the phone rang; it was Lane, who said, "Sorry, I can't be with you, the deal's off." I started to remonstrate but heard a click and the wire went dead. Houghton Mifflin had apparently won, after all, and an announcement appeared that they had acquired a 50 percent interest in American Penguin.

But they *hadn't* won; Lane must have given them a call, too. American Penguin remained the property of Sir Allen Lane until his death in 1970.

Bob de Graff, formerly of Doubleday, that great training ground for publishers, was the man who launched Pocket Books, shortly after Penguin was first started, making them available in drugstores and newsstands throughout this country. From 90,000 to 100,000 outlets carried these handy volumes which sold at twenty-five cents a copy. They were, for the most part, very popular books, largely reprints, which took readers away from the pulp magazines. They made an immediate hit.

Any innovation creates doubters: I recall de Graff calling on Hoyns and me in an attempt to persuade us that Pocket Books would not interfere with the sale of clothbound books, that they would reach an entirely new audience through outlets other than bookstores. He failed to convince us, and for some years we held out against selling rights in any of our titles to Pocket Books. However, as we watched the situation, it eventually became evident that paperback reprints were here to stay. True, they were sold in outlets for clothbound books, as well as on newsstands and in drugstores, and were therefore in direct competition with our publications. Nevertheless, as they were apparently not destroying our market, we finally released some Harper titles to Pocket Books.

As time went by, it gradually dawned upon us at Harper's that we ourselves should play an active part in the reprint business, through the republication of books in clothbound or paperback form *after* their appearance in their original editions. So, when I heard that the firm of Grosset & Dunlap might be for sale and—later on—that Bennett Cerf of Random House was considering its purchase, in association with two or three other publishers, I phoned Bennett and said, "Me, too, please"; we wanted to be in on the deal. In due course, Random House, Harper's, the Book-of-the-Month and Charles Scribner's Sons bought most of the Grosset stock.

Grosset's business differed from that of the so-called original publishers; they would lease the printing plates of the latter and reprint clothbound fiction and children's books at low prices. The reason the purchasing group wished to acquire Grosset stock and thus assure the company's survival was that they feared that otherwise Doubleday would have a monopoly in the field of cheap-edition publishing since they were then the only other important house issuing reprints.

As things turned out, the reason for the Grosset purchase—the maintenance of competition in the low-priced hardbound fiction field—soon disappeared when the advent of paperbacks made such cheap editions of novels obsolete. Nevertheless, the participating publishers had no cause to regret their acquisition of Grosset stock; in fact, this operation turned out extremely well. The Grosset fiction line was simply phased out and the firm concentrated on juveniles and books of reference.

The value of the Grosset stock increased under the very capable management of John O'Connor, who had been appointed president by the participating publishers, and the firm prospered. However, Charlie Scribner, after having been a member of the original purchasing syndicate for some time, decided to withdraw from the group, feeling that the reason for his having joined it had lost its validity. With characteristic generosity Scribner offered to sell his stock to his partners in the enterprise at the price at which he had acquired it.

The paperback revolution spread book reading to hundreds of thousands of people who had seldom read any kind of book before. In this way, paperbacks had the same over-all effect as had book clubs some years earlier—probably an even greater one. For the most part, the early paperbound books were Westerns and mysteries, but gradually the quality of paperbacks improved. An important development occurred during World War II when the clothbound publishers combined to put out special editions in paper covers for the armed services on a nonprofit basis; these books were called Armed Services Editions. Their sales totaled 55 million annually, and it was partly as a result of this enterprise that better reading matter in paperback form was eventually made available to the general public. Nowadays, of course, it is a commonplace to find the classics and books of serious interest on the racks of mass outlets. The paperback revolution has come a long way. This doesn't mean that, because paperbound books are more and more in demand, any title published in paper covers is automatically successful; the market has still to be considered. One title will flourish whereas another will not; one line of books in paper will sell magically and another will die of inertia. And the publisher doesn't always know why.

Yet reprint publishing is more predictable than original publishing, although the vagaries of public taste are an ever-present factor in both fields and the people responsible for selections must have that educated sense of timing which marks the good editor. After many years of experience, I am dubious about any mechanical assessment of the market. I've made it a practice to study the sales records of our old titles that continue to sell. One would think that from these records one could reach significant conclusions about what makes a certain type of book successful and another not. But it's very hard to find guidelines, except the most obvious ones: it is fairly safe to say that a good book of nonfiction is apt to sell if there are not too many titles competing in the same field; that the fresh and unexpected piece of writing will appeal more to the reading public than a capable follow-up. But there are no hard and fast rules. Such maxims are harmless so long as one takes care not to follow them. For example, it was an accepted axiom after World War I that books by Russian émigrés were a drug on the market. One after another was published and they were all flops—no one was interested. Then a biography came along, a really good one, by the Grand Duchess Marie; its large sales went completely against the trend. *The Education of a Princess* was a best seller over many months because its author had the gift of style.

One could go on ad infinitum, citing examples of books that have defied what the experts think they know about public taste. After a long time in the publishing business it comes as a shock to me to realize how very few guidelines are reliable, and to have to acknowledge that a smart book salesman with a year's experience is capable of answering as well, or as poorly, as the experienced editor the riddle of what makes a best seller.

In general, it's more difficult to spot a manuscript with popular appeal than one of literary or scholarly distinction. The latter may not develop into a big seller, though that sometimes happens, but a book of some permanent value—unless its subject matter is highly specialized—should do well. In the popular field one is gambling as wildly as a play producer. One thing I have come to believe firmly: An editor is well advised to watch the author rather than the trend, to stand by his convictions when he believes in a writer's creative talents. This is especially true in the case of novelists, for it sometimes takes years—and several books—for them to find their public; Herman Melville, Joseph Conrad and Sinclair Lewis come immediately to mind; and an editor's faith and backing can be important ingredients in the successful outcome.

Lessons Without a Moral

The lessons that sink in are those learned from personal experience, mostly from one's mistakes. There are some experiences whose lessons are forever elusive, and one can only hope that through constant observation certain insights will be acquired. Publishing is a gamble, with intermittent breaks of good luck. Occasionally, experience may help in recognizing danger signals.

In the late thirties Bernard DeVoto stopped me one day on the street and informed me that Thomas Wolfe had decided to leave his publisher despite the superb editing job Max Perkins had done for him at Scribner's. DeVoto understood that Wolfe had telephoned one of our editors.

Upon returning to the office I asked my colleagues in the book department about this and was confronted with blank stares; no one knew anything. I persisted and, as a last resort, put the question to Lee Hartman, then editor of *Harper's Magazine*. After some moments of thought he recollected having received a call from North Carolina from a person who represented himself as Thomas Wolfe. However, Hartman assured me, the call meant nothing; the man on the telephone, obviously under the influence of liquor, was an impostor. He had felt more than justified in slamming down the receiver after some minutes of fruitless talk.

But it *was* Wolfe, understandably in an agitated state.

The next move in this confused and delicate situation was obviously up to me. All the world knew how close Wolfe and his editor, Max Perkins, had been; Perkins had slaved over Wolfe's massive manuscripts, cut them and helped to give them shape; he contributed greatly to the author's stature as a novelist. Why, then, should Wolfe think of leaving Scribner's? I made some guarded inquiries, and, having satisfied myself that Wolfe was making a change, that his decision was irrevocable, I got hold of him and his agent and arranged for the publication of his succeeding books. They have added much to the prestige of the Harper list; few breaks like this occur in publishing.

Much has been said and written in explanation of the rift between Wolfe and Perkins after their years of close collaboration, and of the reason Wolfe felt compelled to leave Scribner's. The only certainty is that Wolfe, aware of his indebtedness to Perkins, left him in the end, feeling that he needed to assert his independence as a writer. Perkins was a great editor and was beloved by his authors, among whom were Ernest Hemingway and F. Scott Fitzgerald. One day he left his office for lunch and, in his absence, the conservative Mr. Charles Scribner passed Perkins' desk. He glanced at the editor's engagement pad and was shocked to see on it: "Fuck, 3 o'clock." Upon Perkins' return, Mr. Scribner questioned him sharply as to just what he had in mind for the afternoon. Perkins was taken aback, looked thoughtfully at the calendar and said, "Oh, I'm working on Hemingway's new novel and have been cutting down on the author's use of the word 'fuck' to one per chapter."

Mr. Scribner left Perkins' office with relief.

A few weeks after the Wolfe contract had been signed Eu-

The old Harper building on Franklin Square, built in 1855, with the Cliff Street building in the rear

The Harper office in Franklin Square

Sandra Lousada

Mark Gerson

Richard Hughes

J. B. Priestley

Left to right: Eugene Saxton, editor-in-chief; Henry Hoyns, chairman of the board
of Harper & Brothers; and Cass Canfield, president, in 1942

Publishers' Weekly

Aldous Huxley

Ralph Steiner

Julian Huxley

Janet Stone

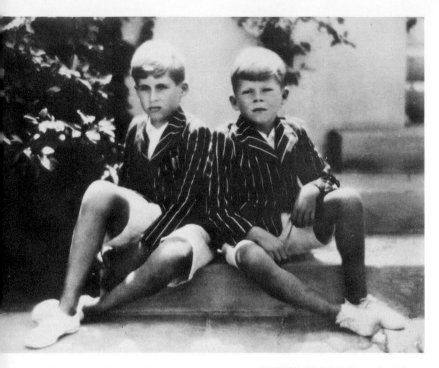

Cass and Michael Canfield

The Hamish Hamiltons

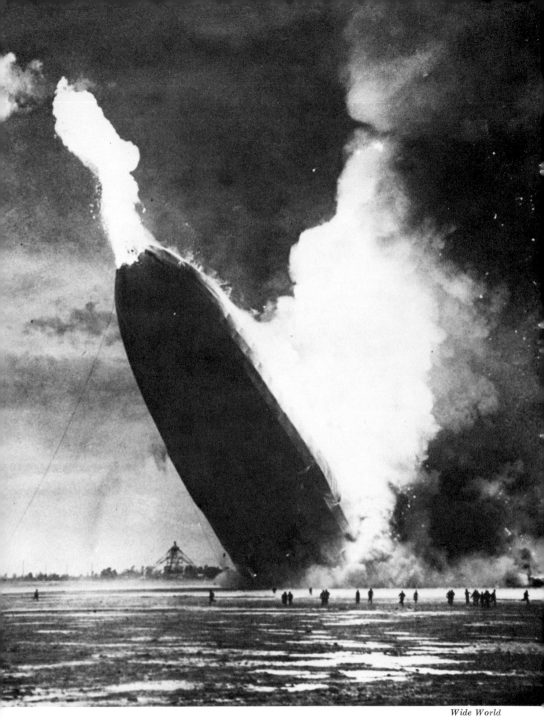

The *Hindenburg* in flames on the field at Lakehurst, New Jersey, May 6, 1937

Jane White Canfield

Ernest I. White

Jane and I with Michael Canfield (front left) and the Fuller children, Sage (rear right), Blair and Jill, 1940

Painting by Felix Kelly, 1947

The house at 152 East Thirty-eighth Street

Cass, Jr. (Army) and Michael (Marines) at Guam, 1944, where they met by chance

Presenting Eleanor Roosevelt with a copy of *This Is My Story,* the first volume of her memoirs. Henry Hoyns in background

Escorting Edna St. Vincent Millay when she received an honorary degree at New York University, 1938

Louis Bromfield at Malabar Farm in Ohio

Maria La Yecona

gene Saxton and I dined with him at Saxton's apartment in Gramercy Square; the conversation at dinner was pleasant but commonplace. It was only when we'd settled down with brandy that Wolfe started telling us the story of his life—partly, I suppose, to give us a sense of the kind of man he was, why he wrote as he did and why he chose certain subjects for his novels. He talked and talked, extremely interestingly—he fascinated us. I recall that, at one point, the nearby Metropolitan Life Insurance clock struck once and I had a feeling that it was either one o'clock or one-thirty. (All of us have, to some degree, a time clock inside of us.) But I was wrong; I looked at my watch, and it was four-thirty!

Wolfe didn't stop talking at four-thirty; he continued for another two hours. We thereupon had breakfast together. So our office work that day was somewhat abbreviated by this most absorbing "evening." Wolfe, as is evident from his novels, was a person of enormous power, and he talked as effectively as he wrote.

The choice of an editor for him at Harper's presented a problem. Wolfe lived at high tension; he was demanding and apt to call his editor at two in the morning to get his advice on some literary problem. Both Saxton and I were involved with so many writers that we felt we could not take on Wolfe, in addition. We therefore asked Ed Aswell, a young intelligent man in our editorial department, whether he'd assume this difficult and time-consuming task. Aswell jumped at the chance and did good work; Wolfe and he got on well together and Aswell became his literary executor.

The dinner with Wolfe was in 1937; the first novel we published by him was *The Web and the Rock*.

Shortly after this Jane and I went to Yugoslavia and, in preparation for the trip, reread Louis Adamic's *The Native's Return,* which Harper's had published. In this book the author described an antique shop in Sarajevo. Some years after the book was written, Jane and I found ourselves opposite this establishment and noticed a handsome young man standing in the doorway. She recognized him as the owner, Omar Alich, mentioned in Adamic's book, and introduced herself; he was pleased to be identified and, in due course, took us to see his father, a venerable Bosnian politician.

No greater contrast could be imagined than that between the son and his parent; the former, Oxford educated and torn between East and West, the latter a white bearded Mohammedan patriarch speaking no English and absorbed in the problems of his own country. We were invited, as the sun was setting, to the old gentleman's house, perched on the top of a high hill overlooking a wide valley, and there, on the terrace, we sat on Oriental carpets and were served attar of roses and black coffee in tiny cups. Behind us we could see, by the light of flaming torches, the house occupied by our host's several wives and daughters.

Mr. Alich talked about the tangled politics of Yugoslavia. At the time, the Croats and Slovaks were at each other's throats; a Croatian peasant leader, Stjepan Radić, had recently been shot as he was making a speech in the senate. No wonder that Sarajevo was the place where the Austrian Archduke had been assassinated! It is a violent city, medieval in atmosphere; in the narrow streets of the bazaars, over which tower the minarets, tradesmen—makers of copper utensils, shoemakers, and so forth —work exactly as did their ancestors for many generations. Nor had their dress changed; the men still wore fezzes and the women, veils—in spite of the fact that in neighboring Turkey Kemal Atatürk had decreed that Mohammedans should wear strictly European dress.

A dilemma presented itself when we published Leon Trotsky's biography of Stalin, a book that took many years in preparation and raised questions about the publisher's obligations and responsibilities to which I still have no sure answers.

Harper's had contracted for the book and the last half of the manuscript was overdue when Jane and I found ourselves in Mexico City early in 1940. Trotsky was living there in exile, and it occurred to me one afternoon that it would be a good idea to call on him and do a little prodding. We found him easily enough in the telephone book and I made an appointment; a taxi took us to the outskirts of Mexico City, to a house in front of which Mexican soldiers were patrolling.

"This is a bit of musical comedy," I remarked to Jane. "I can't imagine that Trotsky's life would be in any particular danger in Mexico City."

We reached a big iron gate and were confronted by an armed guard, who let us in only after we'd shown our identification papers. Thirty or forty feet farther on, we encountered another guard, this one a young Britisher with a large revolver on his hip. Finally, we were introduced into the presence.

The first impression Trotsky made was one of unusual vitality and health; he was rosy-cheeked and bouncy. I was struck with his fine brow and shock of white hair, his strong face and expressive mouth. He was neatly dressed in gray trousers and a white Russian smock. When asked how he managed to keep in such fine physical condition, he surprised me by replying in perfect English, "Oh, I go to the neighboring mountains and hunt game," which conjured up a picture of an Austrian noble-man shooting chamois in Franz Josef's time. In the course of talking to this highly intelligent, engaging but thoroughly dangerous character, I noticed a line of hooks on the wall behind his desk from which were hung our galley proofs of the first half of his biography of Stalin.

Trotsky was affable and provocative. The biography would be completed before many months, he assured us. He said that he had been hampered by the difficulty of obtaining reliable source material in Mexico on Stalin's life and that he got most of the information he required from friends all over the world, some of them in the Soviet Union; I had the impression of a kind of political Voltaire, conducting a vast correspondence.

One question I forgot to ask Trotsky: Just how did Lenin meet his end? I had heard from Louis Fischer, an expert on Soviet affairs, that when Lenin had fallen seriously ill, he had asked various of his political colleagues to give him poison so that he could die quickly. One by one they refused, shocked and unbelieving. How could the Soviet Union survive without its founder, who already enjoyed a saintlike status?

Commenting on Stalin's Russia, Trotsky said that he felt that the Communist Party no longer ruled, that party officials were really rubber stamps for the bureaucracy, as under the Nazi regime. As for the war between the Soviet Union and Finland, which was still going on at that time and puzzling most observers because the Soviet forces weren't making much progress, Trotsky did not doubt the outcome—it was just a matter of time before the Finns would be overwhelmed. The slowness of the Russian advance was explainable, he said, because Stalin had purged the army of many of its best commanders; and the political commissars had such power, the officers being so fearful of them, that military movements were hampered. Also, the Soviet troops, sent to Finland from the Ukraine and southern parts of Russia, were totally unused to the conditions of winter warfare in Finland.

We talked about the world political situation. This was after the Stalin-Hitler pact, which, in Trotsky's view, Stalin had signed because he did not expect Hitler to win the war he knew was coming. Trotsky further believed that Stalin, having secured his front for a period of time, would desert Hitler at the moment of his choice. As we know, the Stalin-Hitler pact failed to achieve its purpose because Hitler attacked before Stalin could desert his Nazi ally. It is amazing how accurately Trotsky had the Nazi-Soviet situation sized up. He pictured Hitler as a master strategist, more formidable than Stalin. Nevertheless, he was confident that Germany would lose the war after a great struggle and that the United States would have to join in and save the Allies. Hitler had successfully invaded Poland when this interview took place, so Trotsky was making these observations at a time when the Nazis were looking very strong.

I asked him what he foresaw at the end of the war. "A ruined planet under American hegemony," he replied. "There will be revolution in the United States, and presumably elsewhere, coming at a time of profound economic dislocation." The British Empire was dying, in his opinion, and he prophesied that her colonies would split off as a consequence of England's lack of vitality, as shown by her policy of appeasement and the Munich reverse.

Not all of Trotsky's predictions were right, but many were;

for me the visit was a telling revelation. Trotsky possessed a naturally inquisitive mind and, perhaps because of his confinement to one place, was eager to learn all he could about what was going on in the world. He asked countless questions and listened carefully to everything we said. This was a response I had never encountered before from a world figure, most of whom like to do all the talking. Trotsky spoke frankly and showed a sense of humor, as when I asked whether he would like to visit the United States. "Indeed I would," he replied promptly, "and I'd be there now if it weren't for 'That Man in the White House.' Mr. Roosevelt knows enough about me so that he wouldn't consider letting me into the country. If you had a Republican President, he would have been less well informed and I would have been able to cross your border."

I inquired what he would be doing if he were in the United States; this was like asking a safecracker what he'd do when he got out of jail. "Start a revolution, of course!" Trotsky answered.

Within a few months of this interview Trotsky was assassinated in his study by Ramón del Rio. In the struggle with his assailant, he was pinned up against the large hooks where the proofs were hung. These proofs, spattered with Trotsky's blood, are now kept in the Houghton Library at Harvard.

With Trotsky dead, it was necessary to find a qualified person to finish the book from his voluminous notes. We chose Charles Malamuth, a Russian scholar, for this assignment, and he performed it well. In a preface he explained exactly how the biography had been prepared. So finally, after years of work, the book was finished. We sent out advance copies on a Friday morning and I breathed a sigh of relief.

The final chapter of this story is concerned with what happened forty-eight hours later, on Sunday morning, December 7, 1941. On that day the terrible news of Pearl Harbor came over the radio. After the first shock I began to think about the publishing problems presented by Trotsky's *Stalin*. It was obvious that, within a few days, Stalin would be America's ally and that he would deeply resent the appearance of this biography by his archrival. On the other hand, we had an obligation to the author—in this case to his estate. It was a sticky situation, as the British would say.

Overnight I pondered this problem, and on Monday morning telephoned three men I knew in Washington, each of whom had access to the President. I needed their advice. The first two were evasive and said, in effect, that Harper's was a private company, that as such we had to make our own decision as to what was best to do in the public interest. By the time I called the third man, I was desperate for guidance. He, too, tended to be indirect, but when I pressed him, he said, "If you want my personal and confidential opinion, I think it would be a disaster if the book were published. The Stalin regime would find it impossible to believe that, with the United States at war, our government would permit publication of an attack on an ally unless it had been officially approved. I can't imagine anything worse, from the point of view of relations with the Soviet Union, than for Trotsky's *Stalin* to be published at this time."

By Monday noon, after discussion with my colleagues, I wrote to the reviewers asking them to return the books which had been sent to them; we then sealed up in our warehouse the substantial first printing of this large volume. There they rested for years—illegally, under the terms of our contract. Mrs. Trotsky's lawyers demanded that we publish forthwith and we received many letters of protest, some of them angry and threatening. We kept the books sealed up until U.S. relations with Stalin had deteriorated to a point, in 1946, where publication could do no harm.

This episode is significant because it raises a vital question: Does a publisher have the right to disregard his contractual obligations in order to fulfill what he considers to be his duty as a citizen? There is no denying that I failed to live up to our publishing agreement and that, with the approval of my colleagues, I set myself up as an arbiter of what was in the national interest, without any instructions from our government. While I believe that I made the right decision, this is certainly a debatable question.

The cloak-and-dagger atmosphere I had encountered on entering Trotsky's house seemed rather absurd at the time, but his assassination proved me wrong. A related incident taught me the same lesson. While working on the Stalin biography, Charles Malamuth was constantly dodging from city to city, avoiding any fixed address. He was no Communist himself, and we couldn't believe that his life was in danger, but Malamuth did. About the same time we had been involved in the publication of a book by Walter Krivitsky, who had been Stalin's chief of intelligence in Western Europe; excerpts from his memoirs, entitled *In Stalin's Secret Service,* had appeared in the *Saturday Evening Post* in 1939 and 1940 and attracted much attention. Like Malamuth, Krivitsky had no fixed dwelling place and would move every two or three days, living under an assumed name.

I remember a curious exchange between Krivitsky and our lawyers on the subject of libel, which points up vividly the difficulties of communication between people whose political and social philosophies are based on widely different premises. Our lawyer was warning us about a passage in which Krivitsky graphically described the cold-blooded murders committed by his associates in the Soviet secret police. Krivitsky, who spoke excellent English, couldn't understand the lawyer's point; it was as if he and our counsel spoke different languages. He kept insisting, "Don't you realize what I am telling you? You say that I'm libeling these men, but they would be immediately liquidated by Stalin if I failed to give them credit for these assassinations." By his reasoning, not only was he *not* committing libel; he was saving his colleagues' lives by telling of the deeds they had performed on behalf of the Soviet state.

After publication of *In Stalin's Secret Service* I kept in touch with Krivitsky. On one occasion Jane and I had him to dinner with Hamilton Fish Armstrong, and I remember that we were all struck by the gentleness, the civilized bearing of this man who had run one of the most brutal secret service operations in our time.

Krivitsky's book was exciting and even sensational reading, but it didn't become a best seller because it was published ahead of its time. People simply could not then believe that the things he set down could be true, that they had actually happened.

One day, some time after the publication of *In Stalin's Secret Service,* I read a headline in the *New York Times*: "Gen. Krivitsky Found Dead; Suicide Finding Questioned." Krivitsky was found in a hotel room in Washington, D.C., and the headline continued: "Notes Convince Washington Police He Shot Himself, but Friends Charge Former Ogpu Officer Was Slain by Reds." I do not know the circumstances, but doubt that he killed himself voluntarily; I am more inclined to agree with his friends that he was shot or that he was forced to commit suicide.

III
WORLD WAR II

Threshold of War

War was approaching for the United States; the country was tense, anticipating the worst. The experts, and they were many, reported the truth as they saw it; sometimes they were right, sometimes not. There was much confusion.

Like most people I became increasingly restless, wanting something meaningful to do and not knowing what. When Mayor La Guardia called for air-raid wardens in 1939, I volunteered and was put in charge of operations in southeastern Manhattan—an arduous assignment for it meant patrolling nights, in addition to working full time at the office during the day. However, I got to know the city community from housewives to undertakers, and this was a compensation. Another satisfaction was working closely with the New York police, for whom I developed considerable admiration. Most of the policemen were Irish, and were lively additions to the parties put on every couple of weeks to boost morale. Patrolman Mike Murphy, who was smart and full of initiative, could be counted on to bring gaiety to any social gathering, and it was not surprising that he rose quickly in the ranks to become New York Police Commissioner not many years later.

Across the oceans things were going from bad to worse as the Germans and Japanese advanced. Returning from a business trip the spring the Nazis were taking Paris, I crossed the Atlantic with Dorothy Thompson, the gifted newspaper commentator and wife of Sinclair Lewis. In the smoking saloon of the ship she was the center of attention, not only because she was a brilliant observer of the political scene and had just completed a survey of Swiss military power, but because she was a vivid character with a vitality which she confirmed by the proud assertion: "When I make love, the house shakes." On the ship's radio we heard, one evening, the voice of Franklin D. Roosevelt informing, and attempting to reassure, the American people about the state of American preparedness. When he'd finished, Dorothy observed that the President's figures showed that our Army and Air Force strength was about equal to that of the Swiss, a situation which we found alarming.

During this period of stress Jane and I attended a dinner dance on Long Island at the home of the John Parkinsons at which Walter Duranty, the expert on Russia and an indisputable authority on world affairs, was also a guest. As the men were having coffee and brandy, Duranty expatiated on the developing Soviet-Nazi crisis of the late spring of 1941, which he minimized. In fact, he argued convincingly that the idea of Hitler's attacking Russia was absurd. This assurance lifted our spirits and the dance went on merrily.

Later in the evening I noticed Duranty sitting at a table enjoying his champagne. In the interval since dinner a pretty young blonde with whom I was dancing had told me some interesting news and, on a wicked impulse, I beckoned to Walter and advised him to cut in on the lady. She imparted to him the report she had heard earlier on the radio—that the Nazi divisions had just invaded Soviet territory. Duranty's reaction would have done justice to a George Price cartoon; he rushed from the dance floor and was off in a flash to the *Times* office in New York.

In such ways the experts managed to keep people shuttling between confidence and despair.

As time passed, it became apparent that the Nazis could not bomb New York; accordingly, air-raid protection became superfluous. I turned to propaganda, to promoting United States participation in the war—a worthy effort but one that, in turn, became unnecessary when the Japanese attacked Pearl Harbor. So, when my friend Thomas K. Finletter, who had joined the Department of State as special consultant to Secretary Hull, asked me early in 1942 to join his staff, I accepted enthusiastically. But it was not to be. A fortnight passed and Finletter telephoned, considerably upset, to tell me that Hull would not permit me to work in the Department of State because he had found my name among the signers of a much-publicized telegram to the President, sent in the spring of 1941, protesting U.S. shipments of scrap iron to Japan on the ground that the Japanese would use the metal to build up their armaments against us. The telegram had infuriated Mr. Hull.

That was that; Finletter next spoke to Milo Perkins, chief of the Board of Economic Warfare. Perkins agreed to take me on as assistant to Paul Nitze in his agency.

Board of Economic Warfare

The BEW was a vital, somewhat reckless organization filled with bright people. Quite a few of them came from Henry Wallace's Department of Agriculture, which probably had more talent in it than any agency in Washington. Vice President Wallace, Chairman of the BEW, was not primarily involved in its operations—rather with broad policy. It was Milo Perkins who was the efficient operating head.

Under Paul Nitze my work was concerned with the purchase of much-needed strategic metals—especially tin—from South America. Nitze, an able man, rose to be Secretary of the Navy and director of the Policy Planning staff of the Department of State. Although I enjoyed working with him—he was an old friend—I unfortunately knew nothing about mining and minerals; so, feeling quite useless, I asked for a transfer. At the request of John Fischer, I was moved to the Office of Economic Analysis of BEW, where my first assignment was economic analysis of Europe and Asia. Here I became involved in what were called blockade and supply problems, which meant trying to cajole and bully the neutral countries—Sweden, Spain, Portugal, Turkey, Switzerland—to ship more of their strategic goods to the United States and less to Nazi Germany. We used every method of persuasion we could think of; for example, in dealing with Sweden, we threatened to cut off her oil imports. Without oil the Swedes could not operate their economy nor maintain their defense forces, and the United States was their source of supply.

The skilled, hard-working individual who had been in charge of economic analysis of Europe and Africa was about to leave BEW for another government agency. Since I was replacing him, I was assigned to work with him long hours for a two-week period during which he crammed me with facts. I learned a great deal and was impressed with the man's striking intensity and his grasp of a complex subject. I had no reason to be suspicious of him, but, some years later, the Communist, Judith Coplon, revealed that this man, whose name was Gregory Silvermaster, had masterminded the Washington spy ring during the war—the group with which Harry Dexter White, key Treasury official, was allegedly involved. Silvermaster had been asked to leave BEW because of questionable intelligence reports about him, yet, despite this, Army Intelligence took him on. There he was in a position to get *really* inside information! Silvermaster's transfer to the War Department is a commentary on the size and complexity of our government structure and points up the confusion bound to exist in wartime because of the pressure of work. The fact that BEW had certain adverse information about Silvermaster unfortunately did not mean that this would ever reach the Army or any other branch of government.

I am convinced that Silvermaster's intensity and zeal were sincere. This was understandable in view of his complete identification, as a devoted Communist, with the objective of winning the war against Nazi Germany. For the Russians, having been invaded, were even more stirred up by the war than we were.

After nine months in Washington I was sent to London with two able associates. On the way, the plane landed at Shannon Airport in Ireland and I spent the night there; it was on a

Saturday and I went to a nearby pub. As the evening wore on, the Irish barflies warmed up and I was amazed to hear an enthusiastic rendering of the Horst Wessel song. Apparently, the place was filled with Nazi sympathizers; a strange thing to come upon among the Irish, whose rate of volunteering for the Allied forces was higher than that in any part of the British Commonwealth during World War II!

Our assignment was to conclude a so-called War Trade Agreement with Sweden. BEW was concerned with the volume of their exports of strategic goods to Germany and determined to effect an increase in their shipments of such materials to the Allied powers. We worked with our British counterparts in the Ministry of Economic Warfare, a most effective organization with only a small staff. From London I was sent to Sweden in the winter of 1942–43, as head of an Anglo-American group of specialists to check up on the Swedish war economy in general and, more specifically, on Swedish exports to Germany—critical materials like ball bearings and machine tools.

There were only four planes flying to Sweden from the east coast of Scotland; they were Swedish planes which carried ball bearings to England. Understandably, the Nazis were not friendly to them, and it was necessary to pick for our flight a dark night when there was no moon so that our plane would not be seen. I remember how startling it was to emerge from the British blackout and from our blacked-out plane into the brilliantly illuminated city of Stockholm. At the principal hotel two bands played to an enthusiastic crowd; one rendering classical music, the other jazz. The jazz band was Nazi, the other, Allied; thus neutrality was preserved. In the hotel's small press room reporters of all nationalities were to be found—Americans and their enemies, the Japanese, working together. Sweden at this time was a divided nation. Half, including the regular and security police, was pro-Nazi; the other half, pro-Ally.

It was the task of our mission to verify the published Swedish export figures and to prepare the way for final negotiation of the War Trade Agreement. In our dealings with the Swedes we met with two important bankers, one of whom negotiated with the Germans while his brother dealt with the Allies. Our mission was greatly helped by the Office of Strategic Services (OSS), whose agents, stationed in the Swedish ports, could use certain methods of persuasion denied to us for obtaining accurate information on shipments abroad. Their activities, and even ours, were embarrassing to the American Ambassador; we were, in fact, really negotiating with the enemy through the Swedish Foreign Office.

I often felt that I was with Alice in Wonderland, and never more so than one evening toward the end of a week of meetings with our Swedish counterparts when I said, on parting with the Swedish Foreign Office man, that I supposed we'd be convening as usual the next day. Obviously embarrassed, he replied, "No, we cannot get together until Tuesday." I reminded him that time was passing, that we required accurate Swedish export figures at the earliest possible moment; he didn't answer me until we were alone. Then he broke down: "Our group is going to Berlin, where we'll be seeing Goering. I'll be back Tuesday morning."

That was the kind of work we were engaged in—a curious experience. We lived in an atmosphere of suspicion and intrigue that made listening devices common on unexpected as well as expected occasions. Our embassy in Stockholm was checked daily for them, as were hotel rooms occupied by Americans; indeed, one could not utter anything but banalities except when walking in the open street.

Eventually the day came when we had all the data we needed and returned to London, where we drafted a War Trade Agreement with the Swedes to replace the existing and less favorable one. The chief negotiator on our side was a clever M.P. with the strange name of Dingle Foot. It was my job to produce the briefs and figures for him and, when all was settled, to draft a cable to our Secretary of State summarizing the text. This I did in a state of some excitement after the long months of preparation. Having finished the 22,000-word cable, I showed it to an odd, rather idle character named Villiers in the British Ministry of Economic Warfare and asked him to read it—for form rather than for content. When he had done so, he returned the cable to me, saying, "I think it's adequate—I suppose you have the figures right. But of course it's not in the English language; so I have taken the liberty of redrafting the text."

Though I was taken aback to be informed that I, an editor, couldn't write, my discomfiture passed when I read his revision. He had transformed a heavy, verbose piece of prose into something readable and had made an economic treatise almost entertaining! I was reminded of my Oxford experience; here was another example of the British gift for expression. The Americans, although not nearly as experienced as the English in blockade strategy and economic warfare, had proved themselves, in time, to be the more thorough in mastering facts by dint of hard work and sheer persistence. But we couldn't match the British mastery of the language.

Toward the end of my London stint I became special adviser on economic affairs to our American Ambassador, Gil Winant, a man with a Lincolnesque look and a quality of greatness. Still, I wasn't convinced that he was as professional as he might have been and found that in my relations with the embassy I got more useful information by talking to the first secretary.

During these months in London I would occasionally visit a room in the Ministry of Economic Warfare where they stored valuable instruments from Switzerland—like theodolites—which were desperately needed by the combined U.S. and British armed forces. These had been smuggled out of Switzerland with great difficulty and at great risk, and the British were rightly proud of their accomplishment. I was sufficiently impressed to inquire about this operation as the war was drawing to a close. By then the room was empty, in spite of the continuing need for these finely made Swiss products. When I asked the reason, I was told that, whereas the British had been able to carry on smuggling operations through the Nazi lines and Vichy France, once the American troops had arrived in the area, the red tape of our Army became so impenetrable that nothing could get through it. Red tape proved to be a greater barrier than enemy vigilance!

I recall another situation which was unusual in that, although I knew from inside information that a certain event was bound to occur—it never did. This was an anticipated big naval battle in the North Sea. I was aware of this because of my attendance at meetings of representatives of our State Department, the British Foreign Office, the British Admiralty and our naval people at which it was decided to take the risk of getting two large ships, filled with ball bearings, out of a Swedish port. We knew that the Germans were fully informed about the ships and their cargo. Moreover, the Nazis well realized how vital were these ball bearings to the Allied war effort at the time. Accordingly, it appeared inevitable that the German Navy would attack when the ships left port under a strong Allied naval escort.

The operation had been decided upon by the end of an afternoon in the winter of 1943. Then, just as the ships were about to sail, the British Admiralty, without consultation with the civil authorities, concluded that the risk was too great, reversed itself and shipped out the ball bearings in some eighteen or twenty fast launches. The Germans, having prepared for battle with a heavily armed British flotilla, were taken by surprise and succeeded in sinking only a few of the unescorted launches. And so the big naval battle never took place; fortunately, my expectation proved entirely wrong.

Not long after the signing of the War Trade Agreement I returned to Washington. There was great confusion at this time over what materials the BEW, which controlled American exports, should allow to be sent to neutral countries. The BEW people felt strongly that many articles being shipped to North Africa, like kerosene, were helping the enemy; kerosene was used for powering every kind of vehicle. On the other hand, the State Department was seeking to appease the French in that area because of our impending invasion of Africa. Incidentally, at least a couple of dozen people in Washington knew about the invasion several weeks before its occurrence and, in retrospect, it seems miraculous that news of the whereabouts of the landing did not leak to the enemy.

One day Admiral William Leahy, FDR's personal representative for over-all strategy, summoned a State Department man and myself. He handed us a directive from the President which read: "Send all materials to North Africa except strategic materials." We asked the Admiral to amplify the statement but could not get a specific answer from him. In consequence, bitter disputes developed between State and BEW as to what was and what was not a strategic material. Since no definition was forthcoming, BEW delayed the departure—from New Orleans to North Africa—of two vessels containing kerosene. This brought matters to a crisis, and a special interdepartmental meeting was held in Tom Finletter's office at which Adolf Berle, an Assistant Secretary of State, accused BEW, and specifically me, of having cost thousands of American lives by denying clearance for these two ships until, in consonance with the North African Accord, two others had left Casablanca bound for the United States.

In the face of such a serious charge, which might well have brought on a postwar Congressional investigation, I made an appointment with General John C. Hull at the newly built Pentagon, he being the officer in Washington responsible for the North African operation. Following our meeting, I drafted a statement of what had been said, and when General Hull had approved it, the document was filed in the Pentagon and State Department records. A few days later, Berle became Acting Secretary of State; during that time, in the absence of Cordell Hull, I was told that he spent most of his days trying, unsuccessfully, to remove this document from his department's files.

The conflict between State and BEW was perhaps unavoidably confused because we in BEW were not kept fully informed about day-to-day foreign policy developments. The State Department people, under the direction of Robert Murphy, were involved in very delicate negotiations with the Vichy French, and it was extremely hard for us to know whether the French, or which French, were on our side in North Africa.

Usually, our wartime discussions in Finletter's office were necessarily grim, but once in a while the unexpected would happen to dispel the gloom. On one occasion a question arose about a large shipment of cobalt, a vital element in the hardening of steel armaments, from a neutral country to Vichy France. We were nervously awaiting news as to whether or not it had been intercepted when a telegram, designed to reassure us, arrived from the U.S. Foreign Service representative in Vichy.

It read to the effect that there was no cause for further tension, that the cobalt was not going to France but was on its way, direct, to Germany! We were astounded by this incredible message and everyone exploded into loud guffaws.

As the days wore on, the situation between BEW and State became impossible. This conflict of interest was known to FDR, and it almost seemed as if he had deliberately created confusion by giving contradictory powers to various governmental agencies. I believe he relished the resulting altercations and that he enjoyed the role of being the final arbiter of bitter disputes. Such calculated confusion seems incredible in retrospect, since Roosevelt did successfully direct the greatest global war effort in history.

My full-time work with BEW ended abruptly when word arrived of Eugene Saxton's death. This was in the latter part of 1943. The loss of Saxton was serious to Harper's and a sorrowful one for me; I was devoted to him and we had worked together closely for twenty years.

In the months that followed I devoted my time to Harper's except for weekly visits to Washington as consultant to BEW. It was in that capacity that I greeted Jack Fischer on his return from India, where he had made an economic analysis for our government which concluded with the statement that, unless the United States made a postwar loan to Great Britain of several billions of dollars without interest, the English nation would collapse, and, with it, the Continent of Europe. He showed his report only to me and to another co-worker before handing it in to the head of BEW. However, the gist of it appeared in Drew Pearson's Washington *Post* column the next day and caused a storm. How Pearson got this information remains a mystery.

Fischer's report was masterly, and I told him, after reading it, that I anticipated three developments: that he'd be fired from BEW when the report was officially submitted, that he'd be offered a job at Harper's, that the report would be printed as the lead article in *Harper's Magazine*. Well, Fischer wasn't dismissed from BEW, but he was demoted; the other two predictions were literally fulfilled. His report appeared as the lead article in *Harper's;* Jack was given an editorial position on the magazine and subsequently became the chief editor of Harper's trade books. Later, he assumed the editorship of *Harper's Magazine.*

Office of War Information

It was about fifteen months after Saxton's death and shortly after the liberation of Paris that Elmer Davis asked me to take charge of the Office of War Information (OWI) in France and North Africa. I could leave Harper's by then as the business was being ably directed by Raymond Harwood, the chief operating officer, assisted by Frank MacGregor, who helped in administration and had the over-all editorial responsibility.

I flew overseas to Paris in December, 1944, while the Battle of the Bulge was being fought; the plane was an old one with tin bucket seats. Before we had reached an altitude of thirty thousand feet oxygen masks were provided, so we should have been comfortable—except that the heating system gave out. And at one point I noticed that two South Americans, sitting next to me, were about to collapse. Though not feeling any too spry myself, I managed to hail the GI steward and point to my companions. As I began to fade away myself, I heard the pilot say to the steward, "Why in hell don't you turn on the valve so they'll get some oxygen?"

Arrived in Paris, I proceeded to a small hotel near the Place de l'Opéra, the headquarters of the OWI mission. Here, about two hundred of us lived and worked, charged with the job of doing everything we could to improve relations with the French, of keeping them informed concerning the United States, of getting information about our war effort into their press, on the radio, and in books. Contacts with French officials were an important part of our duties, and it was necessary, of course, to keep in touch with our embassy, the Army, Psychological Warfare and other government agencies.

Fortunately for us, living on Army rations, the food at our hotel was excellent, far superior to what the French were eating at the time. At the Café de la Paix the coffee was made of acorns, with a corresponding aroma, and the brioches seemed to consist of sawdust.

We worked like fiends—fourteen hours a day. In the evenings I'd read documents in my bedroom, where the temperature was just above freezing. Although I'd turn on the hot-water tap and fill the bath to heat the room a little, I was obliged to wear my hat, overcoat and gloves in order to keep reasonably warm.

The high point in our day was the cocktail hour when we assembled in the hotel bar. The talk would be lively, particularly when Mike Bessie, one of my two principal assistants, would turn up to pour out a torrent of words that held the company spellbound. (Bessie, whom I later persuaded to join Harper's, now heads up the successful book-publishing firm of Atheneum.) My other assistant was William Tyler, who became our Ambassador to Belgium. These two, in turn, were helped by many capable people. The work was demanding and time-consuming—interesting for the most part, but confusing; often we felt that our efforts were futile. On the whole, I found the OWI assignment less satisfying than that in BEW. There was just too much ground to cover and the objectives were less clearly definable.

On one occasion General John Clifford Lee, the COM-Z (communications) commander in France, took us to visit the Normandy beaches. We went in style, in a special Pullman car fitted with bar accessories. I remember, in particular, the return trip from the coast when we intercepted a train carrying badly wounded German prisoners. It was cocktail time and, as we sipped our drinks, a subordinate officer ordered the engineer of our train to delay our departure so that we might linger over our cocktails, thus holding up the cars with the severely wounded men who required immediate medical attention. This was the most shocking episode I witnessed in the war, and I hope that the officer responsible for the outrage now tosses miserably in his bed at night.

Another time, Bill Tyler took me to his mother's château in Burgundy. She was a great lady who had experienced the agony of the Nazi invasion and come through it with her spirit unbroken. A German general had commandeered her château and, in correct Prussian style, had sent his respects to the lady of the house. Mrs. Tyler told his aide that she'd receive the general the next morning in her boudoir at exactly eleven o'clock. He arrived at the appointed time, clicked his heels and got his orders from the lady: "You and your men will be at liberty to use my wine cellar on the west side, but you may not enter the east cellar where the vintage wines are kept. I will regard any infraction of this rule as a serious offense and will take appropriate steps to correct the situation." During the several years of the Nazi occupation Mrs. Tyler's instructions were obeyed to the letter!

During my stay in Paris, Cass, Jr. was doing duty at an airfield on Guam, monitoring incoming and outgoing planes; Michael was serving as a Marine at Iwo Jima, where the casualties were appalling. I was terribly worried and expected, daily, one of those dreaded cables from Michael's C.O. Finally, one came and I thought: This is it. Happily, Michael was only wounded, but his condition necessitated his transfer to a hospital ship bound for California. Michael recovered from his wound and lived for another twenty-four years, until December of 1969, when he died unexpectedly from a coronary occlusion. His heart suddenly stopped as he was flying from New York to England, where he had resided for many years, representing Harper's as I did in the twenties. His family and friends will always remember with delight his charm, his laugh, his wit and his style. At the Garrick Club in London, to which he often went, Michael is missed as few members have ever been. Tragic that this young and attractive man had so short a life. He took pleasure in many things and gave much in return.

We were shocked in OWI, as was the whole world, by the news of FDR's sudden death, which occurred during the night,

Paris time. Within moments, every French newspaper was on my phone; it was as if FDR had been a close relative of people everywhere. The journalists asked detailed questions about a man named Harry Truman; we could not answer them properly because our knowledge of Truman's accomplishments was limited to what we knew of his activities as chairman of the Senate committee examining waste and fraud in military supplies. That night the U.S. Information Service fell flat on its face.

When armistice was declared, I was touring North Africa, examining some financial irregularities in our organization there. The victory celebration in Casablanca was uproarious —parades in the streets, fireworks, incessant shouting and beating of drums. Watching these doings from a veranda overlooking one of the main thoroughfares, we became aware of an Arab just below who squatted, motionless, in the middle of the avenue so that the paraders had to separate into two lanes to avoid crushing him. He never raised his eyes from the ground; to him V-E Day meant less than nothing.

I returned to Paris in time to watch the Victory Parade from the OWI office facing the Place de l'Opéra. Eisenhower was leading it, and I was surprised by his unlined features and placid look as he acknowledged the applause of the cheering crowd. He looked like the coach of a victorious Notre Dame football team rather than the commander of the vast, combined army which had fought its bloody way from North Africa to Berlin. The explanation, I think, is that Ike was a man of great self-confidence, a quality he hid under a bland and genial exterior.

A moving event took place in Paris shortly after V-E Day. Tyler, Bessie and I were in a restaurant on the Left Bank—a boîte—well known as a Resistance meeting place, where the diners were happily making toasts to De Gaulle. At one point the merrymaking was interrupted and we noted with alarm that a drunken American GI had clambered onto a table and was shouting for silence in execrable French. We feared the worst, having had to deal with many unfortunate incidents between American soldiers and Parisians, and held our breath. After much stamping on the table, the GI obtained silence and announced that he was going to sing the greatest song ever written. With that he launched into "Allons enfants de la patrie," and sang the "Marseillaise" straight through in a terrible voice and accent—a disaster, it seemed to us. But the fact that he wanted to sing their national anthem, that he knew the words and sang with feeling, delighted his French audience. The GI was carried high on people's shoulders through the streets, starting a general celebration on the Left Bank. This soldier, with less than a smattering of French, undoubtedly did more to improve Franco-American relations than we'd accomplished over months with the entire OWI apparatus.

There was another episode, less glorious. The American Air Force had been evacuating French refugees from Germany in great numbers, and it came to our attention in OWI that the millionth refugee was about to be returned to France. We sat in solemn conclave and discussed how to celebrate this event, deciding finally to select a typical and attractive young soldier, bring him into Paris and stage a parade. The arrangements were made, a plane was ready to pick the man up, the press had been alerted, everything had been taken care of, when word came from Germany that our boy didn't want to be the star of the celebration. This set us back on our haunches since the man's photograph had appeared in all the papers and his name broadcast. We insisted and he persisted. Although he had a wife and children in France, he'd found a German mistress and was more than satisfied polishing the boots of captured Nazi generals. He liked it fine in Germany and wanted to stay there.

It was too late to change the act so we had to put the screws on him; we dragged him away from the Nazi generals and instructed him to keep his mouth shut. Actually, he behaved well enough and the parade took place on schedule. There must have been a million people watching this disconsolate fellow as he was carried through the streets of Paris. Propaganda takes strange turns.

Some years later I heard De Gaulle make the best kind of propaganda on television when he gave his great speech announcing the newly independent status of Algeria. I was deeply moved, in spite of De Gaulle's wooden gestures, and, returning to my hotel in a taxi, asked the driver whether he had admired this noble speech. He retorted with Gallic wit: "Oui, si vous aimez le Grand Guignol."

It was shortly after the armistice and my return to Paris from Africa that I received a cable with the news of the death of Henry Hoyns. My immediate presence in the Harper office again became necessary, so I had to resign, forthwith, from the OWI.

Looking back over these years of government service with BEW and OWI, I am sharply aware of their value to me as a publisher. Not only did they broaden my experience, make me more knowledgeable about economic and political affairs, but they put me in contact with many individuals who were high in government or who later became so. I learned to speak their language, and this gave me an entree, an opportunity most publishers lacked, for the acquisition of important memoirs for publication. Of direct advantage to Harper's was the employment by the firm of two of my associates in government, John Fischer and Simon Michael Bessie.

IV

YEARS OF CHANGE

Publishing in the Postwar Years

The world that emerged from the war had changed in vital ways, and many of these changes were reflected in publishing. Shortages of paper in the war years had required that all publishers produce small, nasty-looking books with pinched margins; now we could give attention, once more, to putting out books that were pleasing to the eye. Paperbacks had come into their own, helped radically (as I have mentioned) by the success of the Armed Services Editions. In the next two decades textbook publishing was to undergo enormous growth due to the big increase in the college population and to a demand for better education; institutional or library buying, spurred by Federal grants, along with the rapid development and proliferation of college stores, increased sales of all types of books. And the use of electronic devices in teaching challenged old, accepted methods. Another significant development—this in the fifties—was the expanded activity of the American Book Publishers Council leading to a program that promoted book reading.

At Harper's, toward the end of the war and immediately following it, we published a succession of political memoirs which received wide attention. Because of my involvement in government and my particular interest in historical subjects I acted as editor for several books in this field. My young associate, Evan Thomas, gave me invaluable help with a number of them; he also played an important part in the business end of the firm's activities.

One of the first of these memoirs to appear under our imprint was Sumner Welles's *A Time for Decision*. The book was important because it explained the American position on foreign affairs, but, like almost all State Department–trained people, Welles tended to hedge his observations. In working with him over many months, my associate Marguerite Hoyle and I felt it was our job to draw him out; he cooperated fully. When we made a suggestion, he would either say, "Yes, that's good," and question us about it, or would shut us off.

I remember, particularly, one incident with Welles late in '43 or early '44. At the end of a working session in Washington, when he had just completed a couple of chapters, we asked him what topic he was going to tackle next. "Germany," he replied. My next question was: "What are you going to propose—one Germany, two, or several Germanys?" He answered that he really didn't know yet but that he would tell us upon our return in a couple of weeks. I was amazed by this reply since Welles, as Under Secretary of State, had headed up the intergovernmental committee which had been deliberating for eighteen months about Germany's fate, assuming Allied victory. He was bound to be as thoroughly informed about all the possible solutions as anyone in the country; yet at this very late date he hadn't reached a conclusion. In the two chapters covering this subject Welles opted for three Germanys, in addition to the Russian zone, because of his fear that otherwise the German General Staff would, in time, again dominate the country, its foreign policy, its heavy industry and financial operations. He foresaw a tragic repetition of the past.

Another book that was successful and highly relevant to its time was James F. Byrnes's *Speaking Frankly*. Byrnes wrote about American disillusionment with the Soviets, following the end of World War II, and our reasons for changing our policy toward Russia. This former Secretary of State had a very sharp mind and wrote with surprising rapidity. The book, for which we paid a high price in a bidding competition with other houses, sold well.

It was our good fortune to acquire Henry L. Stimson's memoirs because we had brought out, some years before, a book by him on the Manchurian problem. Stimson had some of the aura of Theodore Roosevelt in his energetic attitude toward life. I visited him several times in his house near Oyster Bay and discussed with him and his skilled young collaborator the manuscript of *On Active Service in Peace and War*. His collaborator and research assistant was McGeorge Bundy, now head of the Ford Foundation and formerly one of the most powerful men in Lyndon Johnson's entourage.

The background of Robert E. Sherwood's dual biography, *Roosevelt and Hopkins,* is unusual. I first met Harry Hopkins lying in bed in a hotel in Paris shortly after his return from a mission to Russia, as the war was drawing to a close; he looked haggard and exhausted. Hopkins, FDR's right-hand man, was a very frail, mild-mannered person. He spoke quietly and seemed to enjoy staying well behind the footlights; but Hopkins had a will of iron, strong inner confidence, vision and the courage to make hard decisions. Winston Churchill felt, when he talked with him, that he was dealing with FDR himself. When his death occurred not long afterward, he had made a start in collecting notes for a book of memoirs and, to some extent, had put his papers in order. But he had not begun the actual writing. The question then arose whether to abandon the project or try to find someone capable of dredging something worth publishing out of a mass of miscellaneous material.

Harry Hopkins' widow, Louise, the agents Carl and Carol Brandt and I had lunch together to discuss the problem. The three pros present suggested a number of possible authors, none of whom seemed quite right. Louise then surprised us by bursting out with, "How about Bob Sherwood?" Our initial reaction was lukewarm; although we acknowledged Sherwood's talent, we pointed out that he was a playwright, who had never written a book about politics. But Louise persisted and kept urging Sherwood, emphasizing his close working relationship with FDR, whom he had helped with speeches. The Brandts and I agreed to consider her suggestion because the more we thought about it, the better it seemed.

Accordingly, we approached Sherwood, who accepted the challenge. It was a difficult assignment. Although he was assisted in his work by an able young writer, Sidney Hyman, it took three years to complete the manuscript; when it was delivered to Harper's, we found the writing flawless. *Roosevelt and Hopkins* turned out to be a superlative book, the equal—in my opinion—of Winston Churchill's great memoirs. Certainly this was a case where the amateur, Louise Hopkins, had the right instinct for picking just the writer suited to the task.

Marguerite Hoyle and I had the pleasure of working with Eleanor Roosevelt on several manuscripts. As in the case of Sumner Welles, it was important to draw out the author. Mrs. Roosevelt was most responsive to our prodding and, as we came to know her better, we were impressed—as was anyone who knew her at all well—with the quality and generosity of her character. She was always busy, always working at something. To any question we asked she'd respond promptly, either giving the facts required or explaining that she couldn't write about some particular episode. But to one question she had no satisfactory answer: "Mrs. Roosevelt, you've never talked about your leisure time; what do you do in spare moments to occupy and amuse yourself?" There was a long pause. At last she said, "Oh, well, I suppose I rearrange my closets—and there's always a letter or two to answer." She was a woman who had no leisure and really did not know what the word meant.

Later, I came to know Mrs. Roosevelt as a skillful politician. In 1956, in Chicago, Adlai Stevenson was favored to win the nomination at the Democratic Convention which was to open in a couple of days. Unexpectedly, a surprise movement was then started to draft Averell Harriman in his place. This threw the Democratic Party workers, of whom I was one, into confusion, but when we learned that Mrs. Roosevelt was returning from Europe where she'd been taking a holiday with her grandchildren, we thought we saw a way of rallying the Stevenson forces. A few of us met her plane, told her about the situation on the way from the airport, and escorted her to a gigantic cocktail party given in her honor, where she had to shake hands with hundreds of people—a grueling ordeal after a long transatlantic flight. The party over, Mrs. Roosevelt was put on a national television hook-up and, without preparation, explained why there was only one choice for the convention: Adlai Stevenson. Within an hour of that impromptu speech, clearly and admirably expressed, the problem of who was to be the party's nominee had vanished. An astonishing political feat.

An important postwar book, though hardly a memoir, was *The Silent World* by Jacques-Yves Cousteau. This project originated in an odd way; I was looking at *Life* magazine one day when my attention was caught by a stunning photograph of a shark coming at a man equipped with a device he had invented, of which I had never heard—an aqualung. With the thought that the man in the picture might possibly write an interesting book, I cabled our agent in Paris, Mrs. W. A. Bradley, to look into the matter and give me a report on him. The result, in due course, was the first of several best-selling Cousteau books on life in the ocean depths. Although I initiated this project, the editor who worked with the author in developing the manuscripts was my associate, Evan Thomas.

Cousteau, trained as a French naval officer, is a man of striking appearance, with deep-set eyes in a thin, handsome face. He looks like a poet and, although he writes in prose, is one. He has devoted his life to undersea exploration and has probably discovered more about what takes place under the oceans than any man alive. Through his writings and his famous television programs, he has made people aware of the importance of this major part of the world's surface. His diving exploits have often been hazardous; his contribution to man's knowledge is impressive.

In Paris, Jane and I called on Alice B. Toklas, the life companion of Gertrude Stein, in her apartment on the rue de Fleurus, near the Beaux-Arts. We climbed a long, frigid stone staircase, and her sitting room, warmed by a tiny grate, with magnificent early paintings of Picasso, Picabia, Juan Gris and others who were Stein's intimate friends, was a welcome relief after the unheated entrance.

There was Miss Toklas, with her beautifully chiseled features looking as if she had been carved out of ivory. She talked about her life and about cooking, her favorite hobby; it was this kind of material that she used in *The Alice B. Toklas Cookbook*, a discursive essay with delicious French recipes.

Toklas reminisced about Gertrude Stein and her friends, the outstanding writers and artists of our time—among them

Thornton Wilder, Hemingway, James Joyce and Durand-Ruel, the dealer who discovered the young painters of the World War I period.

It was Mrs. Bradley who sent us to see Toklas, at the suggestion of Joan Kahn, the talented Harper editor. Jenny Bradley has been the outstanding literary agent in Paris for a generation; to have dinner at her apartment on the quai de Béthune is a pleasure one does not forget. Not only is her food superb, but one finds at her table the most distinguished people in France.

Evan Thomas was the editor for John F. Kennedy's *Profiles in Courage,* as he was later for Theodore Sorensen's *Kennedy.* I did, however, have a background role in the negotiations for these books. JFK sent me his first draft of *Profiles in Courage,* partly because my son Michael was then married to his wife's sister, Lee. The draft was sketchy; although it showed evidence of Kennedy's writing ability, there was no doubt that substantial revision and further historical research were required. Thomas, who saw the book's possibilities from the beginning, worked constructively with the Senator, then confined to bed with back trouble. With Ted Sorensen's research assistance, JFK did a vast amount of revision and showed himself to be a meticulous workman. When the book was finished, Evan and I visited him in Washington to go over his proofs. I recall his attention to minute detail, down to commas, and was particularly struck by this expenditure of effort because Kennedy's back was still so bad that he was unable to lean down to pick up the proofs from the table beside him. Ultimately, the book justified all that he had put into it. *Profiles in Courage,* about moments of crisis in the lives of great statesmen, was awarded a Pulitzer Prize and enjoyed a phenomenal sale; it still sells, both in paperback and in cloth.

Kennedy had all the charm one associates with him. I first met him when he was a young Senator; he immediately caught the attention of those around him and gave out an impression of reserve energy. Even then he seemed to have encyclopedic knowledge and had the answer to practically any question asked of him.

Never a Dull Moment, the memoirs of the Countess Cassini, whose father was Russian Minister to Peking in the days of the Dowager Empress, brought back a fascinating bit of half-forgotten history; it was one of the offbeat books which had a pleasant success in the 1950's. Count Cassini had rendered inestimable services to Russia by successfully negotiating for valuable rights in Manchuria, including the Manchurian railway and the cession of Port Arthur, but he was so indiscreet as to marry an actress. When the Czar heard of this mésalliance, he recalled his Minister, ordering him back to St. Petersburg. At the turn of the century the trans-Siberian railway reached no farther than Irkutsk, so the Cassinis—with their daughter —were obliged to make the journey by caravan and sleigh. Later, Count Cassini, who was in wrong with the Czar, was denied the post of Ambassador to France. However, the Czar took into account his distinguished record and forbore dismissing him from the foreign service. Instead, he assigned Cassini to hard labor in a provincial outpost—Washington, D.C.—to serve as the first Russian Ambassador to the United States; this was during the McKinley and Theodore Roosevelt administrations. It was against this exotic background that Countess Cassini told the story of her growing up in the Washington of an earlier day.

The Glitter and the Gold, by Consuelo Balsan, the former Duchess of Marlborough, who had lived in the vast Blenheim Palace and whom I'd encountered as a child in Roslyn, was published at about the same time. Madame Balsan's recollections appealed to a large public, and the author was delighted. At Fishers Island, New York, where we have a tiny two-room house on a beach, she came to tea; we chatted on the terrace adjoining our cottage, and after a pleasant hour she rose to leave. "I've had such a nice time," she said, "and your place is lovely. But *where* is the house?"

My interest in the Kinsey Institute began when I heard that Alfred Kinsey was working on gall-wasps, in whose sex lives and their variations he was absorbed; he later turned to the human species and wrote important books on its sexual behavior which sold in the millions. In addition, he established a private museum of erotic art and literature at Indiana University.

We became publishers for the Kinsey Institute and I visited the museum with my editorial associate, Michael Bessie. Because I'd been with Harper's for many years and was considered an elder statesman, the people in charge of the collection of erotica feared I would be shocked. They were wrong; I was fascinated and looked wide-eyed at everything—the books, the pictures, the sculpture, the paintings. However, after half an hour, I became unutterably bored because the story and the representation of sex have been necessarily the same for over five thousand years. One thing did arouse my interest—the fact that women hardly ever read pornography or create it and that the people who buy it are mainly middle-aged, prosperous men. Kinsey's assistant besought me to persuade my wife, a sculptor, to produce a pornographic work of art because, he said, such a piece of sculpture by a woman would be one of extreme rarity. She refused.

I asked the curator whether the Indiana museum comprised the largest collection of erotica in the world; he said that it ranked second, the first being the Vatican's.

At the opposite end of the spectrum was a collection of sermons we commissioned—the best of the period. These sermons had been delivered by clergymen of all denominations, and one of them was written by Pope Pius XII, whose permission we had obtained for inclusion in our book. As publication date approached, two clever and sophisticated Jesuit priests called upon Eugene Exman, our religious editor. With great courtesy they informed Exman and me that our collection of sermons could not be published if it included one by His Holiness. With equal courtesy we explained that the Pope had specifically granted us permission to do so and that, in any event, the book was on press and thus it was too late to make any changes. "But," our callers said, "Cardinal Spellman will be displeased if you publish. Do you wish to offend the Cardinal?"

A few days later, Exman and I were summoned to the Archbishopric in New York, where Spellman received us affably. After the preliminaries, he told us that we probably lacked knowledge about the customs and traditions of the Catholic

Church and that, were we in possession of such knowledge, we'd realize that anything written by the Pope must appear by itself and therefore must not be included in a volume of collected papers. But, we maintained, we had the Pope's permission to include his sermon; besides, would it not educate Protestants and Jews, some of whom, misguidedly, associated His Holiness with the forces of evil, to read a fine sermon by him in a volume representing all denominations? Spellman's answer was still No, and we were at a deadlock. Finally, after an embarrassing silence, we told the Cardinal that, if he could obtain from the Pope a written statement reversing his position and telling us that we must take out his sermon, we would comply with his wishes. Within a week the Pope's statement to this effect was delivered to Harper's. Spellman had won, and we wondered at the power of the American branch of the Church over Vatican decisions.

This episode recalls a story about a Pope who, in the Middle Ages, suggested to St. Francis that he talk to the birds; Francis did so, as is well known. From this is supposed to have come the expression, "Tell it to the birds."

A Glimpse of Tito's Country

Not all of the books which I saw as interesting possibilities in this postwar period materialized beyond the dream stage. On a trip to Europe, shortly after the war, I took the sadly dilapidated Orient Express from Venice to Belgrade with the object of obtaining Tito's memoirs. The mission failed. I was not able to see Tito, and even if I had, no manuscript would have been available. Now, twenty-five years later, the publishing world is still awaiting his memoirs.

At the Belgrade station stood one ancient taxi, which I

entered on the run after helping the driver push it in order to get the wreck started. Delivered eventually to a run-down hotel, I telephoned Vladimir Dedijer, the Minister of Information, who had been at Tito's side in the guerrilla war against the Nazis, and was informed by him of Yugoslavia's critical military situation at the moment. A Soviet attack against Belgrade might come suddenly, Dedijer said, but it would be repulsed at whatever cost, in spite of the heavy odds against his country. He added that Soviet jets could reach the city in a matter of minutes; as for tanks, the great flat plain around Belgrade offered no defense against them.

Belgrade, at best, is unattractive and dusty; at this time it was most uninviting. Eager to get out of the place as soon as possible, I went to a travel agency where no language I understood was spoken. At that point a young Yugoslav, who had served with the U.S. Army, helped me out; he was delighted to talk to an American and we arranged a later meeting. As I strolled around the streets and gazed at the rather dismal shops, my attention was caught by the signs in the windows. Each item of shoddy merchandise was advertised at three prices: If you were a card-carrying Communist, you could buy a pair of shoddy shoes for $7, but if your standing was only so-so, the price went up to $16. For foreigners and benighted Yugoslavs beyond the Communist pale, the cost was $43. This ingenious price structure was, obviously, an effective political weapon.

At the appointed time I met my friend at a bar; he was clearly under strain and kept looking around nervously. Later in the day we took a streetcar to his apartment, where I met his wife. They were an appealing couple, he an athletic instructor, she a teacher, and their anxiety to be hospitable was apparent. They offered me drinks but no food. An hour and a half went by before I ventured to ask whether I might go out and buy some sausages and sauerkraut. At this suggestion their faces lit up with pleasure—a relief to me because I feared their feelings would be hurt by my offer to pay for the food. The fact is, they were stone-broke. When I left Belgrade, my friend accompanied me to the railroad station to see me off but didn't enter it; with profuse apologies he explained that he couldn't risk being seen there with a foreigner.

From Belgrade I returned to Venice to rejoin Jane. At the border between Yugoslavia and Italy I did not find the pretty local girl who had assured me that on my return she'd be happy to exchange into dollars the thousands of Yugoslav putniks I had been persuaded to purchase from her on the way to Belgrade. I still have the putniks.

Jane was waiting for me at the Grand Hotel in Venice, and, as I drew up in a gondola, I was surprised that she failed to recognize me. The clean, well-dressed, carefully barbered individual who had left her forty-eight hours before had returned from this rough journey an unshaven tramp.

Fruitless scouting trips such as this one are not uncommon in a publisher's life. Sometimes I have spent three exhausting weeks in London seeing authors, publishers and agents with zero results. Then again, with the wind blowing from the right direction, I've gone abroad for just a long weekend and returned with satisfying booty.

The New American Nation

The Rise of Modern Europe series had sold so successfully that I was encouraged, after the war, to recommend to the firm that we initiate another ambitious historical project along the same general lines. I proposed to Professor Henry Commager, the eminent American historian, that he edit a twenty-five-volume history of this country, following—in the main—a chronological pattern. Commager accepted the proposal and even extended the scope of the series, feeling that one covering so much ground should contain not less than forty-five volumes.

It soon became apparent that Commager needed a co-editor for this important project, and it was agreed between us that Richard B. Morris would be ideal; he accepted the assignment. In the twenty years that have passed since this project was launched we have published more than half of the series, and they have had an excellent reception. Recent volumes have appeared both in cloth and in paperback, almost simultaneously. Although the paperback edition, in use by colleges, is priced at $1.85 to $2.45, and the cloth at $7.95, the clothbound sales have increased since the books appeared in paper.

The New American Nation series, like The Rise of Modern Europe, has been a source of great satisfaction. To watch a project of this scope take form involves the editor in the process of creation. As before, I had the invaluable help of my assistant, Beulah Hagen, who has backed up my publishing activities over many years and kept my office functioning smoothly during my long absences, especially those during the war.

Apart from his contribution to The New American Nation series, Dick Morris has added several important books to the Harper list. *The Peacemakers* was awarded the Bancroft Prize; his *Encyclopedia of American History,* which has become a staple selling item, is a brilliant job of editing, and the *Harper Encyclopedia of the Modern World,* of which he is co-editor, is an invaluable work of reference. We have also published a number of notable books by Henry Commager.

A Diversity of Authors

If it appears that my time during these postwar years was taken up wholly by projects in the historical and public affairs field, I have given the wrong impression. There were many authors whose books lent diversity to the Harper list during this period, and in working with some of them I met new challenges.

I didn't know Edna St. Vincent Millay when she lived in New York in the early days of her spectacular career as a poet, but, upon succeeding Eugene Saxton as her editor, I visited her at Austerlitz, New York, where she lived with her husband, Eugene Boissevain. Her marriage was a happy one, and Boissevain's death in the mid-forties came as a tragic blow to Edna, who fell into a state of deep depression afterward. For a while she stayed in a hospital in New York City.

One day a friend of hers telephoned me to say that Edna was anxious to leave the hospital and return to Austerlitz. "I think she should," the friend told me, "but others advise against it because they feel Edna is so melancholy that she might take her own life." The doctor had taken no definite position in the matter, and the problem was left to me to decide. As I thought it over, I, too, came to feel that Edna should have her way and return home. Accordingly, I called for her and drove her to Austerlitz. We talked of various things on the way—about the countryside, her past visits to New York, parties we'd enjoyed together—and avoided intimate subjects. As I left her at the end of the journey, she thanked me, saying, "I appreciate your avoiding probing questions, and I want you to know this: I'm not going to kill myself." She kept her promise and remained at Austerlitz for a number of years—in the cottage overlooking wild hills—until her death in 1950. During this period she continued to write; her later poems reflect her love of nature and of the beautiful country surrounding her house.

In 1948 Vincent Sheean visited Edna at Austerlitz, later including his impressions in a sympathetic book, *The Indigo Bunting*. He described her living room with a big picture window looking out on the bird-feeding station. After her death, he had occasion to return to her cottage, and when he looked for the picture window, it wasn't there; it had, in fact, never existed except in Jimmy Sheean's imagination. Edna, with her intensity and her unconscious talent for magnifying, had made an ordinary farmhouse window seem vast.

Dear Cass Canfield:

It occurs to me with something of dismay, that, if I were dead---instead of being, as I am, alive and kicking, and I said <u>kicking</u> --the firm of Harper & Brothers (Est 1817---and how good is your Latin?) might conceivably, acting upon the advise of a respected friend, alter one word in one of my poems.

This you must never do. Any changes which might profitably be made in any of my poems. were either made by me, before I permitted them to be published, or must be made. if made at all someday by me. Only I, who know what I mean to say, and how I want to say it, am competent to deal with such matters. Many of my poems, of course, are greatly reduced in stature from the majesty which I hoped they might achieve, because I was unable, as one too often is, to make the poem rise up to my conception of it. However, the faults as well as the virtues of this poetry, are my own; and no other person, could possibly lay hands upon any poem of mine in order to correct some real or imagined error without harming the poem more seriously than any faulty execution of my own could possible have done. (I do not. of course include here such hastily-written and hot-headed pieces as are contained in "Make Bright the Arrows" "the Murder of Lidice", etc. I am speaking of poetry composed with no other design than that of making as good a poem as one possibly can make, of poetry written with deliberation and under the sharp eye of an ever-alert self-criticism, of poetry in other words. written with no ulterior motive such as, for instance, the winning of a world-war to keep democracy alive)

As for sonnet XlV from "Epitaph for the Race of Man", let me assure you now (because I know that you are deeply troubled about this matter and in a mood to accept from a friend whose learning you respect, a suggested alteration in one of my poems) let me assure you that your friend has brashly leaped to an ill-considered conclusion, and that in this instance he has made a complete ass of himself.

This particular sonnet is guilty of a serious fault, but from the point of view of sonnet-structure, not from the point of view of either fact or mythology. The octave is written in the pure Italian form, whereas in the sestet the rhyme-scheme (ccddd) is improper. This is very bad, of course. Yet I do consider this particular bastard sestet to be sometimes as in this sonnet, for instance, not ineffective.

As to what this sonnet actually says,- well, it seems to me that any bright boy in the eighth grade, who cared for poetry, and was not too lazy to look up a few words in the dictionary, would have little difficulty as to its literal meaning. If this poem makes any statement at all which it does, than the substitution of the word "Ixion" for the word "Aeolus" would render the whole sonnet utterly ridiculous, confusing and meaningless....

I would not, if I were you, in the future, pay much attention to any suggestion made to you by this acquaintance of yours on the subject of poetry, for which, it would seem, he really cares little, and concerning which, even more seriously, he knows even less. He is not, in any case, a thorough going student: he is a pouncer upon details and his scholarship - if indeed it exist at all - is bumpy and uneven.

Sincerely yours, and with every good wish for the New Year,

Edna St. Vincent Millay

January 8th, 1946.

Edna St. Vincent Millay, writing in 1946, declares in no uncertain terms her exclusive right to correct her own work.

Edna Millay was unique, enchanting to look at, with a crystal-clear mind. She could have been a great scientist or a distinguished lawyer, had she not turned to poetry. Her books sold like ice cream cones, many of them over fifty thousand copies. What struck me most about Edna was her attention to detail; we made small changes in her manuscripts at our peril. Once, when I thought that she had misquoted a classical phrase, I made a correction. To my letter about this she responded with a hurricane of correspondence, and six months elapsed before it died down. One just didn't tamper with Millay's work.

Another example of her meticulousness, of her conscience as a poet and a writer: Occasionally she would be asked to serve as judge in a poetry contest—the kind of routine chore most writers perform from time to time. Instead of letting assistants weed out for her the obviously inferior manuscripts, she would read every one—sometimes hundreds of them—and if a young poet showed the slightest promise, she'd write him or her in great detail; these Millay letters are models of good critical writing. She was a highly professional person who took her craft with extreme seriousness.

Shortly after my visit to Miss Millay in Austerlitz I went to Washington, D.C., to call upon Millicent Todd Bingham, who had in her possession many unpublished poems by Emily Dickinson—a notable find. But on my way back to New York, I felt depressed, as I realized the poems probably could not be published because their copyright was in question. Indeed, there was every reason to believe that a lawsuit with Little, Brown & Company, which had brought out Emily Dickinson's previous work, would be inevitable should we or any other firm produce a volume of the poems in Mrs. Bingham's possession. On the other hand, Mrs. Bingham, through her mother, Mabel Loomis Todd, who was Dickinson's first editor, had a strong claim to their publication, based on physical possession —a claim which dated back many years. The complicating factor was a bitter feud involving the Dickinson heirs and Mrs. Todd, which had been passed down in the families with undiminished intensity. It was a Gothic drama of classic proportions. My problem concerned only the poems, a great literary heritage not be kept from the public because of excessive timidity on the part of a publisher. Did I dare to take the risk for Harper's?

In my low state of mind that evening on the train I treated myself to a couple of Scotches and little by little my courage returned. I startled my fellow passengers by exclaiming, "Am I a man or a mouse?" No one in the car said, "Mouse," so I concluded I was the former. Accordingly, I decided to risk a lawsuit and committing the firm to the probability of incurring a large financial liability. *Bolts of Melody* was published in 1945, to the acclaim of the public and critics. Although the lawsuit never materialized, it was a recurring threat for years. For the successful outcome of this publishing venture I owe much to Elizabeth Lawrence, my co-editor, who took the brunt of untangling an intricate situation.

At this time I saw more of Aldous Huxley, and I was struck by his amazing visual perception despite his very bad eyesight. When he admired a painting, he would look at it with a magnifying glass, examining it inch by inch; once he took part in a symposium of the world's leading art critics, organized by the Museum of Modern Art in order to explain to the layman the significance of the work of the great abstract painters. In an account of this, printed in *Life* magazine, Huxley's findings were the most imaginatively acute of all the comments.

He was unusual, like his brother Julian, for the diversity of his interests. Whatever subject might arise—overpopulation, scientific research, the problem of diminishing water supply, literature, art or Oriental philosophy—Huxley would bring to it precision and penetrating observation. And his vision of the future, described in *Brave New World,* which was written in 1931, has proved to be disturbingly prophetic.

Jane and I took a walk in the desert with Aldous and his wife, Maria, when they were living in a small, plain house not far from Los Angeles. After a simple, vegetarian lunch we set out; we looked at the arid stretch of stone and sand and started reluctantly. Maria flew ahead like a tiny bird, discovering minute and wonderful little flowers or a small bird's nest in a cactus; while Aldous gazed at the line of distant hills and

3276 Deronda Dr
LA 28
Cal
August 30ᵗʰ 1956

Dear Cass,
I have just heard from someone
who has seen an advance
copy that there is a 35¢ edition
of <u>the Genius & the Goddess</u> on
the market. Is this so? I don't
remember your telling me of it
Also my informant tells me
that it has a cover representing
a young lady putting on (or taking
off) her drawers!
    I hope <u>tomorrow</u> & <u>T. & T</u> is
getting under way satisfactorily
Incidentally, how did <u>Heaven & Hell</u>
make out?
    I expect to be in NY for a
few days from Oct 10ᵗʰ & hope
to see you then Yours
                    A Huxley.

740 NORTH KINGS ROAD • (LOS ANGELES 46 • CALIFORNIA

32 76 Deronda Drive
Tel: Hollywood 7-0152.
Thank you for the copies
of the G & G in paper covers.
The lady in underclothes is not
too bad after all. Above is
the new address — reminiscent
of George Eliot, Daniel Deronda.
Aldous H.

The late Aldous Huxley expresses qualified approval of a lady in underclothes.

the colors of the sunset. Finally, we came to an old, gnarled peach orchard in blossom, once irrigated and tended, but long since abandoned and forgotten. Aldous stood still and exclaimed, "How moving that is—the old trees still valiantly bringing forth blossoms in this desert wilderness!"

Aldous told us about a journey he had taken through Africa in the course of which he had visited a "medical center" on the West Coast—the Johns Hopkins of the continent, where witch doctors from all over Africa assembled to learn the tricks of their trade. Huxley was one of the few Westerners ever to have been permitted to enter the sacred precincts. One day he witnessed an extraordinary sight: He saw a man cut in two, after which the victim walked away, smiling. Aldous could not explain this exhibition of black magic except in terms of hypnotism.

In a lighter vein: a writer-artist I knew and loved was Ludwig Bemelmans; self-exiled from Germany after the First World War, he had a varied and colorful career in this country. At one time he worked as a bus boy in the Ritz kitchens under Oscar, a waiter who rose to become maître d'hôtel of a famous restaurant. The top-dog headwaiter at the Ritz, who seldom deigned to visit the kitchens, chose one of his rare occasions to do so during the 1914 War against Germany and was so rash as to praise the Kaiser. This nettled young Bemelmans, who happened at the moment to be carrying a tureen of soup. Reacting instinctively, Bemelmans threw the steaming soup into the face of the headwaiter, thus abruptly terminating his career at the Ritz.

Many years later I invited Bemelmans to the Pavillon restaurant. There he encountered Oscar, whom he'd not seen since the time he had worked for him as a bus boy; the two men embraced each other and had a grand reunion. Our lunch was perfection, with a fine Chablis, and when the overwhelming bill was presented, Ludwig insisted, over my protestations, on paying it, although it was for me, as host, to pay. As we were leaving the restaurant, Bemelmans remarked casually, "I'm a little short of cash and wonder whether Harper's would loan me five thousand dollars." Without hesitation I replied, "Of course, Ludwig." This substantial advance on a future book was outstanding for years, but after having been treated to such a magnificent lunch a few thousand dollars seemed to me picayune.

Bemelmans was full of humor and told stories with gusto. For years he cut a lively figure in the art and literary world of New York; the Crazy Horse restaurant in the East Fifties which he decorated was long one of the city's eye-catching landmarks.

George Orwell was another writer whose early career included service as a kitchen boy in a Ritz hotel—this one, the Paris Ritz. He wrote about it in *Down and Out in Paris and London,* a book which didn't sell at the time of its publication but contributed to the author's reputation. Orwell taught me two things: not to put uncritical trust in a reader's report and to hold fast to a writer whose work you admire. After *Down and Out* Orwell wrote *Animal Farm.* The finished manuscript appeared on my desk in New York a couple of days before my departure on vacation and I asked for a quick report. The reader damned the book, taking the view that its fantasy was unconvincing, that *Animal Farm* fell between two stools; she felt it was not suited either to children or to adults. So we declined the manuscript—and the book has become a classic. The rejection of *Animal Farm* was disastrous, and this goof taught me to read a manuscript myself when there is the slightest question about its merit. However, occasionally a reading is impossible because the editor must make a publishing decision on the basis of an outline, sometimes on the basis of no more than a title and the author's name. As bidding for potential big sellers has become more and more frantic, this kind of situation occurs more and more frequently. There have been cases where up to a million dollars have been guaranteed to a famous political figure for his memoirs, sight unseen.

Among my intimates are Emily Kimbrough and Edward Streeter, both serious people who write with infectious humor. Streeter, famous for his *Father of the Bride* and *Chairman of the Bored,* is a phenomenon—a highly successful banker who, by back roads of understanding, has managed to illuminate with humor areas of behavior peculiar to the establishment: a sort of reluctant rebel. Emily Kimbrough is a rebel of another sort; she expresses her rebellion against the restraints of her environment by fleeing from it. Starting with *Our Hearts Were Young and Gay,* which she wrote with Cornelia Otis Skinner, she has produced a succession of books about her travels in various countries which reflect her wit and understanding.

To recollect one's author friends is a pleasure. Cecil Woodham-Smith, a rare person, who wrote a life of Florence Nightingale and *The Reason Why,* is one of the most distinguished biographer-historians of her time. A reserved, witty lady, she combines meticulous research with a very human approach to her subjects. Her forthcoming *Queen Victoria* will be magnificent.

From earliest days I have known and admired Glenway Wescott; among his books *The Grandmothers* is his best novel. Although he was not the first writer of quality to evoke the American past, he brought unusual freshness to a kind of personal narrative that has grown in popularity over the years. Glenway's brilliance in conversation matches the quality of his literary style. Once president of the National Institute of Arts and Letters, he's an important figure in American letters; his writing style is a model of distinction. I hope that, someday, he will permit the publication of his vast correspondence for he's one of the great letter writers.

I was very fond of the late John Mason Brown, a person of special wit; author, dramatic critic, lecturer. His conversation sparkled and I remember one of his observations when he attended a party given by a famous collector of modern art. Confronted by a massive sculpture by Arp, with a large hole in its middle, Brown exclaimed, "Ah, a womb with a view!" His frequent contributions to the *Saturday Review* and his books, particularly his biography of Robert E. Sherwood, have interested and entertained many readers who remember Brown and his writings with nostalgia.

John Garraty is a man I admire. After he had completed

a biography of George W. Perkins, a Morgan partner, I persuaded him to undertake an ambitious project—a history of this country for college students. The book has been a pronounced success; being both readable and authoritative. Garraty has written a number of other books, and his next, *The Columbia History of the World,* which he is editing in collaboration with an eminent associate, Peter Gay, will be a worthy successor to H. G. Wells's *Outline of History.*

Gustav Eckstein, a diminutive person, sets a room quivering like a strong electric current. Intimate of the Alfred Lunts, the late Alexander Woollcott and Ned Sheldon, he is loved by everyone who knows him. His conversation is original, like his books. A lady told me that on one occasion he burst out with, "My dear woman, if you don't like pigeons, I have no further use for you." His life has, in fact, been devoted to pigeons and to canaries; besides, he is an outstanding physiologist-philosopher. His genius reveals itself in several books, of which *The Body Has a Head* is perhaps the outstanding.

A Publisher's Day

I am still learning—I hope—and still attempting to close the gap between what one hopes for and what is attainable. It's impossible for editors to live up to their expectations; we stagger along from day to day, solving problems as best we can and trusting that our judgments will stand the test of time.

What—I have been asked—does my working day consist of? The key adjective for any publisher's day is "fragmented." One starts with the shaving process, a productive interval; it is then that the half-formed ideas of the night are adopted or discarded. During breakfast the *New York Times* often suggests a possible book. By the time one arrives at one's desk, the thought process is replaced by routine until the office quiets down, late in the afternoon, though at lunchtime—a vitally important event in the publisher's day—an idea or two may come.

The almost total absence of creative thought during office hours is caused by the constant interruptions, by callers, office associates, the telephone and conferences. The caller may be anyone from an old lady referred by a friend, who seeks publication of her poems, to an insurance salesman, or a young person looking for guidance about publishing. The neophyte publisher can be taken care of quickly, for when you tell him that the best introduction to the business is for him to go on the road and sell books, he generally disappears; what he wants is to be an editor—at once. Many of the telephone calls are from authors complaining that their books, which may have been out only a few weeks, are unobtainable at the major bookstores. While this unhappy state of affairs is sometimes exactly as reported by the author, we often find, on checking, that the complaint is unfounded, although many booksellers have a maddening way of letting even new books go out of stock. This habit, which depresses the author and drives the publisher to his wit's end, has been growing; in fact, though the number of bookstores has increased, there are now fewer booksellers carrying a representative stock of publications than twenty years ago.

Another author gripe, sometimes justified but usually not, is that his book has not been properly advertised; he's convinced that one more big ad will start the ball rolling. This is seldom the case. Moreover, it's unhappily true that advertising usually fails to have any discernible effect unless a book is already moving quite rapidly out of the stores. Much publishers' advertising is done to please the author—an expensive pastime and one that eats into profits. Trade book publishers spend many times as much advertising money, based on sales volume, as do department stores; only jewelers and dispensers of perfume match them.

Conferences—editorial, sales, advertising, financial—take a lot of time and there seems to be no way of eliminating them, although at Harper's we encourage editors to make their own decisions about what to publish, since we distrust the committee, compromising approach. Our editorial meetings consist mainly of reports on books which have been accepted and general discussion of future projects.

I spend some time every day with our advertising and sales managers going over advertising copy and plans; jackets must be approved by them. This is only one of the many steps in producing a book: First, the manuscript is copyedited for grammar and punctuation. It is then set up in type and the galley proofs are sent to the author, who has usually already approved the format. Subsequently, the editor and the salesmen establish a sales quota upon which the first printing is based. At this point the publicity and advertising people come into the picture—television and radio appearances are arranged and the advertising budget is established. Finally, the book is published and the author awaits the reviews, just as a playwright tosses in bed waiting to see the notices on his show in the morning papers.

The last thing most people are inclined to do is to buy a book; many enjoy reading them but will resort to anything— beg, borrow or steal—rather than buy. This is not because books are overpriced; when clothbound novels sold at $2 in the twenties, it was just as true. It's hard on the authors, for they get nothing for years of work when their books are borrowed from a friend or taken from a library. Yet people complain about the high prices of books, although they have gone up less than theater tickets or Fuller brushes.

But I do understand the annoyance of a person who buys a book and then finds he doesn't like it. How can he or she know whether a particular title is worth buying? Not from reviews, nor from the recommendations of friends, because everyone's taste is different; yet first-rate reviewers, like Edmund Wilson and Elizabeth Hardwick, can recognize quality. In addition, the publisher's imprint is a useful signpost, although few readers bother to look for it.

One might conclude that enthusiastic reviews and comments from well-known people (obtained by the publisher) would automatically guarantee a book's sale. That helps occasionally, but not always. On the other hand, when Prime Minister Stanley Baldwin endorsed an obscure novel in the twenties, *Precious Bane* by Mary Webb, the sales suddenly soared. So reviews and comments are apt to affect sales, especially in a periodical like the *New York Times Book Review*. But even this statement must be qualified, for when the prestigious London *Times Literary Supplement* ran a long, front-page review of *The Disappearance of the Earwig* from the Swamps of Northumberland* (in four volumes), this opus failed to sell. Hard to believe?

Obviously, a publisher who fails to pay attention to reviewers deserves extinction. Since all editors are more than aware of this, some of them pursue the reviewers, taking them out to lunch and seeking to do them favors. Nothing so surely guarantees omission of a review from the pages of the *New York Times,* although friendly relations and frequent contacts with the critics are useful. With them, as with booksellers, the publisher's imprint counts, so that a book published by Random House, Knopf, Viking or Harper—to take random examples—is likely to receive at least some notice. Perhaps one in every twenty books achieves a review of more than a few lines in a metropolitan paper.

As noted earlier, a publisher's lunch and his evenings are usually devoted to business. At the midday meal he entertains an author or an agent; dinner may be spent trying to entice an author to publish with the firm. And that brings up the thorny question of what is, and is not, considered fair publishing practice. If I admire the work of another publisher's author, am I free to proposition him or her? The answer to that question is probably more a matter of common sense than of ethics. Obviously, only a fool poaches on his neighbor's property unless his chances of success are good, for failure to snare the bird arouses the man across the road just as much as success—and leads to reprisals. Furthermore, it is apt to be bad business to buy an author on the auction block from another house; the required advance or guarantee is likely to be excessive. But ethics do enter

---

* A creature known only to the most avid bird-watchers.

in, as when a woman tries to lure away her friend's cook. When an author is satisfied with his publisher, it is foolhardy, as well as questionable ethics, to try and entice him away. On the other hand, when he is dissatisfied, he's fair game. Sometimes one casts a fly and it is not until many years later that the big fish is caught.

I often hear it said that in the years before World War II publishing used to be a gentleman's game; this was in the days of Tom Wells, who would remark caustically that it was foolish to maintain that a man could be a gentleman and a businessman at the same time. Competition, certainly, was keen in the twenties, and large advances were paid for potential best sellers; in England the literary agents were already an important factor, although in this country their influence in boosting advances was negligible as compared with today. I don't fully agree with Wells's sardonic axiom; after all, a gentleman-businessman may be rare, but, unlike the dodo, he is not yet extinct. On the whole, I would say that publishers in 1971 are more business-oriented than they were forty years ago, and consequently, the book industry has become more commercial, with the result that the tender feelings of competitors are largely ignored. The end result is fiercer competition.

Author dissatisfaction may arise from many causes. I used to have difficulties with my very good friend Louis Bromfield; we would battle over repetitious passages in his manuscripts, which he maintained were put in for emphasis. However, after a tussle, he would quickly forget his objections. Bromfield could also become infuriated by the copyeditor's corrections.* However, when mutual friendliness and professional respect exist between author and publisher, when it is acknowledged that the author is the final authority and the editor knows at what point to give in, serious conflicts do not arise.

In this connection, Betty Smith comes to mind. She, too,

---

* By "copyediting" is meant the correction of faulty punctuation, grammar, construction and the like. It is a very tricky and skilled operation, and over-zealousness on the part of a copyeditor can lose you an author overnight. On the other hand, a perceptive copyeditor can complement and enhance the work of the editor.

presented editorial problems; nevertheless, as in Bromfield's case, she'd accept justifiable criticism. Her original manuscript, submitted in a nonfiction contest and reported on favorably by a first reader, was then read by Elizabeth Lawrence, who was touched by its human quality but felt that the book did not quite come off. Miss Smith herself was uncertain of her intention; she was writing about the family she "wished" she had had. She responded readily to Elizabeth's suggestions for turning the book into a novel; the result, after much work and amiable cooperation between author and editor, was *A Tree Grows in Brooklyn*.

Rarely is money, per se, a major issue between the author and his publisher. Although we have often failed to cover advances to authors by sales of their books, and although we have lost possible authors who demanded unreasonable financial guarantees, I cannot recall any instance of a break over money. However, the late Stanley Rinehart, head of the firm of Farrar & Rinehart, did have some difficulty with his famous mother, Mary Roberts Rinehart, whose novels he published. When he became aware of her dissatisfaction, Stanley asked her for the reason. She replied, "I understand that my books sell very well but, in spite of that, I cannot recall when I last received any money from your company." Rinehart checked his records and found that large royalty checks had been mailed to her regularly, and he couldn't understand what was going on in her mind. How could he satisfy her?

In the middle of the night he had an inspiration. He bought a big strongbox and filled it with thousands of one-dollar bills. He then tied a red ribbon around it, embellished with sprigs of holly, and had the precious package sent to his mother at Christmas. In great excitement, Mrs. Rinehart called her son on Christmas morning: "Stanley dear, can you guess what I've just received from Farrar & Rinehart? It's unbelievable—a real treasure chest brimming over with crisp, new dollar bills! Why, this is a fortune, and I'm worried that your poor firm will go bankrupt. What a bonanza!"

The good lady had paid no attention to the royalty checks she had received; they had meant nothing to her. But dollar bills were real money.

I have digressed from what takes place in a publisher's day, but this is in the nature of the day itself, which, more often than not, proceeds by a series of interruptions. I can think of only a few occasions when there has been opportunity to read a manuscript in the office—even for half an hour; reading must be done at home. Sometimes it is seven o'clock in the evening before one has a chance to read the day's mail.

What Makes a Good Publisher?

A publisher's day having been disposed of, it is fair to ask: What makes a good publisher, one interested and active in both the editorial and business ends of publishing?

It is dangerous to generalize, but I believe that a good publisher is born, not made. In a word, the successful trade book publisher should possess:

A nose
A kind of animal instinct for spotting the prey—the writer
   —before he has displayed his full talents
A sense of figures
Pertinacity
Receptiveness—an interest in almost any subject
A gambling instinct
A sense of timing
Some educational background but not too much

I have already mentioned the indispensable nose. It is not only a matter of having one for books, for subjects and for what people want to read, but a nose for authors, for gifted individuals likely to write well but who haven't yet proved themselves. I stress this quality because, too often, for lack of it an editor fails to hold an author of talent. After taking on a promising first novel an editor may decline the author's second

—a mistake because, even if it does not measure up, the publisher should take a long-run view if he believes in a writer's talent; he should be prepared to take on one book—maybe several—for which he lacks enthusiasm. Otherwise, the talented writer will find another publisher willing to take a long-range gamble. This is what Alfred Knopf did when he worked for Doubleday in his early days. Knopf believed in Joseph Conrad and kept insisting that Conrad would one day be acclaimed as a great novelist, in spite of the fact that his early books failed to achieve public acceptance.

The phrase "a sense of figures" explains itself. No matter what delight he may take in literature, a publisher is in business to make a profit. The better he is at figures, the more he can indulge his literary tastes.

Pertinacity is important. And the publisher needs an acquisitive instinct, although he should not let this appear on the surface. If he has an idea he believes in, or if he thinks someone can produce a first-rate book, he should continue to press for it, just short of making himself a nuisance. Often, surprisingly, a book may come into being long years after it was first discussed. The story of John Gunther's *Inside Europe* is an example; persistence pays off.

By receptiveness, I mean that the publisher, who must combine the qualities of editor, gambler and businessman, should always be on the receiving end. He should take an interest in almost any subject and be content to remain anonymous, letting the author take center stage, being the creative person. The publisher, in his capacity as editor, must be the catalyst and draw people out as does an effective reporter. He should also be an attentive listener and, if he has a valid idea for a book, should make a present of it to the author, laying no claim to it himself.

A good suggestion came to me from a taxi driver named Charlie. He was exhausted, having spent some hours at home trying to keep his large brood of young children amused. And as we chugged along a country road, he told me about his wearing experience and exclaimed, "I wish someone would write a book describing a thousand ways to amuse a child!" His despairing remark ignited a spark, and I told him that the words he had just uttered would yield him $100 from Harper's. He was mystified until I explained that it was our custom to pay this sum to anyone suggesting an acceptable idea for a book project. We parted happily at the end of the taxi ride, and, in due course, Harper's published *838 Ways to Amuse a Child* by June Johnson, a successful book that has sold over many years.

It goes without saying that without a gambling instinct and a taste for hazardous adventure a man should never hang out a publishing sign.

As for a sense of timing, it is as essential to a publisher as to an art dealer. The most perceptive art dealers in the 1890's had spotted the French Post-Impressionists, but they were too far ahead of the public taste to be able to sell these paintings with any profit. In contrast, the dealers of a later decade made fortunes, having caught the new wave of taste at the right moment. The same thing happens in publishing: The publisher who thinks in terms of the past is finished, but if he anticipates public taste too far, he's in equal trouble. We all know of conventional publishers who have failed and whose passing evoked little regret; it is for the business failures of pioneers like Thomas Seltzer, Ben Huebsch, Pat Covici and Robert Haas that we have sympathy, for they first published writers of the stature of D. H. Lawrence, James Joyce, Thorstein Veblen, Sherwood Anderson, John Steinbeck, William Faulkner, Robert Graves and André Malraux. Martin Secker of London is another example of a publisher who lived in the future and consequently had to sell his firm. In the twenties he had acquired an impressive group of writers, but he'd discovered them too early.

The final attribute of a successful trade publisher is a curious one: some educational background but not too much. To illustrate: Had I been knowledgeable about sixteenth-century biographies, I wouldn't have combed Oxford for a life of Elizabeth I; I would have known that, in the opinion of scholars, an excellent life of her was still in print. But in, and perhaps through, my ignorance I got results. I knew just enough about the period to be able to discuss it and consequently picked up—if such a term can be used respectfully in connection with A. L. Rowse and Hugh Trevor-Roper—two first-rate historians for the House.

An example of a publisher who was first-rate and yet had little educational background was a man who started his career at the turn of the century as a salesman for Harper's little establishment in London. Jonathan Cape did not attend a university, but if ever there was a man with a nose and the indefinable capacity for spotting authors, he was the example. In his prime, in the twenties and thirties, Jonathan Cape was *the* outstanding new and imaginative publisher in London.

I have already indicated that I distrust analytical evaluations where publishing judgments are concerned; the public's taste defies analysis. In my opinion, when an editor chooses a book because he figures out that it will appeal to a large popular audience, he usually guesses wrong. His only safeguard, in the exercise of literary judgment, is to have the kind of mind that shares the reactions of the crowd; what interests and amuses the mass book audience must be what interests and amuses him. Sometimes, admittedly, the public chooses fiction that is vulgar and "corny," but sometimes not. When Harold Latham of the Macmillan Company enthusiastically accepted Margaret Mitchell's *Gone With the Wind,* he did so, not because he had analyzed the public taste, but because he was carried away by this wonderful story and was sufficiently representative of the average reader to pick a great best seller. Similarly, in the case of *A Tree Grows in Brooklyn,* it was the editor's identification with the public's taste that was the determining factor in the choice of the book. Miss Lawrence's emotional reaction was that of the typical bookstore customer.

I have suggested that the editor's evaluation of his readers' reports is a complicated business. Some publishers establish rules, which I suspect, like the automatic declination of a manuscript which has failed to get an expert's approval. I doubt the value of such a routine process because the editor must be the final judge on the publication of a book. It is up to him to decide whether a given expert's opinion may be prejudiced or may express too technical a view. For example, a manuscript is submitted—say, a biography designed for popular consumption;

although it should be factually accurate, it cannot, by its nature, be all-inclusive, nor encompass the amount of detail and cover all the sources a scholar might demand.

The editor's decision must govern, and it is the major responsibility of the management of any publishing company to ferret out good editors. The Oxford University Press succeeded in this aim when they picked the editor, Philip Vaudrin, who spotted Rachel Carson's talent. Miss Carson was almost unknown at the time—she was a civil servant in the Department of the Interior with only one book, *Under the Sea Wind,* to her credit, and that had been a publishing failure. Vaudrin and his associates found themselves absorbed by a new manuscript by Rachel Carson and were so certain about its quality that they contracted for it immediately, ignoring the fate of her previous book. The manuscript was *The Sea Around Us,* which will, I believe, be read as a classic when all of us are dead.

Obviously, the publisher must depend considerably on the reports of his readers, although he will not be effective unless he reads endlessly himself—at home, on trains, wherever he can find a few minutes without interruption. In evaluating his readers' reports he must take into consideration their prejudices and tastes as well as being aware of his own; in addition, he should take care to distinguish between the opinions a reader is qualified to give and those he is not. To illustrate: In 1920 a historical manuscript of obvious importance was submitted to Harper's, and the editor decided to obtain an expert reading from James Harvey Robinson, one of the best-known historians of the day. Robinson reported the book to be an outstanding contribution to current thinking but concluded that it was not one for a commercial house to publish in view of what he considered its limited, scholarly appeal. The editor made the mistake of disregarding Robinson's opinion, as a historian, of the book's quality but accepted his estimate of its salability, which Robinson, a scholar, was not qualified to make. The rejected manuscript was Oswald Spengler's *Decline of the West,* now a standard work. It is the *fairly good* manuscript which presents a problem to the editor; the distinguished book is quite easy to spot. And while one might think that an editor's course of action was clear when he's been presented with a strongly adverse report on a manuscript, that is just the time to watch one's step, for a violent reaction from a reader is apt to mean that the book he has been reading has an explosive quality and hence will create controversy—and probably sales.

The life of a publisher, as is apparent, is full of ups and downs. At best it is stimulating and absorbing, for he must be in contact with the best minds of his time; this is challenging. On the other hand, his work is full of detail, often tiresome detail. And the matter of declining manuscripts is a continual headache, always depressing and sometimes extremely painful; finally many authors, being creative people, are difficult to deal with. The editor stands or falls on his ability to persuade his authors to accept the changes and revisions he proposes to them —or makes himself. Again and again, particularly when an editor lacks tact, the author will leave him and seek a more sympathetic publisher. In many such cases he will eventually make the very changes proposed by the first editor; when this happens, the original editor may derive some melancholy satisfaction from having helped to improve a manuscript, even though in the process he lost an author.

How does a good editor edit? He does this by attempting to persuade the author to revise his manuscript. That is the secret, for the author knows more about his book than anyone else. The editor can make intelligent suggestions, but, when these are not carried out, the editor must get to work on the manuscript himself and put it into shape. He must strive to see the book as a whole and show the author how to make changes in the beginning, middle or end of his manuscript that will make it a more effective piece of writing.

I have known many good editors; some of them have become quite well known—others, not. Frequently, the most publicized editors are those who contract for a large number of books carrying big advances, and, despite the fact that many of these advances remain unearned and that many of the manuscripts selected by them turn out publishing failures, these individuals have retained their reputations as great editors.

One of an editor's functions is to help his authors to find

attractive titles for their books. A title should catch the eye, it should arouse curiosity, it should suggest clearly the contents of the book, it should be brief and memorable. Sometimes the title of a book has none of these attributes, but if the book sells, it's all right.

So long as he can survive his trials, a publisher gets certain satisfactions, although he's bound to be plagued by the mistakes he has made. He will keep his reason only by repeating to himself that trade publishing is no more predictable than horse racing; only one book in three makes a profit. He should not be discouraged even when his average falls below one in three for, often, the editor who picks a succession of flops is the most valuable—provided he also finds some best sellers. In contrast, the editor who contributes a succession of mediocre books with satisfactory sales may be only mediocre himself.

At the present time, over four decades from the start of my publishing career, it is a delight for me still to be editing books by E. B. White, Thornton Wilder and John Gunther, authors who remain as fresh as when they started writing in the twenties. When he died, Gunther had completed only a fifth of his projected *Inside Australia;* the manuscript, with the invaluable help of Jane Gunther, who accompanied her husband on the Australian journey, has been completed by William H. Forbis.

I have made the ideal publisher-editor sound important and have meant to do so; he is indeed important, but should remain the catalyst. For the great book can be produced by only one person, the man or woman who writes it. The editor can sometimes suggest and provide a spark, he can help and support the writer, but he is—and must continue to be—the anonymous, sometimes essential, man behind the scenes. His only monument can be the publishing house where he has worked.

Having described the ideal editor, I suppose I should take a look at myself and see how I stack up; I consider myself *average* because my likes and dislikes are those of the crowd. Like a Mack truck I keep moving at a maddeningly even pace under all conditions. A plodder? Yes, but I hope that I possess other, less deadly, qualities such as curiosity and interest in the future rather than the past. A bit of an actor, an optimist, something of a show-off, an enjoyer of life, a lover of the world, I swear by Shakespeare's observation:

> There is a tide in the affairs of men
> Which, taken at the flood, leads on to fortune;
> Omitted, all the voyage of their life
> Is bound in shallows and in miseries.

Travel—Near and Far

Travel, all my life, has been a necessity as well as a pleasure; I have traveled more than most and enjoy the stimulation of new places and people.

One of the strangest foreign places is Hollywood, where many potentially good novelists have ended up as scriptwriters in order to maintain their swimming pools and elaborate houses. In Hollywood there have always been many talented authors who wanted to write fiction but who could not because of their financial obligations. Many years ago I offered one of them a $5,000 advance—quite a handsome sum for a second novel—which he accepted, and so everything was set for the eventual delivery of a manuscript. But the arrangement didn't stick. His monthly expenses came to $5,000 and he was forced to go back to the scriptwriting he disliked. He was one of many; not only among scriptwriters, but today among television people and advertising copywriters as well. They are apt to be a sad, disillusioned lot, trapped by their way of life.

I have yet to go to a first-class restaurant, anywhere, without finding a publisher at the best table, and in Hollywood there are many fine eating places. On one trip there I was royally entertained over a long weekend by a Harper author who also wrote

Thornton Wilder

G. D. Hackett

John Gunther

Erich Hartmann

E. B. White

James Thurber

Adlai E. Stevenson with Albert Schweitzer in Africa, 1954

Glenway Wescott

Peter Deane

Sir Winston Churchill presenting the Duff Cooper Memorial Prize to Alan Moorehead for his book, *Gallipoli*

Eric Hoffer on the waterfront

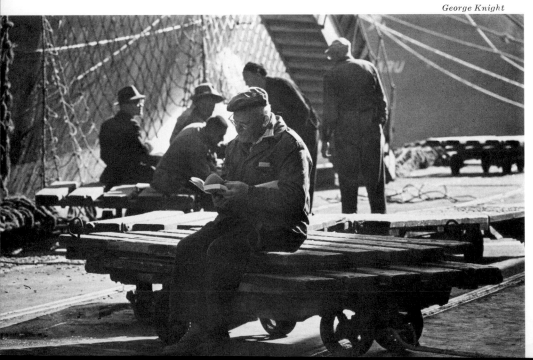

George Hoyningen-Huene

Consuelo Vanderbilt Balsan, 1942

Svetlana Alliluyeva flanked by Edward Greenbaum and myself at the publication party for *Twenty Letters to a Friend*

Linda Moser

Jill Fuller Fox

Sage Fuller Cowles
and John Cowles, Jr.

Gabriella and Cass Canfield, Jr., with their son, Temple

Michael Canfield and John F. Kennedy
in Jamaica in 1957

CC on a cruise through
the Greek islands, 1969

CC at his Harper desk, 1970

Paul Wilkes

movie scripts. The time had come for a reciprocal gesture, so I took him to a well-known restaurant. In due course the check was presented and, as I reached for my wallet, my guest beat me to the draw. This bothered me no end, but, when I protested, he told me that it would damage his reputation around town if I were seen paying the bill. He pointed to a gossip columnist at a nearby table, who would know that he was dining with a New York publisher and would be bound to write stories about him, picturing him as down and out. That was Hollywood in the golden era of the big studios.

From there Jane and I motored to Pasadena to see Mrs. Zane Grey, who had kept her late husband's study exactly as it was in his lifetime; she treated the room where he wrote with the reverence due to a Shakespeare. Zane Grey was a genuine "original"; first a bush league baseball player, then a dentist, he came to consider himself one of the two greatest American writers—he and Mark Twain. It didn't faze him that critics wrote ironic comments about his books; he *knew* that he was the best. He did deserve some fame, for his early novels were good of their kind.

Harper's published forty Zane Grey books, including about twenty of the manuscripts left at his death. His novels were translated into twenty languages and helped materially to perpetuate the legend of the Wild West. It is a wonder to me that Westerns continue to attract millions of readers and moviegoers, considering that the Old West disappeared with Custer's Last Stand. But then it is a wonder, too, that spy stories absorb vast audiences in a time when satellites can uncover more secrets than any number of CIA agents, Mata Haris or James Bonds.

It was in Aspen, Colorado, on a later trip west, that I took part in a seminar which made a deep impression on me. Najeeb Hallaby, then head of the Civil Aeronautics Board, was asked to prosecute—in a mock trial—the case of the Athenian Senate vs. Socrates. Was the great philosopher guilty of corrupting the young men of Athens by inciting them to dissent against the State? Hallaby, though convinced of Socrates' innocence, argued brilliantly that he was guilty, with the result that when the case was put to the jurors, the vote condemning Socrates was 8 to 7, precisely the same ratio as that in the Athenian Senate nearly 2,500 years before! The incident gave me pause then, and does now. Through all the centuries of change so much remains the same.

My wanderings in these postwar years took me several times to Mexico and frequently to England and the Continent. In Paris I met Nancy Mitford, well known for her witty novels and distinguished biographies. She was in a mood to make new publishing arrangements so that my visit was fortunate and timely. Miss Mitford, a good friend of Art Buchwald, would often see him in Paris, and one day he lent her a copy of *The Day Lincoln Was Shot*. A week later Buchwald asked this aristocratic lady how she liked the book. "Oh," she said, "I found it fascinating, but, you see, I have always had an irrational dislike for Abraham Lincoln. I couldn't wait to finish the book; I knew that he was going to be assassinated but was kept in suspense for fear that something would happen to change the end." Buchwald printed this story in his *Herald Tribune* column, with the result that letters of protest poured in from Lincoln fans all over the country.

In London I arranged with Alan Moorehead for the publication of his books. At the time they did not sell particularly well in this country, but, as the years passed, his gift was recognized so that his books about the Gallipoli campaign, Australia and the Russian Revolution achieved the wide recognition they deserved. His *The White Nile* is a vivid picture of a land and its people.

Another fine British author we acquired much later was Harold Macmillan, the British Prime Minister, who is now completing his impressive memoirs in five volumes. I recall having lunch with this great man and the editors of the London *Times*. At first, Macmillan disappointed me; in inaudible tones he made feeble jokes. But, as lunch progressed and the wine circulated, a light came into his eye. He then spoke clearly and brilliantly; he might, in fact, have been addressing a session of the House of Lords or the House of Commons.

Eric Hoffer, the former San Francisco longshoreman, is in striking contrast to these two distinguished Britishers. Outgoing and bluff, he appears to be a simple person but, below the surface, is a complicated character. Of his many books I still admire most *The True Believer*. Eisenhower did, too, and I've seen a copy heavily annotated with Ike's handwritten comments. Hoffer, who, after several years of blindness as a boy, educated himself, is a fresh interpreter of American life. He is a unique figure in contemporary letters.

Round the World Again

One day in the fall of 1952, when our relations with Russia were deteriorating, I received a phone call from my friend Tom Finletter, then Secretary of the Air Force, inviting me to accompany him on a round-the-world flight to inspect U.S. airfields which had been built or were under construction to offset Soviet military power. I accepted eagerly, and we were off within the week; the party included a number of generals and Finletter's wife, Gay. We flew south from Paris over the lush, green Burgundy country, which contrasted sharply with the dryness of the brown Spanish landscape; indeed, from Burgundy on, we saw only occasional, sparse patches of green until we reached Thailand, halfway around the world. Our Air Force plane put down wherever we had military airfields. A network of them was being constructed, at Finletter's insistence, in great haste, and consequently at great expense. He believed—and I feel he was right at the time—that, unless this country encircled the Soviet Union with air bases, we would be in grave danger, since the United States and its allies were no match for the vast Russian ground forces.

In Spain I encountered John Masters, one of our authors,

who made an interesting observation. From watching the Spanish women near the U.S. base, laundering clothes in washing machines, observing their children in cowboy suits drinking Coca-Cola and the men playing baseball, he reached the conclusion that, except for the Romans, no civilization has ever been able to impose its native characteristics on another to the extent of the Americans. Certainly, not the English who, in the Middle Ages, controlled half of France but, in departing, left little trace except for the French sporting types who drink *le weeski et soda*. Not the French, for, despite 1066 and the lovely ladies they contributed to many royal households, nothing remains to mark their influence in England except for a few French restaurants in London.

As our plane was landing in Marrakech, Finletter received a radio message reporting an unidentified flying object (UFO) sighted nearby. He radioed back that we wished to meet the captain who had made the observation; accordingly, upon our arrival, the general in command of the base brought the man to lunch, against his will, because the last thing he wanted was to be considered eccentric. Nevertheless, he told his story. With two technical sergeants, and equipped with the proper instruments, he had spotted an object flying at two thousand miles per hour, a speed then unobtainable by any known plane. It turned sharply, at a ninety-degree angle; it was round, like a saucer, and emitted a strange light. Unbelievable, but there it was, a UFO, attested by qualified experts.

Back in our plane, General Norstad, commander of NATO, and his brother officers explained to me that the phenomenon must have been caused by swamp gas or something of the sort. However, after dinner, the talk loosened up, and in a free exchange of opinions one of the officers burst out with: "Wouldn't it be funny if we were all wrong and the object was actually a flying saucer? The truth is that we really know nothing about this subject."

Our hottest stopover was Bahrein, at the head of the Persian Gulf, where we maintain a big oil installation; the heat there can be nearly as intense as that of a sauna bath. To welcome us, a squad of pathetic, undersized Arab soldiers appeared, scarcely able to lift their rifles. In sharp contrast, the smart, British-trained Pakistani guard at Karachi were strikingly precise, and when their band played "God Save the Queen," it was very moving.

From Hong Kong I was sent on, alone, to Formosa. As the little plane was about to land there, I was surprised to receive a message to the effect that the U.S. Army and Air Force commanders would meet me at the airport; I didn't realize that they even knew my name. Within a few moments I had regained my cool—and my vanity. It seemed to me perfectly understandable, on reflection, that these generals should be anxious to meet an "expert" on airfield construction who had been traveling with the Secretary of the Air Force. Upon landing in the darkness I prepared to salute the waiting honor guard and was disappointed that the guard and band were not to be seen.

But the generals were. Without a word they escorted me to the shed that served as the military airport, making sure that all the doors and windows were securely closed. Thereupon a torrent of abuse was heaped upon me: "We understand that, at Bangkok, Finletter's party was welcomed by fifty Thai jet fighters. Goddamn it! We haven't received *one* jet for the Nationalist forces here although we've trained fifteen hundred Chinese pilots to fly them! And"—more cussing—"after being in office for several years, Truman sends, not the Secretary of State, not Finletter, but *you!*" They went on to add that they'd received no reinforcements nor supplies. After an overnight stay with these gentle creatures I flew to Tokyo and rejoined Finletter, to whom I related the generals' complaints. Possibly as a result, some fresh military supplies were sent to Taiwan.

From Tokyo we visited the front in Korea, flying in helicopters at treetop level in order to avoid enemy fire. We walked around the front-line trenches, from which we could see Panmunjom, seat of the endless peace negotiations. The trenches were manned by a United States Marine battalion which had suffered casualties up to half its strength in the preceding few weeks.

On the final leg of our journey we reached Anchorage in

Alaska. Knowing in advance that we would stop there, I'd thoughtfully brought a bright red flannel hunting shirt which I felt would be suitable in that cold climate. It was decidedly not, for we were rushed to an elaborate luncheon at which the generals' ladies were covered with orchids. Mrs. Finletter's luncheon partner asked her who was the strange-looking character in the red hunting shirt, and she quickly replied, "Oh, he's a rather queer artist we took along to do a portrait of my husband."

The late Mrs. Finletter was delightful and talented, with a ready wit that sparkled in her conversation as well as in her books, *From the Top of the Stairs* and *The Dinner Party*. Over the years, as a member of Washington's official society, she developed a special technique which she found useful for holding the attention of her dinner companions. To some minor official seated next to her she would say, "I hear that you're slated to be Under Secretary of State"—or Labor, or Interior, or Agriculture—whatever might fit the circumstance. At this, the young man would stammer out the reply that she must have been misinformed. Then, recovering confidence, he'd admit that there *had* been talk of a shake-up in his department and that anything might happen.

In this way the Washington rumor factory gets its supply of misinformation.

Adlai Stevenson

It was at a dinner given by the Lloyd Garrisons in the winter of 1955 that my wife and I had the opportunity of talking to Adlai Stevenson, whom I'd seen only once or twice previously. Over coffee and cigars he described a projected tour of Africa, where he was going on legal business. We showed such lively interest in his plans that he suggested we and the Garrisons accompany him on the trip, with Bill Blair—then his aide and later our Ambassador to the Philippines. We accepted on the spot.

A fortnight later we all met in Nairobi. The opening hour, I recall, was rather stiff as we took each other's measure as traveling companions. Stevenson was tired from a long flight and, when lunch was over, retired for a nap after asking Garrison and me to come to his sitting room at five o'clock, when Professor Louis Leakey, the famous anthropologist and authority on East Africa, was to call. Garrison and I showed up on the dot of five, as did Leakey. The conversation lagged; Stevenson was very sleepy, very tired, and reacted indifferently to the questions addressed to him. After a few minutes, during which Adlai's replies to Leakey were almost inaudible and there were awkward pauses, I decided to try my luck with the distinguished professor. Some leading questions from me soon got him going and things went splendidly for about an hour. As he got up to leave, Leakey thanked me for a delightful interview, adding, "I have a book for you, Mr. Stevenson, which I've inscribed." I gracefully accepted the volume, with a glance at Stevenson, who gave me the wink.

Stevenson had law business in South Africa, and this gave him a reason for touring the continent. He loved to travel, to learn about people, and he was sharply observant. He would conserve his energy by relaxing at will, and whenever there was a wait—ten minutes or an hour—Adlai would take a quick nap.

Our trip, starting in East Africa, continued through the Rhodesias, Johannesburg, the Congo and, finally, up the west coast to Accra. In Nairobi the Mau Mau outrages were still going on. Looking out our bedroom window into the big courtyard, we watched Africans at work, going about their tasks cheerlessly, with fear in their eyes. This was not surprising because in Mau Mau country the African was in far greater danger than the white; for every Britisher murdered, a hundred black men were killed.

As we wandered about the city, we saw, everywhere, evidence of the terror. Here were African workers living in barbed-wire compounds built to protect them from the Mau Maus; nearby, the fenced-in convict enclosures contained hundreds of Mau Mau prisoners, sullen, determined and full of hate. Out in the country, we found the non-Mau Mau natives herded together for safety in fortified villages, dominated by wooden watchtowers some fifty to sixty feet high and surrounded by moats. Within these armed camps squads of native home guards drilled in dilapidated shorts, proudly doing the manual of arms with rifles supplied by the British.

Nairobi, according to John Gunther, boasts eight golf courses and seven lions. We visited the wild animal park there and found a small pride of lions; we went close to them, protected by our Land Rover. The game warden, who was very proud of his lions, told me of a recent event which had shocked him deeply: A French *père de famille* was looking out of the window of his house, watching his young children at play, when a lion appeared with hungry eyes fixed on his progeny. "Can you imagine what he did?" the game warden asked. (Well, I could.) "He shot the lion!"

A reminder that everything is relative.

John Gunther's reports on the country were very helpful. He had supplied Adlai with a set of galley proofs of *Inside Africa*, and we read them avidly, for they contained more information about the continent than we could ever have learned at first hand on a short visit. Our itinerary was marked by a trail of these sheets, which were constantly flying out of our car windows.

Stevenson, at the time of this journey, was already an international figure. He was received as such everywhere we went; we accompanied him to lunches and dinners given by the governors of the various colonies. I was struck by Stevenson's impact on the Africans. In Uganda we visited a black college, Makerere, and as we were walking toward our cars through a dusty little campus, hundreds of students suddenly appeared. They thronged around Adlai, asking him to speak to them; he did so, off the cuff, with a grace and an understanding that delighted them. This sort of thing happened several times on the trip; he was the best extemporaneous speaker I'd ever heard.

It was one of his winning traits that he would become completely absorbed in what he was doing and seeing. Markets in Africa fascinated him, and he'd spend hours wandering about them, talking to the natives through an interpreter.

A tragic incident occurred in Uganda. We were motoring down a straight road when a drunken African on a bicycle swerved out in front of the car. We watched, horrified, as the man and his bicycle were hurled over the radiator against our windshield; looking back, we saw him lying motionless in the road, entangled in the wreckage of his machine. The road was deserted, but, within moments, a crowd of Africans appeared out of the bush, attracted instinctively to the scene; many of them were drunk. We were out of the Mau Mau country, but Uganda was, nevertheless, a land of smoldering discontent directed against the British. In the agonizing wait for medical aid to reach us we did our best to put up a good front, to look confident and in control of the situation as the onlookers swarmed around the victim, who was barely breathing and obviously in bad shape. A woman started to wail, and her hysterical lamentations were taken up by the other women. The situation looked very ugly, and had it not been for the composure of our African driver, violence might well have broken out.

After what seemed a long time, during which we expected to be attacked momentarily, an extremely young, blond British official arrived on the scene with first-aid equipment, armed only with a small swagger stick. His natural manner and the words he addressed to the crowd in their own language turned the tide; the wounded man was carried away to the hospital in Kabala. This was a striking example of the cool confidence of British officials in Africa and of their remarkable hold over the natives.

Because the color bar was absolute in British Africa, we were in for a surprise when we entered the Belgian territory of Ruanda-Urundi. The Catholic bishopric there is a large brick building set on a hill just across the border from Uganda, and here we waited for the African bishop to receive us. He entered the anteroom after a few moments—a tall, impressive

Watusi giant, accompanied by two Belgian priests. To our amazement, the white officer accompanying us knelt down and kissed his hand. This was one of those staggering contrasts frequently encountered in Africa. Though the Ruanda-Urundi countryside appeared similar to that of British Uganda, the Belgians operated on a wholly different concept. Here the African native was not barred from high office when he was qualified to hold it.

South Africa, the sorest spot on the continent, where the white population is entrenched, although outnumbered almost four to one by the blacks, offered other surprises and disturbing contrasts. The situation there was impossible to evaluate. In spite of the antagonism between the races, they depend on each other, the Africans as laborers in a booming industrial economy, the whites as managers and organizers. It is hard even to speculate about what can be done in South Africa to achieve stability; one thing only seems reasonably certain: The intensive drive by the South African Nationalist Party to impose a complete color bar, to achieve absolute separation of the races, is leading to disaster.

Certain incidents stand out vividly, sometimes incongruously, from the events of those five crowded weeks. In Swaziland, Adlai presented to the King a fine art book we had brought for the occasion. The King thanked us in a speech delivered in such perfect English that we were doubly astonished when, a few minutes later, the Crown Princess entered the room on all fours—in deference to His Exalted Majesty. At sundown we had "tea" with the Queen Mother in her thatched kraal and were served a nauseous concoction from a bowl which was passed around for all of us to share.

From South Africa we flew to the Belgian Congo. The citizens of what was then Léopoldville are proud of their live, bustling city, and it was natural that one of them should insist that we visit their brand-new stadium. Since we'd seen quite a number of such structures elsewhere, we murmured about the heat and made excuses, but it was useless to protest; the stadium was a center of civic pride and we were going to see it and like it. After our experience of South Africa, the sight was quite overwhelming; several hundred African boys and girls were being trained by white-clad Catholic nuns in great dance formations. A large native band produced lively music and everyone looked happy and absorbed. This just couldn't be true; it was an unbelievable scene after the sullen, angry crowds in the native locations of Johannesburg. The market in Léopoldville came as another heartening surprise; the natives there were laughing and shouting at one another. We had forgotten, in South and East Africa, about the black man's great capacity for gaiety. There was color, too, in that market, in contrast to the drabness of other areas, where Africans wore European dress. Here the barefooted women, happily selecting fried caterpillars and monkey meat from the foodstuffs on display, were attired in gorgeous calicoes. On their heads they carried brilliantly colored trays matching their elaborate costumes.

The Belgian Congo, at the time of our visit, had come a long way from the days when, as the personal property of King Leopold II, the country was the scandal of the age. Yet the great revolutionary explosion took place there rather than in South Africa. Was it because, unlike the South Africans, the people of the Congo knew something of the taste of freedom; because their spirit had not been deadened by extreme oppression from the white population?

We ended up at Accra, where we saw the handsomest and best-dressed women in the world; their diaphanous, flowing garments and vivid turbans would make Christian Dior green with envy. Although these native ladies lived in mud hovels, they were spotless, for Accra is on the dirt line dividing the filthy Mohammedan north of Africa from the clean, black south.

It was a wrench to leave Adlai when our journey came to an end; with his delight in everything he saw, he had been a gay, stimulating companion. Only once on the trip had American politics been mentioned. Stevenson was then debating whether to make himself available again for the Presidential nomination, and, as he seemed to want our views, Garrison and I expressed the opinion that he should not run a second time—the chances of his winning against Eisenhower seemed too slim. To this Stevenson replied that we were undoubtedly right and that he appreciated our advice. However, the problem as he saw it came down to a very simple issue: If the party really wanted him to represent it, and so insisted, he felt that he had no choice but to accept. This incident was significant to me because Stevenson has so often been accused of indecisiveness.

My Foray into Politics

Later that year Lloyd Garrison, who had long been active in Democratic Party affairs, asked me whether I'd be willing to take part in the Stevenson Presidential campaign of 1956. I didn't have a ready answer. On the one hand, I liked and admired Stevenson, and I am a Democrat by persuasion. Moreover, I have long been interested in politics and have always welcomed the challenge of working in a new field. On the other hand, I knew it would be difficult, in terms of available spare time, to combine political activity with publishing. Furthermore, I hesitated, as an editor, to become involved in politics because I believe that a publisher should maintain a nonpartisan position.

I debated with myself, at length, and finally concluded that in this case I was bound to help out so far as I could. Accordingly, I agreed to take on the job of chairman of the executive committee of the Volunteers for Stevenson in New York State. This was in the fall of 1955.

The people with whom I worked most closely during the following months were Tom Finletter and Anna Rosenberg; they were my superiors in the political hierarchy. Finletter was an old friend, but I hardly knew Anna Rosenberg. As chairman of the executive committee I was quite surprised when she took over our meetings. However, she knew the ins and outs of Democratic politics in New York as I did not, and she's a woman bursting with ideas and vitality. So I was glad to have her take the lead.

During a twelve-month period I devoted several hours a day to the Stevenson campaign. I learned something about the workings of a political organization and found that, in contrast to the relative orderliness of a business operation, politics is a disorganized kind of activity. The confusions of working with volunteers, the unexpected crises to be dealt with—such as raising money at the eleventh hour to pay for television time—required adaptability and infinite patience. Somehow we all survived, and I must say that the volunteers, the majority of them women, were remarkable. In particular, the selfless concentration of Marietta Tree, who did splendid work and never pushed herself forward, impressed me.

We—Finletter, Anna Rosenberg and I—had dealings, of course, with the regular Democratic organization, with Carmine De Sapio, then head of Tammany Hall. There were no difficulties that led to unpleasantness, but we found it hard to correlate our activities with those of De Sapio; though he talked of cooperation, and though we did our best to work with him, real teamwork was never achieved. The regular Democratic organization just didn't cotton to the volunteers, and the Tammany pros probably thought that, if the volunteers became too powerful, the reform movement would gain momentum. Their attitude, although understandable, was disheartening.

Altogether, I enjoyed this political job and learned a lot; it was a good deal like being in show business on a large scale. Of course, the end of the campaign was a letdown because our candidate was badly beaten. In a way we had expected defeat; but once one becomes involved in a campaign one becomes infused with enthusiasm and belief in victory. Even Adlai Stevenson, who was experienced in politics, responded to the tremendous receptions he was given, and, to some extent, was carried away. True, he became depressed sometimes and would then lose touch with his supporters. This occurred when he was speaking, early one morning, to some West Virginia miners about the problem of the Chinese offshore islands. One of his pro advisers, Jim Flanagan, put it bluntly when he snorted,

"The miners thought he was telling them about breakfast foods—talking about Quemoy and Matsu!" Another time, after a day of hard campaigning in Brooklyn, Long Island and Westchester, Adlai ended up with an address at the town hall in White Plains. He was exhausted, the sparkle that could hold an audience with the hypnotic power of a John Barrymore had left him, and he read listlessly from a prepared speech. He was a flop and he knew it, but his ebullient and humorous spirit could not be curbed for long. Later that evening Jane and I drove him to our house in Bedford, and as we turned into the driveway, which is dominated by tall spruces, Adlai stepped out of the car to address the noble trees in ringing, oratorical tones: "Friends, Romans, countrymen, lend me your ears. . . ."

At the wind-up of the campaign an incident occurred which impressed me with his detachment; it showed him magnificent and unruffled in defeat. There was the usual farewell party for the candidate in the ballroom of a large hotel in New York—a depressing affair, in view of the election results, for all of us who had worked for Stevenson. He then flew to Chicago, and the next morning a few of his friends followed to spend the day with him. At the Blackstone Hotel there was still a good deal of excitement—reporters, television cameramen and the like crowded around Stevenson, and we spent an interesting day discussing what the Democratic Party should do next. In the evening we had dinner with Mrs. Edison Dick, a close friend of Adlai's; we were about twenty-five people at a buffet supper, and it happened that a few of us were gathered at one end of the room with the Governor. Mrs. Dick had provided a magnificent claret which Stevenson enjoyed, and, as we sat together for several hours sipping the wine, he did most of the talking. He touched on many subjects, from classical Greece to the meaning of history, but never once in the course of the evening did he mention politics. An amazing performance for a man who had just gone through the beating of weeks of intensive campaigning.

Later, when Stevenson worked at the United Nations, I saw a good deal of him; we would play tennis together, and occasionally he'd stay with us in Bedford. Although he sometimes spoke of current problems, of his difficult position in the UN, where he was obliged to reflect the Washington view, which was often not his own, he was inclined to choose his own topics of conversation. He never shared confidences which might, for example, have revealed how he and President Kennedy differed about the Bay of Pigs invasion—the subject, of course, of Stevenson's most famous UN speech.

One is tempted to contrast Stevenson with John F. Kennedy. I didn't know JFK as well as I did Adlai, but when Kennedy was a young Senator, he impressed me with his reserve power. However, he did not quite have Stevenson's wit. In comparing these men I would say that Stevenson was more interested in ideas, Kennedy more concerned with action. If asked to assign them positions in a publishing business—to put them in a context I know about—I would make Kennedy the president of the company and Stevenson the chief editor.

Would Stevenson have made a good President? There's no answer to this question, any more than there was in the case of Lincoln before he took office. Certainly Stevenson was a states-man, an intellectual, orator and poet. And it must be added that if there were any truth to the charge that Stevenson was in-decisive, it might apply to his handling of small decisions—such as his reluctance to make up his mind until the last moment whether or not to accept an invitation to dinner. He also found it difficult to decide on his plans for a short vacation. On the other hand, when a question of substance had to be resolved, such as our role in Vietnam or our policy toward China, Steven-son's opinions were definite, firm and consistently held. And as Governor of Illinois he made an outstanding record. Without question, he was one of the most gifted men ever to have taken part in our national politics.

What I cherish most about Adlai Stevenson was his in-fectious zest for living, despite the demands upon his energies and the frustrations he must have experienced in his UN career. Shortly after his death Sir Julian Huxley observed that he had the gift of friendship—and, more than that, the gift of loving and being loved. This was very true. Adlai's own moving words about Eleanor Roosevelt apply to him, also: "She would rather light candles than curse the darkness, and her glow warmed the world."

Sputnik and the Revolution in Education

I have mentioned the changes in publishing in the wake of World War II; the greatly increased need for textbooks was a major development. Our population was then growing by leaps and bounds, young men were returning from war to re-enter college, more mature than college students of former years. This created a demand for better education, a demand that, in my opinion, received its full impetus from Sputnik. Although the effect of a single event can be exaggerated, the Soviet launching of Sputnik was a dramatic turning point which made Americans realize that they were not ahead in education, but behind. Sputnik was the shock that destroyed our smugness and spurred us on to improve our educational tools. One significant new trend was the introduction into the college curriculum of trade books to supplement the basic texts. Currently, the student in a superior college is exposed to the best books on any given subject, and this policy is spreading to the less advanced institutions. More and more, the need to read outside the required curriculum is being emphasized. In consequence, the increase in the institutional buying of books has been very marked in recent years; this in spite of the fact that Federal grants to libraries and schools, which were an important factor in postwar publishing, were severely cut for several years. Publishers have come to depend more and more upon sales to libraries and other institutional sources; in the case of Harper's, about 50 percent of our adult trade books, and about 75 percent of our children's books, are sold to institutions.

Book departments in college stores have grown enormously, again in large part because of the popularity of paperbacks. In selling paperbacks, many of them for use in specific courses, the stores found that they could also sell selected clothbound books as the dividing lines between trade and educational titles, adult and children's books, became blurred.

The use of electronic devices in teaching is another new factor in modern-day education and publishing. Some fear that this will lessen the value of books and authors, but I take an optimistic view. Like fire, the machine can be a benefit or a disaster, depending upon the use to which it is put. That there exists today a tendency toward standardization is apparent; the mass media of communication give ample evidence of it. But this does not mean that the use of electronic devices in teaching cannot be adapted to individual needs, nor does it mean that the machine will supplant books and the people who write them. I believe that electronics will necessarily be confined to certain teaching areas where factual presentation rather than intellectual concepts is involved. Because of the novelty of the new methods we are apt to exaggerate their importance, forgetting that a computer is of value only to the extent that an excellent program is fed into it.

No doubt the role of the author in the academic field will change; he will be concerned with creating programs as well as writing books. But he cannot be replaced. For much the same reason I believe the publisher's function in the future will be fully as important as it is today. Techniques of conveying information will alter and develop, yet no one but the creative author can produce the required educational material and no one but the good editor can help him do so. There is excellent evidence to support the view that the book is not only a necessary source for teaching programs but the best, and probably the only, tool where complicated subjects are involved. And, so far as the general public is concerned, the book offers a unique variety of stimulation and interest.

Threat from the Mass Media

Many factors have contributed to the public's interest in books as a source of information and diversion. The American Book Publishers Council, in enlarging the scope of its activities, has played a considerable part in fostering this trend. I served on the board of the ABPC in 1950, when an expanded program of services led to the establishment of what we named the Committee on Reading Development. This committee evolved from an informal dinner at my house, arranged so that a number of publishers could get together and exchange views on problems of mutual interest. The group included Harold Guinzburg, head of Viking Press, Douglas Black of Doubleday, Alfred Knopf, Stanley Rinehart of Rinehart & Company, and Henry Laughlin of Houghton Mifflin. All of us were concerned about new developments in mass-media communication that posed a competitive threat to books, and Guinzburg talked persuasively on the subject, emphasizing the danger that books might be swamped by television. He described an impressive program designed to promote awareness of the value of books, the program to be channeled through schools and libraries. His plan impressed me, and I suggested to Harold, half-jokingly, that he devote the next three years to carrying out his ideas, during which he might delegate to others the operation of the Viking Press. This was, of course, impossible for him to do, and at the end of the evening we had reached no conclusion about what action to take.

But I kept thinking about Guinzburg's proposals; I felt that the information-promoting campaign he had outlined should be implemented. Someone had to be found with the necessary intelligence and drive to do this. After considering various possibilities it occurred to me that a young man named Theodore Waller might be the right person. I'd known Waller for years; he had done effective work in Washington promoting world political cooperation; and it seemed to me that he had the qualities we needed. Accordingly, I recommended him to my associates on the board of the ABPC. In due course he was taken on. In this way, with Waller in charge, the Committee on Reading Development (CRD) came into being. In four or five years Waller became the executive head of the Publishers Council, and it was through his efforts that the CRD evolved into an effective force in stimulating wider reading.

Other projects were developed by the Council under Waller's direction. The National Book Committee was formed, a group consisting of well-known citizens mostly from outside the book business, who devote considerable time to promoting public awareness of the benefits of reading. The committee established the annual National Book Awards, and from this new activity developed National Library Week, which has had an impressive effect in spreading the word about the importance of books. All this represented progress, but, despite such efforts to promote reading habits and despite the public's lively response to educational programs inside and outside the classroom, trade publishing remains a risky business. Fortunes are made from paper products such as milk containers, paper cups, Kleenex, paper towels, and the risks involved are relatively small. But the moment paper is covered with print, trouble starts and profits shrink. Every trade book is a new and individual product which must be sold in the market place, untried. In consequence, the trade book publisher who makes a profit on sales is fortunate, even though his "old" books, which he seldom has to advertise —those which have been on the market for over a year—account for nearly 50 percent of his sales volume. His profit must derive from subsidiary income, from book clubs and paperbacks, on which he normally receives a half-share. Including this special income, which cannot be depended on, the trade publisher's net profit averages only 2 to 3 percent.

The trouble is that, as in play producing, the trade publisher guesses wrong more often than he guesses right; if he could always pick best sellers and reject the turkeys, he'd be in fine shape. Unfortunately, no genius with this capacity has appeared in two thousand years. So one must figure on averages. If a book, fiction or nonfiction, sells 7,500 copies, it is doing better than two-thirds of all the general books published. At this sales figure the result for the publisher in terms of profit is exactly zero. So I feel that my observation about the profitability of selling paper which is not covered with print holds water.

The trade publisher is also faced with a dilemma when he has to decide on the size of the first printing of a book. Should he gamble on, say, fifteen thousand copies or should he play it close to his chest and print only half that quantity? If he does the latter, he will pay a high price per copy for production and take the risk of his book's going out of stock. If, on the other hand, he elects to print the larger quantity, he may see truckloads of the volume returned by the booksellers. The disposal of these truckloads means a loss; the books may be sold to what is known in the trade as a "remainder house" (these are the titles one sees displayed in cut-price outlets at bargain rates), or the books may have to be destroyed as of no value.

Pornography and Censorship

Pornography and the attitude to be taken toward it has long been one of the most controversial of publishing problems. To begin with, the term "pornographic book" requires definition. Does *Lolita* qualify? Does *The Story of O?* Opinions vary, as they do about what is humor. My feeling is that *Lolita* belongs to literature because the writing is distinguished and the novel is concerned with a human failing that is not uncommon; on the other hand, *The Story of O,* which I have used as an example of "dirty" fiction because the book is typical of its kind, seems to me worthless—without a redeeming feature. It should never have seen the light of day. My reaction to pornography is necessarily an individual one. I am not a moralist and do not believe in the publisher's setting himself up as an ethical arbiter; yet he certainly has the right to reject what is distasteful to him. Taste and standards vary greatly from period to period—witness the contrast between Restoration and Victorian attitudes; today anything goes, and this compounds the problem of pornography for responsible publishers and citizens in general.

There are always publishers looking for a fast buck, although, according to a recent *New York Times* survey, the profits from pornographic publishing are far less than generally supposed. When irresponsible people publish books that have no purpose except to shock, there ought to be some way of invoking restraints. At the same time, none of us wants censorship affecting the freedom to publish. The perfect answer to the dilemma would be to educate children so that dirty books would not hold their interest for long, but this is an ideal unlikely to be realized. The Supreme Court has attempted to exercise control by passing upon the manner in which books are presented to the public and advertised; this has been of only limited benefit. Price can be another controlling factor: The expensive book is less likely to get into the hands of the impressionable young than cheap, mass-produced ones. But these methods of control only nibble at the fringe of the problem. There are so many factors involved that I find it impossible to take a definite position. I can only state that I favor as little censorship as possible, and that by the courts rather than by the police or the Watch and Ward Society.

There are no fixed boundaries here, as is shown by a book dealing with a sex problem—the case of *The Well of Loneliness,* which Harper's declined to publish. By an editorial vote of two to one we decided to pass up this novel which we knew would sell, and did sell all through the 1929 depression, when we, and every other publisher, desperately needed profits. Today this decision, for which I voted, is hard to believe. An important consideration in reaching it was our feeling that, if *The Well of Loneliness* were brought into the courts, as it was in England, we could not conscientiously defend it as a work of outstanding literary merit. The subject matter of the novel also affected our attitude; it deals with lesbianism, and two of us felt that its publication would initiate a trend toward greater acceptance of lesbianism and homosexuality. It did, but we made the wrong decision back then. Homosexuality is now accepted almost to the extent that it was in classical times, and this is a healthier situation than keeping the subject under wraps.

Lady Chatterley's Lover, by D. H. Lawrence, was another novel which stirred the waters in the post-World War I period. Opinion on this book was sharply divided, and, of the reviews of it I have seen, a British one that appeared in *Field and Stream* in 1959 certainly took a most original viewpoint:

> Although written many years ago, *Lady Chatterley's Lover* has just been reissued. This fictional account of the day-to-day life of an English gamekeeper is still of considerable interest to outdoor-minded readers as it contains many passages on pheasant raising, the apprehending of poachers, ways to control vermin, and other chores and duties of the professional gamekeeper. Unfortunately, one is obliged to wade through many pages of extraneous material in order to discover and savor these sidelights on the management of a Midlands shooting estate, and in this reviewer's opinion, this book cannot take the place of J. R. Miller's *Practical Gamekeeping.*

A Time of Change

Within the House changes were taking place in the fifties and sixties. Raymond Harwood was made president, Frank MacGregor became chairman of the board, and I was appointed chairman of the executive committee. Over many years Harwood had demonstrated his business ability; his knowledge of the operations of the firm was thorough, and he was both liked and respected for his fair-mindedness. As president, subsequently, of the American Book Publishers Council, he made an enviable record. When Harwood became president of Harper's, Evan Thomas was relieved of some of his editorial responsibilities so that he could help with administrative work. He was appointed executive vice president, a position he held until he left Harper's to go to Norton a few years later. His move is one I shall always regret.

It was during these years that Harper's became preoccupied with starting its own line of paperbacks to supplement our indirect interest in paperback publishing through stock ownership in Bantam Books. Melvin Arnold, then a religious-book editor under Eugene Exman, undertook to develop Torchbooks, an attractive-looking and carefully chosen series designed to appeal largely to college and graduate students. Torchbooks achieved immediate recognition and success and two other paperback lines were soon added: Perennial and Colophon, both of them aimed at a less scholarly and younger audience than Torchbooks. Although Perennial is now a fast-selling line, it ran into serious difficulties after a year or two due to overproduction, and when Arnold assumed general management responsibilities for Harper's, Cass, Jr. was chosen for the difficult task of getting our paperbooks back on the rails. He achieved this with firmness and skill so that Torchbooks, Perennial and Colophon books, the three Harper paperback lines, are now very profitable. With them Harper's had become involved in almost every kind of publishing except elementary and high school textbooks, law and sets of reference books. The stage was set for further expansion, and the next step was to enter the field of elementary and high school (El-Hi) publishing. We investigated the possibility of starting an El-Hi enterprise of our own but found that this would involve a large expenditure of capital and would take many years. Moreover, we'd had our fingers burned by an unsuccessful venture into this field some years before. So, discouraged in that direction, we looked around with a view to arranging a merger. We started negotiations in 1962 with Row, Peterson of Evanston, Illinois, a long-established El-Hi firm with an excellent reputation, particularly in the elementary field. The merger was duly consummated, and our firm name was changed from Harper & Brothers to Harper & Row.

Too many mergers have recently taken place, in my opinion,

for publishing firms are most profitable and contribute most when managed by men who know books, rather than by accountants, no matter how able. However, the combination of Harper & Brothers and Row, Peterson has been successful because it offered distinct advantages to both parties and kept the operations in the hands of people familiar with the book-publishing business.

Through the merger, Harper's succeeded in rounding out its important textbook list, and Row, Peterson, which Gordon Jones had built up from a small concern to a large one, gained strength by its alliance with Harper's. The two offices, in New York and Evanston, are maintained as before, and each concerns itself with its own area of publishing.

The problem of combining books with machines has led to the acquisition of publishing concerns by huge electronics companies. Mergers such as those of Random House with RCA and of Holt, Rinehart with CBS were designed to achieve a combination of editorial know-how and the technical facilities needed to prepare the programs for what can be broadly described as teaching machines. Actually, the merging process is not the only solution since the great electronics concerns like RCA are already making arrangements with important, independently owned publishers for the use of their editorial material. Besides, many small companies manufacturing electronic devices have been started, so the machines can be purchased from them by the publishing firms.

When the merger with Row, Peterson took place in 1962, Harwood was still president of our company. Since he had expressed a wish to take things easier, we looked around for a new chief executive; our choice fell upon Mel Arnold, who became president in 1967. Two years later Harwood announced his wish to retire, and John Cowles, Jr. was elected chairman of the board, Gordon Jones chairman of the executive committee.

The world goes around and, as it does so, the world changes; so do publishing organizations, including Harper's. The most recent change in our firm was the election as president of Winthrop Knowlton, a young man with a splendid record both in government and in Wall Street; this took place in April, 1970, when Arnold expressed the desire, as I had, to devote all his time to editorial work.

In the sixties *Harper's Magazine* became independent after Cowles, who is president of the Minneapolis Star and Tribune Company and married to my stepdaughter, talked to me about wanting to enter magazine publishing and about the possibility of buying a periodical. He mentioned two or three publications which seemed to me doubtful. After some discussion I said to him, "If you're interested in extending your publishing activities, why don't you consider buying stock in Harper & Row?" The merger was by then an accomplished fact and Harper & Row stock was being sold over the counter. I saw an advantage in having it held by a person like John, who would contribute ability as well as financial resources to the firm. The upshot was that the Minneapolis Star and Tribune Company became a substantial minority stockholder in our company, and this led to their total acquisition of *Harper's Magazine*.

More recently, the book-publishing firm, Harper's Magazine Press, was formed; it is jointly owned and operated by *Harper's Magazine* and Harper & Row. With the addition of Basic Books, under the direction of Arthur Rosenthal, which we acquired by merger, and the establishment in 1970 of the Canfield Press in San Francisco, which specializes in textbooks designed for junior colleges, Harper's range of publications is now as diversified as that of any firm in the business.

Old and New Interests

While many changes were taking place in publishing, I found myself unexpectedly caught up in a new and challenging interest—planned parenthood. My involvement, in fact, became so great that I had to sever my connections with other nonprofit organizations with which I had been associated, like New York University, the N.Y.U.-Bellevue Medical Center, the Phoenix Repertory Theatre, the New York State Council on the Arts and various foundations.

It was Jane who was largely responsible for my involvement in planned parenthood. In 1959 I accompanied her to New Delhi where she was attending a world-wide conference on birth control as a director of the International Planned Parenthood Federation (IPPF). My role there was that of observer-reporter. The conference was impressive; representatives of the leading nations were present, and Nehru delivered the opening address, accompanied by Margaret Sanger, then an old lady but an extraordinarily vital one. In the World War I period she had been sentenced to a jail term in New York for advocating birth control and operating a clinic. Subsequently, on the advice of friends, she left the United States for England, where she was welcomed by such men as H. G. Wells, Julian and Aldous Huxley and Havelock Ellis, who joined her cause. In this manner, through Margaret Sanger's initiative, a world-wide movement was started, although IPPF was not organized until 1952.

India is the tragic showplace of the world for overpopulation, misery and hunger; in the streets of its great cities men, women and children lie on the pavements, day and night, too weak to move. I had long been concerned with the problem of excessive population growth, and this visit to India convinced me that planned parenthood was an activity in which I should take part. First, as president of the American Federation; then, as chairman of the governing body of IPPF, of which I am now honorary chairman, I have found the work most rewarding. I feel that, in order to avoid doubling the number of people on earth by the end of this century, population control is not only essential but also a problem that is soluble.

Of the planned parenthood organizations in various parts of the world (IPPF is established in seventy countries and is working actively in many others) the U.S. branch is one of the most dynamic. Measurable progress is being made; yet, even in this rich and favored land, more than four million women—

mostly among the poor—still lack access to birth control information and aid. It will be years before the situation can be remedied with the help of public health agencies and hospitals. Here and elsewhere there are roadblocks: the Catholic Church, taboos, the worship of sex in certain countries like India, inertia and a persistent tradition in rural areas that many children are desirable—to work and care for their parents in old age. Whether such opposition helps or hinders the birth control movement is debatable, but there's no doubt that in the past few years the public's change of attitude has been striking. Changed, too, is the attitude of governments, which are spending millions on population limitation and contributing substantial sums to IPPF. The United Nations now gives practical help and is an important factor in the progress of this movement which is so closely related to the problem of pollution.

In regions like Latin America accurate statistics are difficult to obtain; the best estimate is that for every three children born there is at least one illegal abortion, involving sickness and loss of life because of the unsanitary conditions under which the operation must be performed. To the Catholic Church abortion is a mortal sin as well as a social evil, but, in spite of this, many priests see the need of legalizing it so as to cut down the deaths resulting from unskilled and unscrupulous medical attention. In the last year there has been impressive progress in removing the obstacles to abortion. As of the spring of 1970 fifteen states in this country had liberalized their abortion laws and three of them—New York, Hawaii and Alaska—had repealed all statutes forbidding the performance of abortions and made the conditions for them a matter of consent between a woman and her physician. However, the battle is not yet won, for in thirty-four states abortions were still virtually outlawed and it was a criminal offense to perform one except to preserve the life of the woman.

Until recently the dollar appropriation from our government for basic research in human biology and birth control was less than the amount spent on researching hoof-and-mouth disease! This absurd situation is being corrected, but a much greater effort is needed. Basic research by the government and by private foundations, like the Rockefeller, has been stepped up considerably, and, within the next few years, new contraceptive devices will be on the market. Among developments in an experimental stage are the "morning after" pill and reversible vasectomy.

Recently, Pope Paul has reaffirmed the Church's rigid position regarding birth control and the pill; in doing so, he has lost his liberal following. While such setbacks are disheartening, they do not cancel out progress in limiting the current birth rate which results in sixty million more people on this earth each year. Over the past decade the annual budget of International Planned Parenthood—now $20 million—has increased by a ratio of 400 to 1. Accordingly, I look at the future with some confidence and believe that, particularly in the underdeveloped countries, excessive population growth will be better controlled so that in these areas adequate education and housing, and an increase in the present pitifully low per capita income, can be achieved.

The Manchester Affair

What has come to be known in publishing circles as the Manchester Affair was, for me, a distressing experience. It was painful because the lawsuit brought against Harper's by Jacqueline Kennedy and Senator Robert Kennedy was bitter and prolonged; it was especially painful because I have known Jackie Onassis for a long time and like her.

The Bouvier sisters are very appealing, and both Lee, who was married to my son Michael, and Jackie have natural good manners. No wonder that President De Gaulle was attracted by Jackie's intelligence and charm.

Jackie has ability, too; as a girl in Washington she wrote a column for one of the newspapers there, reporting vividly on what she saw and heard in the streets of the city. She has the capacity to get what she wants and demands the best. Her impeccable taste was apparent in the redecoration of the White House which she supervised. She always insists on the best—in the people she has around her, in the works of art she collects and in the music she listens to.

When JFK was President, Jackie entertained Jane and me at the White House, receiving us in her sitting room, where she was surrounded by photographs of her father, Jack Bouvier; obviously, she had been devoted to him. In the course of conversation I asked her what she was planning for the weekend, and at this her face lit up; she was going fox hunting in Middleburg. It was clear that hunting was what she liked above all— the White House was a burden to her.

Jacqueline Onassis is a complicated character, with a theatrical streak; her roommate at Farmington (Miss Porter's School) was often baffled by Jackie's quick changes of mood. One morning, as she was walking with Jackie on the way to a class, she asked her, "Who are you *today*?"

The trouble over William Manchester's book on the assassination of John F. Kennedy began late in 1966 when Jackie and Robert Kennedy brought suit, first against *Look* magazine, then against Harper's. It was hot news and the press made much of it, so it is unnecessary for me to go into familiar details; I shall confine my comments mainly to matters John Corry did not mention and probably did not know about when he wrote that interesting book, *The Manchester Affair.**

Corry wrote: "If Manchester's book, which was authorized by the Kennedy family, contained an unpleasant picture [of Lyndon Johnson], it was not unlikely that Johnson would be offended and make it difficult for Bobby Kennedy at a national convention." That passage sets the stage for the drama that was to unfold.

Evan Thomas, with whom I worked throughout the crisis, was the able editor of the book. He deleted and changed certain

---

* *The Manchester Affair* by John Corry, G. P. Putnam's Sons, 1967.

passages derogatory to LBJ as well as to others; also passages giving Jackie's intimate, personal reactions to which she might object. Evan took infinite trouble over the manuscript and asked four Harper editors to mark passages which might disturb her; he then showed these to Pamela Turnure, Jackie's secretary. All this took place before the manuscript was seen by *Look* and serial publication arranged for; also, before any legal action was taken.

Corry: "While Harper & Row would not profit at all from the sale of the [serial] rights, the publishing company had some loose connections with Cowles Communications which [owns a number of television stations, newspapers and magazines and] puts out *Look*."

In our agreement with Robert Kennedy relating to *The Death of a President* Harper's profit was limited to 6 percent on the first printing, which was initially estimated at 100,000 cloth-bound copies, with no share in any other rights. The first edition turned out to be 600,000 copies and the book was selected by the Book-of-the-Month Club, which paid $250,000; in addition, a million-dollar offer was made for paperback rights, but the paper edition was published under our imprint and marketed by Popular Library. *Look* paid $665,000 for serial rights.

The reason for Harper's self-denying ordinance was that Thomas, when making the profit-sharing arrangements with Robert Kennedy, insisted that we did not wish to make more than a nominal profit from a book describing the tragedy of the assassination. We stipulated that the profits, over our modest share, go to the Kennedy Library; to date these have amounted to more than one million dollars.

Corry (quoting John Harding of *Look*) : ". . . the manuscript of July 18th in which [*Look*] purchased first serial rights was approved by Robert F. Kennedy, acting for all members of the Kennedy family . . . and the sale of first serial rights in the manuscript at this time was similarly approved."

A curious background for a lawsuit against *Look* and, later, against Harper's. Part of the explanation is that, as time passed, the whole situation became more and more confused as an increasing number of Kennedy advisers became involved with the manuscript.

Corry: "[Richard] Goodwin at various times had been in touch with nearly everyone [in the Kennedy circle]. . . . Along with the Senator himself . . . they drew together to consider one great question: Should we sue?"

Goodwin was named by Jackie to be her primary representative; she had several others—among them, John Seigenthaler, Edwin Guthman and Pamela Turnure—all of whom read the manuscript. Thomas had advised Jackie not to do so; he felt that Manchester's vivid account of the assassination might be too painful for her.

Goodwin was said to be difficult (Corry refers to him as Machiavelli), but I found him cooperative. For instance, one evening after our lawyers had refused to meet with Goodwin, Thomas and I noticed him dining at the restaurant where General Greenbaum—senior partner of Greenbaum, Wolff & Ernst, counsel for Harper—Evan and I were having dinner. We suggested that Goodwin join us, but Greenbaum said No; nevertheless, when Goodwin had finished his meal and was passing our table, I asked him to have a brandy with us. The result was constructive because Goodwin cooperated at a time when the opposing lawyers—Simon Rifkind and his aides on the Kennedy side, and General Greenbaum, Harriet Pilpel, Maurice Greenbaum, Roger Hunting, Nancy Wechsler and Alan Schwartz on ours—were hopelessly at odds. After several sessions in Rifkind's chambers, they could not agree where to meet because each legal line-up wanted the other to come to their office: shades of the four-sided table in the Vietnam negotiations!

Corry: "They [the Kennedys] wanted a truly authorized history, perhaps not an inaccurate one, but one that just omitted part of the history. . . . A few days after [Mike] Land [a *Look* editor] met with Manchester, Cass Canfield and Evan Thomas met with Mrs. Kennedy."

I recall that at our meeting with Jackie Kennedy in her Fifth Avenue apartment Burke Marshall, one of her legal advisers, was present. The occasion of this meeting, which took place some days after Manchester's session with Mike Land, was our request that Jackie write to Manchester, who had departed for London, and ask him to make the changes she wanted in the text—changes in addition to those already agreed to by the author, involving personal matters she'd had put on tape for him alone. Jackie asked Thomas and me to deliver her letter to Manchester. Its tone was rather commanding in spite of the fact that we'd pleaded with her to make it appealing; we were certain that Manchester would do anything to please Jackie, provided she would take some trouble to please him.

The next day Thomas and I flew to London, where we talked to Manchester in the office of his London agent, A. D. Peters. We had marked up his page proofs with the changes which we insisted upon as a matter of good taste, changes relating to Jackie's personal experiences during the assassination as well as to matters affecting LBJ. Although Manchester was not well—was ill with pneumonia—he appeared at the Connaught Hotel just before our departure for New York. There was no time to examine his changes, which were in addition to those he had previously made, but he assured us that they were "numerous and substantial." This satisfied us.

To our surprise, Manchester offered to accompany us to the London airport. At that point the gods intervened. Our plane, starting at Frankfurt, was delayed on account of mechanical troubles and we were told that it would not leave until 2 A.M. As this seemed late, I decided to take the morning flight and went with Thomas to the BOAC hotel. We were quite touched that Manchester, although ill, had come to see us off and failed to realize that he might have done so because he didn't wish us to examine the last changes he had made and perhaps raise further questions about his much-edited book.

In the hotel that night we reread the proofs and found that, while Manchester's alterations were numerous, they were unimportant. When we telephoned him late that night, he repeated that he was feeling unwell, adding that he could make no further changes, since his manuscript had been revised and altered by half a dozen of the Kennedys' advisers. He put down the receiver, but a few minutes later we called back and told him that unless he made the alterations we had stipulated we wouldn't publish the book. This meant that *The Death of a President* would not appear in print since we had the contract for exclusive publication and Manchester, therefore, could not legally offer the book to another house. At that point Manchester gave in. We had won, and the final changes, insisted upon by Thomas and myself, were incorporated in the page proofs.

At Kennedy Airport, the next day, I was paged at the passport desk by Harriet Pilpel of the Ernst firm; she said that my presence was required immediately at Judge Rifkind's office. I objected, saying that I'd had no time to make notes of the recent conversations with Manchester. But she insisted, pointing out that Jackie would be present at the meeting; so I agreed, reluctantly, and took the helicopter to town. There they all were, including Judge Rifkind. I reported that Manchester had made the revisions Thomas and I had demanded, that they were both numerous and substantial, adding that I'd been obliged to invoke the publisher's "ultimate threat"—not to publish unless the changes were satisfactory.

Corry: "With a flourish, Canfield left the office, arm in arm with Mrs. Kennedy."

Jackie was delighted. That night, in the early morning hours, she wrote me a warm, affectionate letter.

A few days later, in the middle of December, she telephoned me early in the morning, asking to see the latest Manchester changes. Unfortunately, however, as Manchester had insisted that they be kept confidential and had made Thomas and me agree not to show them to the Kennedys—an understandable demand in view of the fact that he felt no compulsion to make further revisions—I was obliged to tell Jackie that I couldn't do what she asked. She hung up, and later that morning, in association with Senator Kennedy, brought legal action against Harper & Row. Bobby had not wanted Jackie to bring suit but, in loyalty to her, agreed to join her in the action.

Corry: "It has never been quite clear when Mrs. Kennedy read the manuscript. Her partisans say she never read it at all. Yet she read at least a large part of the material that *Look* wanted to serialize in a meeting one Saturday morning [in December] in an attorney's office on Wall Street. She emerged from the meeting in tears, not because of the manuscript. She was annoyed because there were two reporters outside and she had thought that the meeting would be secret."

241

Indeed, Jackie's tears were not shed over the book; in fact, the changes made by Manchester were more extensive than she'd been led to expect. Anyway, her cheeks were dry when she rode in a steeplechase the next day in Bernardsville, New Jersey. A superb horsewoman, she finished with the first half-dozen riders, and was flushed with pleasure.

At last, on December 27, a few hours before the hearing was to take place, the case was settled. Bobby and Jackie had been summoned to testify on that day, and it was probably this that made them take the decision, since every word spoken at the hearing would have been featured in newspapers throughout the world. Hundreds of thousands of dollars had been spent in legal fees; a total of only seven pages had been deleted from the book, the text of which ran ultimately to 647 pages. Through acting courageously and decisively, by insisting that the hearing should not be postponed, General Greenbaum had saved the day. His brief was a masterpiece; his argument, had it been presented in court, would have been exceedingly hard to refute.

A day or two after the settlement I appeared on a national television hook-up and made this statement:

My experience in connection with *The Death of a President* has been the most trying and distressing one in a forty-year publishing career and Evan Thomas, the editor of the book at Harper & Row, shares my distress. We take great pride in having published President Kennedy's *Profiles in Courage* as well as books by Senator Robert Kennedy. When the Kennedy family asked us to issue the Manchester book and we agreed to do so, they were asking us to assume the responsibilities of a publisher—a function we have exercised honorably and professionally over nearly one hundred and fifty years.

I wish to stress how very badly I feel that Mrs. Kennedy, for whom I have deep regard and respect, is so disturbed about *The Death of a President*. The principals involved in this dispute are all people for whom Evan Thomas and I have deep regard; Manchester's book is a moving, sincere and outstanding piece of writing. He has been subject to many repeated pressures for many months; he was asked to prepare for publication an accurate account of the events of the assassination and was assured that his role as an author would be respected.

Understandably, the members of the Kennedy family were unwilling to read the manuscript themselves; hence they designated representatives to do this for them. Had they read it, the legal action might have been avoided.

Harper & Row was not motivated by profit when it undertook publication; on the contrary, all Harper profits will go to the Kennedy Library except a small return to Harper's on the first printing. In no event will this limit be exceeded. Mr. Manchester is also making substantial contributions to the Library from his earnings on the book.

In the interest of historical accuracy and of people's right to know the true facts of the awesome tragedy—this right to know which led the Kennedy family to request Mr. Manchester to write his book and us to publish it—we join with him in defending the book's right to live.

The Manchester Affair was closed.

The legal fees charged by the opposing lawyers were formidable and this expense seemed unnecessary; moreover, the suit did not help Bobby Kennedy's political chances. Commenting on a public opinion poll at the time, Corry wrote: "They preferred Lyndon Johnson to Robert Kennedy by 59 to 41 percent, while people who did not follow the controversy wanted Kennedy rather than Johnson, 54 to 46 percent."

Svetlana

The furor over the Manchester Affair quieted down, but we had hardly recovered our breath when, as I was about to fly to South America, I received a phone call from General Greenbaum. He wanted to know when he could see me and I explained that, unfortunately, I was scheduled to leave for Lima, Peru, within an hour. He insisted that the matter he wished to discuss

243

was urgent; he had just returned from Switzerland and said that he wished to meet with me at once. So I asked him to come to my house immediately and requested Evan Thomas to be there also.

Eddie Greenbaum's eyes shone with excitement as he told Evan and me of his very recent talk with Stalin's daughter, Svetlana Alliluyeva, in Switzerland. News of her having written *Twenty Letters to a Friend* had leaked out, and she had received many offers from publishers. Greenbaum was in a position to sell these memoirs and, because of restrictions imposed by the Swiss government, had to do so quickly and quietly. In answer to our inquiry about price, the General said that he required a large sum for U.S. book rights, which sounded rather steep to Thomas and me, but we told him that, if we could obtain an encouraging opinion on the Russian manuscript from someone whose judgment we trusted, we'd meet the offer. Two days later George Kennan gave us a highly favorable report. Evan made the deal for the book as I was crossing the Andes.

I met Svetlana shortly after her brilliant television appearance upon her arrival in this country, when she charmed everyone with her friendliness, modesty and directness. Later, she stayed with us in Bedford Village and proved to be a fascinating guest, but she was obviously worried and distracted. At the time, her *Twenty Letters to a Friend* was appearing serially in the *New York Times,* as well as in magazines and newspapers throughout the world, and Svetlana had been told that only one chapter of the book would be used. Instead, all of it had been abridged. She was also distressed by the use of photographs stolen from her home in Russia by the secret police. In spite of these harassments she did look forward to publication of her book in the version she had written.

When I suggested that Harper's give a party to celebrate the occasion, she first rejected the idea. But, later on, she began to ask questions: What kind of a party? How big? Would the guests be friendly to her? When I reassured her, she became enthusiastic and finally exclaimed, "A party would be wonderful. I've never been given one in my whole life!"

The Harper cocktail party for Svetlana at the St. Regis was

"Can you direct me to Harper & Row?" *Drawing by Mischa Richter;*
Copr. © *1967 The New Yorker Magazine, Inc.*

a great success; about a hundred people—critics and booksellers
—came. Afterward, a few friends, mostly members of General
Greenbaum's firm and of the Harper office, entertained her at
dinner. On this occasion Svetlana, shy as usual, declined to
speak, but, as the evening wore on, she rose to her feet. In
simple, appealing words, similar to those in her book, she
talked about the Russian countryside, the white birches, the
children, and pointed to similarities between the places she had
known as a child and those she'd seen in America. She wanted
us to know that she felt she had "come home." We were all
deeply moved.

On New Year's Eve of 1968 Svetlana planned a party of her
own—a surprise party—for the friendly policemen who protected her house at Princeton which she had rented. The prep-
arations completed, the table set and ready, she rang the special
alarm that had been installed, and in a trice the policemen
whirled into her driveway prepared for an emergency. Looking
very pretty and dressed, as always, in perfect taste, she greeted
her guests, only to be met with a rebuff: "Sorry, ma'am, we're on
duty and can't have a drink, or spend any time here." Sadly,
Svetlana put away the glasses and dishes, wondering why the
policemen had failed to understand her joke.

Twenty Letters created a great stir; the reviews were excellent and the book enjoyed a large sale, although considerably
less than it would have had there been no serialization before
publication. *Twenty Letters* was overpublicized, overexposed.

Svetlana's second book, *Only One Year,* tells of her departure from Russia and her journey to the village in India bearing
the ashes of her husband, Brajesh Singh. She had a happy time
there and became deeply attached to the people in the village—
happy except for the Soviet surveillance of which there was no
end. Finally, the time came when she could stand it no longer
and she determined to escape. One evening, while a party was
in progress at the Soviet Embassy, Svetlana seized the moment.
Hailing a passing taxi, and carrying only a small suitcase, she
told the driver to go to the United States Embassy, where she
was met by a Marine who was at a loss to know what to do with
this Russian lady seeking sanctuary. He referred her to the

officer on duty in the absence of Chester Bowles, our Ambassador, who was ill with the flu. Bowles, reached on the phone, told the duty officer, "Get her off to Switzerland just as soon as you possibly can." As it happened, there was a direct flight to Rome once a week and, fortunately, this was the right night. Accompanied by an embassy aide, Svetlana caught the 2 A.M. plane; the aide got her a room in a hotel in Rome and saw that she was kept there, incognito, during her stopover of forty-eight hours. The next destination was Switzerland, where she stayed in a convent with the Mother Superior.

The day after Svetlana's escape, Bowles encountered the Soviet Ambassador to India, who complained to him bitterly: "I thought you and I were friends; over the years I've always tried to cooperate with you in every possible way." Bowles replied that he regretted the Svetlana incident, patted his diplomatic colleague on the shoulder and said, "Look, old man, if you ever want to escape yourself, I'll do you the same favor that I did for Svetlana."

Madame Alliluyeva has been chided for leaving her children, an unfair criticism because her son and daughter are grown up, the son a doctor and married, the daughter in the university. Svetlana misses them greatly, but, as she explained to me, it was impossible for her to return to the Soviet Union from India since she knew that she would have been forced to work for the party, a thing she could not, would not, do.

Only One Year appeared in the fall of 1969; the excellent translator was Paul Chavchavadze, a Russian of noble family. It is interesting that Stalin's daughter should have had such a congenial relation with this representative of the old regime. The book won immediate acclaim from critics and the public; it was considered—and is—an important, distinguished work. The late Louis Fischer made the observation that Svetlana's story of her escape from the Soviet Union, with its flashbacks to her life in Russia, explained more about the Stalin regime and told more about her father than we are likely to know for a generation. *Only One Year* is a remarkable work which reveals the iniquities of her father's rule; it refutes the author's contention that she's not a natural writer. She is, in fact, a fine stylist and writes with simple directness; her prose accurately conveys what she feels.

In the spring of 1970 Svetlana married William Wesley Peters, a noted architect. He is vice president of the Frank Lloyd Wright Foundation which maintains an architectural concern and a school of architecture at Taliesin West in Arizona, and at Taliesin East in Wisconsin.

V

FOOTLOOSE

By Sea and Air

Adventure still offers itself when I least expect it: two unusual trips in recent years, one by sea and the other by air.

In the summer of 1967 I was invited to be one of a party of ten civilian observers on the aircraft carrier *U.S.S. Coral Sea,* bound for the waters off Vietnam on a combat mission. It was after midnight when we boarded ship in San Francisco and made a grim passage through the hangar deck to our cabins. The *Coral Sea* is a maze for the visitor, and only a bloodhound following a scent could have found its way around it. However, several briefings and an exhausting tour of the carrier that took us up and down perpendicular ladders,. ad infinitum, provided us with information which dispelled our ignorance and confusion. We learned that the vessel carried about a hundred planes of various types and that they were expected to fly ten thousand missions over Vietnam. On the previous tour of duty twelve airmen and twenty planes had been lost—evidence that the enemy defense was getting tougher. The *Coral Sea,* built when the Kamikazes were at their peak of activity and completed in 1947, is a fifth of a mile long, with a tonnage of 63,000 and a crew of 4,200. A huge, floating machine shop, honeycombed with watertight compartments and operated by incomprehensible dials, it is one of the larger United States aircraft carriers.

My civilian companions—reporters and broadcasters from all parts of the country—were a bright lot. Jim Bassett, editor of the Los Angeles *Times-Mirror,* who had been PR officer for

Admiral Halsey in the Pacific, was my cabin mate, and it was our good fortune to be attached for the duration of the trip to the Grey Foxes air fighter squadron, a group with a fine *esprit de corps*. It was interesting to listen to their special jargon and to observe the pilots, most of whom had had battle experience. Bassett and I became very fond of the Grey Foxes and used their briefing room as we would a club. They were a high-spirited lot, yet serious—sort of Hemingway types: tough on the surface but romantic underneath. They seemed to belong to the World War I generation and were a far cry from today's hippies.

The crew of the carrier consisted largely of technicians, who took justifiable satisfaction in the excellent performance of their jobs. In addition, about forty Marines guarded the atomic weapons and acted as ship's police; they were as tough as they come and the sailors hated them. I wondered about the men's attitude toward the war. One of them asked me what I thought of it, and though he did not express agreement with my dim view of the conflict, I gathered he was not enthusiastic about the Vietnam assignment and guessed that many others felt the same.

On the third day out we heard news of a disaster on the carrier *Forrestal*. Early reports had minimized the number of casualties, apparently caused by an exploding gas tank, but later ones established the figure at around two hundred, of which two-thirds were fatal. The personnel of the *Coral Sea* took this news grimly and with little comment. One felt that they were thinking, "It could happen to us." The *Forrestal* accident added a note of urgency to the fire-fighting, atomic and other daily drills on our ship.

The accuracy with which planes took off and returned to the carrier was astounding. Four wires stretched across the aft deck at intervals of about forty feet; to make a perfect landing an incoming aircraft plane had to catch the third wire with its hook, and most of them did. As part of our indoctrination we were shot off the carrier in a plane, seated facing backward to minimize the shock of take-off and return. To be catapulted is an exciting experience. It reminded me of a similar one in a small mail plane on which I was a passenger, launched from the *S.S. France* in 1930 on a 250-mile flight to Paris. My account of this amazed the Navy men, who couldn't believe that an airplane catapult had existed before most of them had been born. Actually, it was made of some elastic material and was very primitive.

The catapult chain on a modern carrier is about 125 feet long and the plane shot off it attains a speed of about 100 mph as it leaves the flight deck. At the start of the run you hear a loud report like a cannon shot; then, in a moment, you're airborne. Landing on the ship was relatively easy; we had expected a tremendous jerk when we hit the wire, but it wasn't severe.

In five days the *Coral Sea* reached Hawaii, where we were given top treatment and encountered admirals at every turn. We were briefed at Headquarters Pacific, and the talks, or lectures, illustrated with slides and maps, were usually excellent. They gave us an over-all view of the whole Pacific operation; the strategy involved a vast field of action of which Vietnam is only a part. We received other briefings from which emerged facts, both interesting and terrifying, about the instruments of modern atomic warfare. One impressed me particularly. The Polaris submarine, of which we then had thirty-two, can deliver atomic missiles up to 2,500 miles and hit any target with a margin of error of one mile. Manhattan Island, by this reckoning, could be destroyed by one hydrogen bomb from a sub. A machine of inconceivable power, the Polaris is designed as a deterrent and, as one officer remarked, "If we ever have to use it, we shall have failed."

At Pearl Harbor we were taken aboard *Flasher,* an atomic attack submarine and, after an excellent lunch, embarked upon a five-hour trip. The ship is a beautiful piece of mechanism, manned by experts—about one hundred of them—all volunteers. We were told that thirty-six months were required to train officers for this service, following their Annapolis course, and thirty-five months to train enlisted men.

After surfacing outside the harbor, *Flasher* dove to four hundred feet. Except for the tilt of the ship and the seeming abscence of motion after submerging, one couldn't tell when this silent creature went under. It was like being inside a huge shark—no vibration, just silence and a feeling of effortless power. The instrument room, filled with sonar devices, was beyond our comprehension. We listened to the sounds heard when a sub runs into various kinds of marine life—the hissing of shrimps like butter in a frying pan, the mating noises of porpoises and the sounds made by whales. Science fiction! In this room one imagined the sensation of hearing a noise that *might* announce the approach of an enemy sub. According to our informant, it is not possible to distinguish, positively, between the sounds made by an approaching submarine and those of a whale, nor can the object's exact location be pinpointed. The vision of two subs circling one another in the middle of an ocean, like two men out to kill each other in total darkness, made one shudder.

We were allowed to take over the controls, as delicate as those on a plane. I held the stick and turned *Flasher* sharply to the right and left, tipping the ship ten degrees in the process. I dove her from two hundred to four hundred feet, then brought her back in a climb. Thus did a little boy's Walter Mitty dream come true.

At a Marine training ground in Hawaii we witnessed an exercise in fire power, including a simulated guerrilla attack on a make-believe Vietnam hamlet guarded by our men. It was very realistic, complete with tanks, helicopters and support planes. We were also given a demonstration of guerrilla weapons and walked through a simulated jungle filled with crude but horrifying booby traps, like those used by the Vietcong. Many of them were made of pointed bamboo sticks poisoned with human excrement, traps skillfully hidden with nails driven in at an angle, so that the struggling victim, attempting to extricate himself, would only drive the nails more deeply into his body. The ingenuity of these homemade devices is appalling, many of them being adaptations of animal traps.

In the early hours of the following morning, feeling beaten down by the rapid succession of events and impressions, I was engulfed by the apparent futility of our great military apparatus. One is bound to be impressed by the ingenuity and organization that go into the huge Pacific Army-Navy-Marine operation, but, after a while, revulsion sets in and one's mind begins to go in circles. For this vast military setup is undoubtedly a necessary asset; without it we would not survive as a nation in today's world. One can only hope that, because weapons have become so deadly, another world war on the grand scale may be avoided.

Our tour at an end, we civilians boarded a comfortable propeller plane, complete with bunks, for the ten-hour flight to San Francisco. As we were about to take off, we heard that the enlisted men of the *Coral Sea* had distinguished themselves in Honolulu by consuming ten thousand bottles of beer in the enlisted men's club, leaving the place in shambles. Dozens were arrested and taken back to the carrier in police wagons, no doubt to be subjected to punitive exercises, supervised by pitiless Marine sergeants, on the way to Vietnam.

A First to Moscow

It was in July, 1968, just a year after the *Coral Sea* junket, that I was invited by Najeeb Hallaby, president of Pan American Airlines, to take a joy ride to Moscow. The flight was to inaugurate the first commercial air service to the Soviet Union, and I was one of a party which included some twenty newspaper publishers from different parts of the country.

On arrival at the Moscow airport we were entertained with vodka and cakes, and Charles Bohlen, who had served as our Ambassador to Russia, made a brief speech. Although the Russians were polite and correct, it was clear that we were not being overwhelmed with hospitality.

John Cheever, whose books Harper's had published, had asked me in New York to look up a woman who had translated his work into Russian, so I inquired of a member of our embassy staff how I could get in touch with her in Moscow. His reply was discouraging: "You stay in the bus group; it's not worthwhile to take unnecessary chances." I did as I was told and didn't pursue the matter further. A great Russian writer whom I wanted to see, but couldn't, was Alexander Solzhenitsyn, author of *The First Circle*, which we had recently published. Last year, Solzhenitsyn, surely one of the great writers of our time, as well as one of the most courageous in his resistance to Soviet persecution, was awarded the Nobel Prize for Literature.

I thoroughly enjoyed our three-day tour in the Soviet Union. But Moscow is a grim-looking city; Leningrad, in contrast, is beautiful, and the circus there was the best and liveliest I have ever seen. With Leonard Lyons I visited GUM, the huge Moscow department store—a depressing experience for the shoddy merchandise was high-priced and there were long lines of dejected-looking people waiting to claim their purchases. On the other hand, the crowds one met on the streets from all parts of the Soviet Union, including many Orientals, seemed quite cheerful.

On my previous visit to Moscow, thirty-five years before, there had been much excitement about the wonderful new subway which was about to open. Its promise was now fulfilled and the stations, with their colorful mosaics, were impressive. Like the cathedral at Chartres, the Moscow subway represents a great joint effort, a building achievement to be enjoyed by the people, as are the towering skyscrapers, designed in Riverside Drive 1914 style, which house tens of thousands of university students. Other monuments include a vast heated swimming pool in the center of Moscow and the astonishing Hotel Moskva. This huge caravansary boasts five thousand rooms but only about a dozen elevators, from which the guests must walk miles in order to reach their cell-like, but adequately furnished, bedrooms.

This trip to the Soviet Union was too brief to warrant my drawing conclusions about the state of the country and its economy, but there were many signs of improvement since my last visit over a generation before. One got the impression that the mass of Soviet citizens were well cared for and, aside from the intellectual or professional classes, which are violently in revolt against the rigid government controls, that they were seemingly satisfied with their lot.

The flight east and the landing at the excellently managed Moscow airport took place without a hitch. In contrast, there was a considerable delay in landing at Kennedy, and I asked the board chairman of Pan American the reason. He said that it was caused by a slow-up of the airport's personnel who were on strike—something which the Russians found difficult to understand since their planes are invariably on time. My informant went on to say that we were very lucky to have reached Moscow at all in view of the Czech crisis at the time. Pan Am had been trying for years to inaugurate commercial flights to the Soviet Union but, due to one complication or another, they had always been canceled.

Last Lap

The game of Likes and Dislikes brings out the characteristics of the players; some people can write down their five dislikes in a trice, others are hard put to find five things that displease them. The same holds true for likes. I belong to the cheerful group and can scribble any number of likes in a moment: wine, women, song, sport, pictures, reading. Hates take longer for me to enumerate: stuffed shirts, idleness, negativism, waiting—and people who keep recalling the "good old days."

What was so good about them? True, there was more leisure before the gasoline engine and movies and radio; *Life with Father* was pleasant on the whole, but how many lived it? Perhaps one in a hundred; the rest had to scrabble for their daily bread and spend a large part of their existences in sweatshops and dark factories. Although today's world is a very uncertain place to live in, the world always has been so.

Having reached the age when many men retire, I talked to Joanna Maravel in my office about my future, about which I took a dim view. "You can never tell what's ahead," she observed. She happened to be right, for the recent years have been full of interest. With new books from Svetlana Alliluyeva, Chester Bowles, Lady Longford, Gustav Eckstein, Alan Moorehead, J. B. Priestley, E. B. White, Nancy Mitford, and many others on the way, my editorial plate is piled high. Too high, it has seemed at times, and had it not been for invaluable help from my two assistants, Beulah Hagen and Joanna Maravel, I would have sunk without trace, long ago. Well, almost sunk—my wife, Jane, would have come to the rescue. During the thirty-two years of our married life she has been an essential collaborator—not only in the matter of evaluating manuscripts but also in that of keeping authors happy.

In recent years big changes have taken place in Harper & Row. Although they have caused some dislocation, I believe that in the long run they will strengthen the operations of the firm. One of the profound satisfactions of my career is that my son Cass, who publishes a large and important list of authors, is associated with me in Harper's and that my son-in-law, John Cowles, Jr., has taken such an active part in the business. John is making a signal contribution as chairman of our board of directors.

In this period, which I have found full of surprises, new interests have given me great satisfaction; for example, I have started a collection of drawings by both American and foreign artists. This activity is a delight; searching for fine drawings is an adventure. Travel, also, has been endlessly fascinating, and the writing of these memoirs—which I approached reluctantly —has been absorbing. But, after all, Coleridge's sailor was right: one's life is a tapestry seen from the wrong side—without pattern.

Up and Down and Around was begun in the spring of 1969 when Jane and I were cruising in the Ionian islands. We visited unfrequented places and anchored in small harbors where we swam several times a day. On one of these occasions I was standing some hundred yards from a beach and noted with lively interest—as I invariably do—a lovely young woman with a charming figure coming out of the sea. I kept my eyes on her until she came closer so that I could discern her features.

It was Jane.

Bedford Village, New York
February 1, 1971

Index

71 72 73 10 9 8 7 6 5 4 3 2